The
Secretary
of
State

The
Secretary
of
State

♦ The American Assembly
Columbia University

A SPECTRUM  BOOK

Englewood Cliffs, N. J.
PRENTICE-HALL, INC.

PRINTED IN THE UNITED STATES OF AMERICA

79748-C

Preface

This volume served as background reading for the Eighteenth American Assembly, a national meeting on the *Secretary of State* held at Arden House October 6-9, 1960. It is also intended to encourage informed discussion by the American public and to provide a basis for deliberations and independent findings by regional, state and municipal sessions of The American Assembly.

The Final Report of the Arden House Assembly begins on page 191. But each reader may form his own opinion of the responsibilities and opportunities before the Secretary in his complex role today. Individual views expressed by the authors are not endorsed by The American Assembly, by Don K. Price, who organized the volume, or by the Rockefeller Foundation which generously supported this program.

Henry M. Wriston
President
The American Assembly

Table of Contents

3   The Secretary and the Development and Coordination of Policy   51

Robert R. Bowie

4   The Secretary and the Management of the Department   76

Henry M. Wriston

5   The Secretary and Congress   112

William Y. Elliott

The
Secretary
of
State

Introduction:

A new look at the Secretary of State

♦ Don K. Price

Editor

The first Secretary of State of the United States of America, Thomas Jefferson, went on to become President. Each of the next three Presidents—Madison, Monroe, and John Quincy Adams—had also served as Secretary of State. Since then, however, that position has been no road to political advancement, even though it has retained by tradition the highest rank in the Cabinet. Indeed, in recent years the Secretary of State has seemed to be the official scapegoat for a nation which resents the sacrifices of two world wars and the frustration of the idealistic hopes which carried it to victory but failed to establish a firm basis for peace.

1

◆ DON K. PRICE, Dean of the Graduate School of Public Administration of Harvard University, was formerly Vice President (for international programs) of the Ford Foundation, and Deputy Chairman of the Research and Development Board of the Department of Defense. In 1945, he was a member of the Budget Bureau staff for the study of the State Department requested by Secretary Byrnes, and in 1948 an assistant to former President Hoover in his study of the Presidency for the Hoover Commission. He is a member of the President's Advisory Committee on Government Organization.

As a nation, we have first been jolted out of our comfortable isolation, and then forced to realize that our troubles had no short-term or easy solution. The Secretary of State has been obliged, therefore, to call on a nation that supposed itself at peace to continue to make sacrifices, and accept restraints, that had been thought tolerable before only in time of war. And all this came at a time when the new nature of international relations had radically changed the nature of diplomacy, and we had to face antagonists, and deal with allies, who did not share our basic cultural and political traditions. It is perhaps surprising only that the job of the Secretary has not been an even more crushing burden.

To consider the position of the Secretary of State is to open up an inquiry into some of the main constitutional and political and administrative problems of the government as a whole. The Secretary, of course, has from the beginning been not the head of an independent agency, or an officer with duties prescribed in detail by law, but an extension of the President's responsibility for the conduct of international affairs. Nothing can make this point more plain than to quote the Act of 1789 which provided that the Secretary of State:

> . . . shall perform and execute such duties as shall from time to time be enjoined on or entrusted to him by the President of the United States, agreeable to the Constitution, relative to correspondences, commissions or instructions to or with public ministers or consuls, from the United States or to negotiations with public ministers from foreign states or princes or to memorials or other applications from foreign public ministers or other foreigners, or to such other matters respecting foreign affairs, as the President of the United States shall assign to the said Department; and furthermore that the said principal officers shall conduct the business of the said Department in such

manner as the President of the United States shall from time to
time order or instruct.

The essays in this volume, therefore, consider the position of the
Secretary in a broad perspective. Mr. Nitze discusses the ways in which
the fundamental changes in the nature of nternational relations have
changed the ways in which the Secretary executes foreign policy. Mr.
Acheson deals with the Secretary in his most important personal and
official relationship: with the President. Mr. Bowie describes the role
of the Secretary in the coordination and formulation of policy within
the Exective Branch, and Mr. Wriston, the Secretary's management of
the Department of State and the Foregn Service. Moving from the
problems within the Executive Branch to the broader setting, Mr. Elliott
writes of the Secretary in relation to the Congress, and Dr. Dickey, of
the Secretary's relationship with the public and pressure groups. Finally,
the editor tres to outline what seem to him the major lessons to be
learned from these six chapters.

At the outset, one thing is clear: in recent months the President of
the United States, the Senate Committee on Foreign Relations, and
leaders of both political parties have expressed concern in various ways
regarding the ability of or government, as presently organized, to
develop policies with the wisdom and reflection, and to carry them out
with the energy and dispatch, that our predicament demands. To look
searchingly at the problems of the principal officer whose energies are
concentrated on our international affairs may well be worth our while
at this juncture in history.

1.

The Secretary and the execution of foreign policy

◆ Paul H. Nitze

This chapter addresses itself to the Secretary of State in his specific role of executing this country's foreign policy. Other sections in this volume deal with the Secretary in his relation to the President, Congress, public, and as a participant in the top national policy formulating bodies. These are obviously critically important aspects of the role of the Secretary of State. In dealing with the Secretary only in his role of executing foreign policy, one must therefore deal with an abstraction which is less than the real man.

On the other hand I propose to treat of this role in a sense which is in some respects larger than that of any specific individual. There is a series of functions to be performed by something which one can think of as the office

4

♦ PAUL H. NITZE, after wartime service in the Office of the Coordinator of Inter-American Affairs, the Board of Economic Warfare, and the Foreign Economic Administration, moved to the Department of State in 1946 and served from 1950 to 1953 as Director of its Policy Planning Staff. He is now President of the Foreign Service Educational Foundation.

of the Secretary of State, even though at times they may be carried, at least in part, by a President who acts as his own Secretary, or by an Under Secretary of State whom the Secretary permits to assume these functions.

In any successful enterprise of importance and complexity one can generally find a focal point of executive, as distinguished from top policy, responsibility. This point is not generally at the summit of authority. In most New England textile companies, it was the treasurer who occupied this focal point of executive responsibility. In many modern corporations, it is the general manager, not the president or the chairman of the board of directors. In most military organizations it is the chief of the staff, not the commanding general.

What I shall concentrate on is the "general manager" function of executive direction of the conduct of our foreign affairs. To my mind, the executive function of the Office of Secretary of State is to see to it that the foreign policy of the United States operates in all its essential parts, that the show stays on the road, that whatever would throw the show off the road is taken care of, surmounted, managed, or avoided. This "general manager" function includes, but is by no means limited to, administration; its primary concern is with the management of substantive policy and its execution.

It is the role, then, of the Office of Secretary of State as general manager in the execution of foreign policy to which this paper will be addressed.

The approach to this subject will be to set a target rather than merely to describe. It will attempt to set forth, not so much what the role of Secretary of State has been, as what I think it should be under the circumstances which seem to be emerging over the horizon.

The Evolution of the Task

Prior to World War I the State Department and the Diplomatic and Consular Services were conceived as having two primary functions. One was to help American citizens and businessmen in their travels and dealings abroad. The other was to act as a channel of information and communication, and as a repository of files, records, memory, and experience for the President and Secretary of State in the conduct of our foreign relations. The Congress expected the combined operation to be self supporting; passport and consular fees should (and did) exceed costs of the Department and the two Services.

That all this has changed in the course of some thirty to forty years is obvious. That it will change further in the years ahead is probable. If we are to have some insight into the nature of the task the Secretary of State is likely to face in the future, it is worthwhile briefly to review some of the significant facts which have brought about the change already taken place. Furthermore, in selecting what is significant it is necessary to start with some view as to what our foreign policy is about.

The fundamental purpose of the United States is laid down in the Constitution. It is:

> . . . to form a more perfect Union, establish Justice, insure domestic Tranquility, provide for the common defence, promote the general Welfare, and secure the Blessings of Liberty to ourselves and our Posterity. . .

The object of our foreign policy derives from this purpose. It is to promote and secure conditions in the world under which a nation, with such purposes as ours, can live and prosper.

We assume that the lesson of the two world wars and of the postwar period is that the United States has become too important a factor in the world to be concerned merely with its narrow national interests in a system the nature of which is to be left largely to the responsibility and will of other nations. In other words, our position is now such that we must bear a major share of responsibility compatible with our development as the nation we are and believe ourselves capable of becoming.

A few words of expansion of this point may be appropriate.

One possible viewpoint in considering the aims of United States foreign policy is to emphasize United States interests, United States security, and the direct threat to that security posed by the hostile power and intentions of the Soviet-Chinese Communist bloc. From this point of view, allies are important to us only because of the contribution they can make to our interests and our security, and the object of our foreign policy is basically defensive. It is to keep the Russians and Chinese Communists and those whom they control from expanding into areas that would threaten our direct interests and our security as a nation.

The alternative is to regard United States interests and security as directly dependent upon the creation of some form of world order compatible with our values and interests. The establishment and maintenance of such a system calls for a protracted and creative effort on the part of the United States—an effort including, but going beyond, mere holding operations against communist encroachment. From this viewpoint, the object of policy is focused more directly on what it is we are trying to construct, and to defend while we are constructing it, rather than merely upon reaction to communist encroachments.

From this second point of view, it is useful to take a brief look at the last preceding historical period during which a considerable degree of world order and stability existed.

The century from 1815 to 1914 was such a period. During those hundred years the balance of power among the European states operated to preserve a large measure of international stability. No single power could realistically aspire to dominate the world. England, with firm control of the seas, acted as a check on the ambitions of any of the land powers. England was not strong enough and did not aspire to dominate the European continent. She acted as a wheel to preserve the balance of power between the European continental land empires. No nation outside Europe had the command of modern technology or an industrial base sufficient to make plausible a general challenge to European leadership. Economic institutions based on the gold standard and centered on the London capital market provided an economic framework within which large portions of the world, including the United States, were able to make tremendous forward strides in developing their economies. The principles of the common law and of political institutions based on the notion of public responsibility began to spread out to the far corners of the world. Above all, wars up to 1914 were kept limited in their geographic extent and in the objectives of the participants.

The two World Wars and the progress and spread of modern technology shattered this system. The balance of power in Europe, and the very empires on which it depended, were destroyed. The power of England was weakened. The significance of sea power was diminished by modern weapons systems of great range and potentially overpowering destructiveness. The primacy of the European powers was cast in doubt. A strong United States and a bitterly hostile Russia came to the fore.

From the second point of view, the fundamental issue in the international arena is not merely that of United States security; it is the question of who will be the builder of a new international order, appropriate to today's world, to take the place of the one that was shattered in the two world wars. Since 1946, we have been trying to resolve that question, whether or not we have always been fully conscious of it, by contesting with the Soviet Union and its allies whether it would be they, or we and our allies, who would succeed in constructing such a new system.

What are the main elements of the structure we have been trying to erect since 1946, and to defend while it was being erected?

This new structure had to have its political, its economic, and its military parts. It had to provide for certain world-wide functions. It had to foster closer regional institutions within the world-wide system. A unique role in this system had continuously to be borne by the United States because we alone had the resources and the will to tackle the job. And it had to be constantly defended against the hostile and destructive efforts of the Soviet-Chinese Communist bloc which was dedicated to the construction of quite another system.

An important part of the structure was its economic sector. This had its world-wide aspects geared into the United Nations structure. The International Monetary Fund provided an institution looking toward greater stability of the world's currencies necessary for the financing of world commerce. The International Bank for Reconstruction and Development was to provide a pool of capital to flow to those areas needing capital and able to make sound use of it. The arrangements under GATT (the General Agreement on Tariffs and Trade) were to move toward the reduction of administrative barriers to international trade. These international institutions were reinforced by regional and bilateral actions such as the Marshall Plan, the Organization for European Economic Cooperation (OEEC), the European Payments Union (EPU), the technical assistance program, and the Colombo Plan. We supported these international, regional, and bilateral approaches through United States economic policies generally consistent with our new role as the world's leading creditor nation and its principal reservoir of capital and of technology.

In the military sphere a similar structure compounded of international, regional, and individual arrangements had to be got underway. The heart of these military arrangements had to be strength at the center, strength in the United States itself. Supplementing strength at the periphery, through the Organization of American States (OAS), the North Atlantic Treaty Organization (NATO), the Southeast Asia Treaty Organization (SEATO), through the mutual defense assistance program, and through our bilateral arrangements with the Republic of Korea, the Chinese Nationalists, and Japan. Many of the noncommunist parts of the world outside the alliance system were given a substantial measure of protection through the strengthening of world acceptance of the principle of restraint against the use of aggressive military force—and our active support of that principle.

These economic and military measures have found their place within a political structure, the broadest aspect of which was the United Nations Organization, but the heart and driving spirit of which has been United States responsibility. A pattern of political relationships emerged, characterized by exceptionally close collaboration between the United States, England, and Canada, spreading out through close, but not as close, relationships with France, Germany, Italy, and Japan, and shading off to cooperation on certain basic matters with uncommitted but free countries such as India and Burma.

The object has been to create a structure sufficiently flexible in its arrangements and sufficiently dynamic to house the diverse interests and requirements of the entire noncommunist world. Even with respect to the communist world it was hoped that the structure would have something to offer and would, by its attractive power, either give room for maneuver and draw off portions of the communist world, as it did in the case of Yugoslavia, or result in a weakening of the bonds within the communist world, as it did in the case of Poland but failed to do in the case of Communist China.

This broad view of the purpose and aims of United States foreign policy, and of the range and scope of the objectives and programs which it implied, did not come into being all at once.

At the end of World War II, the great majority of Americans were awake to the fact that the United States had new responsibilities in the wake of victory in that war. They did not then have in mind a narrow pursuit of national interests or of security. They wished their leaders to lay the foundations of a new order that was compatible with the basic interests of free people everywhere. It was in this spirit that the United States took the initiative in establishing the United Nations, sought to assure the right of free elections and democratic institutions for the peoples of Eastern Europe, sought prompt and generous peace treaties to restore the defeated nations to the world community, and put its influence behind the early emergence of the colonial peoples to self-government. These policies were urged on their merits and not as a mere reaction to what later came to be recognized as the threat of Soviet and communist hostilities and expansionism. In fact, it was originally expected by many, and hoped by nearly all, that the great victors of the war, especially the United States and the Soviet Union, would be able to continue their wartime cooperation into the peace and keep their wartime enemies or any new aggressive powers from disturbing that peace.

The prompt and uncompromising demonstration by the Soviet leaders that they had no intention of continuing such cooperation and were in fact set upon establishing a world order of their own—an order diametrically opposed to any concept of justice and equity understandable to us—did not alter the basic American purpose, but it radically changed the character of the grand strategy by which it now had to be pursued. The cold war arose in a clash between two antagonistic and, so far at least, incompatible views as to how the world was to be shaped. It developed into a struggle in which the survival not only of the United States, but of the free world as well, was at stake.

There was, thereafter, no longer a valid place for the utopian view that all the United States had to do was to suggest organizational and political arrangements designed to be compatible with the basic interests of free peoples everywhere, and then give a shining example of its own disinterestedness by demobilizing its military forces and those economic and political instruments by which its power could be effectively brought to bear as a discriminating tool of policy. It soon became evident that quite another strategy was called for. All the means of influence and power—military forces as well as the economic, ideological, and moral strength not only of ourselves but of all those other nations in the world who saw the problem as we did—had to be mobilized and thrown into the contest. The important place that had to be given to military policy and power came as a shock to many at home and has been exploited abroad to create the false image of a militaristic America.

The necessities of defense against the grave threat of Soviet and communist expansionism forced the United States to modify the character of its relations with the nations of the free world. Persistent and arbitrary Soviet use of the veto destroyed the potential utility of the United Nations Security Council as a body competent effectively to determine violations of the Charter and to command appropriate collective action. The United States had to modify its original hope that it could pursue its security and other political interests within the United Nations framework and restrict its non-U.N. actions to peaceful collaboration with all nations looking toward economic and cultural reconstruction and development. Instead, alliances for collective defense had to be established with allies often chosen, not because their institutions and values corresponded with those of the United States, but because of the contribution they could make to the cause of common defense.

These developments occurred, moreover, at the very time the world was entering the nuclear age. At first, the full impact of this circumstance was obscured by the fact that the United States enjoyed a monopoly of nuclear weapons. It was always recognized that the monopoly would be temporary. It was presumed, however, that the United States possessed a technological edge that could be expected to give it a possibly commanding strategic advantage over the Soviet bloc for an indefinite period.

Serious problems of relating military force to our policy and strategy arose even during the period of our atomic monopoly. As stated earlier, there had been no basic shift in our basic objective of creating and maintaining a compatible structure of world order. Our national strategy had had to be amended concurrently to take account of the reality of Soviet hostility and intransigence. The problem we faced in the realm of military policy and strategy was therefore twofold. On the one hand, we had to have the military forces appropriate to back up with force and authority the principles and standards of international behavior implied by that system of world order that we and the free world, supporting the United Nations Charter, were attempting to work out. On the other hand, we had to have military forces adequate to balance the military power of the Soviet Union and its associates. The first function of military force was somewhat analogous, in the international field, to the police power in the domestic field. Police power to be effective should be unchallengeable, should be coupled with a high degree of community consent determined through accepted procedures, and should be of a kind that restrains the culprit but does not destroy the community. The second function of our military forces, that of balancing Soviet military capabilities, implied a capability of influencing the choices open to those directing the Soviet Union so that Soviet military forces would not be used, or of destroying those forces should deterrence fail.

During the period of our atomic monopoly, it appeared that our conventional forces should be adequate for the first function and that the added weight given by our atomic capability should make our military forces as a whole adequate for the second function. It soon became evident, however, that most of the issues deemed by us to involve a violation of the principles of the UN Charter and therefore to call for collective corrective action would be challenged by the Soviet bloc. The two military strategic problems therefore appeared to coalesce into one problem. If this were so, then the weapons and forces appropriate to the one function should be appropriate to the other. That this is not entirely true has become evident every time we have actually had to face issues involving the use of military force but not involving the actual commitment of full Soviet military capabilities. Atomic weapons, and a fortiori large thermonuclear weapons, have not been deemed to be appropriate in any such situations as have arisen in the past, viz., Korea, Indochina, Suez, and Quemoy.

Obviously the difficulty of finding an appropriate military posture to support the complex objectives of our foreign policy increased after the ending of our atomic monopoly and the rapid further strides made by Soviet military technology.

To many it seemed that the military, financial, and psychological burdens which our foreign policy entailed were excessive. It is hardly astonishing, therefore, that some came to despair of the possibility or desirability of the course on which the country had engaged itself, a course that in their minds would overextend the resources of the United States and could lead to disaster.

One group advocated retrenchment, a policy of Fortress America, by which the United States would disengage itself from commitments to preserve the independence of nations on, or close to, the Eurasian land mass. A second group more or less openly toyed with a leap forward into preventive war which would put an early end to the struggle by removing the instruments of military power from those who opposed us. Most American people have stood against such advice.

Withdrawal to the Western Hemisphere would place the rest of the world at the mercy of the Soviets and turn the United States into an island in a sea of communism. A preventive war would violate the very principles on which the United States is seeking to base a new order and would alienate the very forces in the world whose cooperation is imperative if progress toward such an order is to be accomplished. Both policies would run counter to the idea of responsible leadership as understood in this country.

If the burdens and risks of the main line of our foreign policy appeared excessive and if no escape could be found through withdrawal or preventive war, it was only natural that great attention should be focused upon hope of an accommodation between the noncommunist and communist worlds through negotiation. This view has been strongly supported not only in this country but also among our allies, particularly the British and the Canadians. Adlai Stevenson in discussing negotiation with the Russians has stated the extreme position clearly. He has used the phrase "negotiations that are vital to our survival." A strict interpretation of this view would be that if we fail to agree with the Russians about the fundamental issues of foreign policy, war will become inevitable and our survival impossible. The logical corollary would seem to be that if we can't get them to agree to our point of view, we must then accept theirs if we are to survive. Only the Bertrand Russells and the pacifists fully accept this corollary. The underlying attitude is, however, widespread and has some support in the facts of the situation. At a minimum, it is part of the real world with which the Secretary of State must deal.

With the collapse of the Paris summit meeting, and evidence of a shift in the Soviet line, perhaps to a position somewhat closer to the Chinese Communist emphasis on implacable hostility and revolutionary struggle, the full magnitude of the task facing the Secretary of State becomes evident.

The Tools Available

Charles Burton Marshall, in *The Limits of Foreign Policy*, emphasizes the obvious fact that foreign policy deals with matters outside the jurisdiction of the United States and therefore beyond its control. But the United States does have tools with which it can make its influence felt. The task of the Secretary of State in the execution of foreign policy is to see to the development of those tools and then to their judicious use in the support of policy.

The tools which may be effective with those who share our basic points of view are quite different from the tools that can be effective with those hostile to us or undecided as to how they think.

It may therefore be convenient in discussing the role of the Secretary in the execution of foreign policy to do so under four different headings:

    a. in relation to the Sino-Soviet bloc
    b. in relation to the other members of the Western coalition
    c. in relation to the new nations of Asia and Africa and other uncommitted nations and
    d. in the world forum as a whole, and in the United Nations, where every stripe is represented.

Subsequent sections will attempt such a treatment. In this section some general discussion of the tools of diplomacy and foreign policy as they have evolved in the modern world may be appropriate.

Many students and analysts of foreign affairs have stressed the impact of technology upon communication between peoples. The telegraph; then the radio and television; the world-wide circulation of newspapers, magazines, and trade journals; and the increase in speed, ease, and volume of travel—all have obviously created a world quite different from that which existed even as recently as the nineteenth century. It is probable that most people in the world outside remote rural areas had heard of the U-2 incident within a week of its occurrence. Some analysts have expressed the wish to see relations between nations restricted to a small professional elite, known to each other, and sharing a unique experience and thus a sense of responsibility to certain traditional patterns of diplomacy. This simply is not possible today.

Private diplomacy, though it may preserve to itself a hard core of exclusive responsibility, must compete with mass public reactions to events and the interpretation put on events; these greatly limit its freedom and scope of action. This seems obviously true as to democratically organized states; it is probably also true to a considerable though lesser degree in the "people's democracies."

Other analysts have stressed the impact of modern industrial technology on the economic relations and thus on the political relations among countries. As George Liska has pointed out in *The New Statecraft*, foreign aid, like so many other seemingly revolutionary innovations in international politics, is a mixture of immemorial principle and new scope. The Athenians levied subsidies from their lesser, dependent allies. For the Spartans to acquire new allies was to gain in economic strength. In their subsidies policy the Athenians behaved more like the Soviet land empire, collecting tribute from the satellites, than like the United States. But with the rise of the merchant princes of the Renaissance, the alliance of finance and diplomacy entered the modern age never to leave it again. The economically stronger states often found it useful and effective to subsidize weaker allies. The shortcomings of such a policy also became clear. Machiavelli said that "the friendship which is gained by purchase and not through grandeur and nobility of spirit is bought but not secured. . . ." And as Liska points out, it is not friendship.

From the days of Louis XIV onward there has been a continuing further evolution of the relationship between economics and politics. Examples of almost every conceivable linkage between economic benefits and diplomatic action can be found in the diplomatic history books. The element new to this day and age is that a number of countries have made, and almost all countries aspire to make, the transition from a pre-industrial to an industrial economy. Thus there has been added to the panoply of economic tools not merely new methods of granting subsidies, and of assuring markets, credit, and means of exchange and sources of supply, but a third element—that of assisting in a complete transformation of pre-existing methods of production. This last factor has immensely more important repercussions on the internal politics of the country involved than would more traditional forms of economic assistance. The impact on the external political relations of the country is also likely to be deep and basic.

Other analysts have stressed the revolutionary impact of military technology on the tools available to support diplomacy. Until World War I, it was universally accepted that the ultimate sanction in international politics was war, that wars of lesser or greater violence were bound to follow each other with considerable frequency, and that to secure alignments favorable to one's country's interests in these wars was the very heart of serious diplomacy. Under such circumstances it was clear that the greatest benefit states could confer on one another was a commitment to side together in the event of war.

The advent of long-range strategic weapons has had two major effects.

First is that whereas in the past military forces interposed themselves between the civilian populations and it was only in the event of defeat of the military forces of one side that its population was subjected to direct physical violence or coercion, now civilian populations could be included in the initial attack. *Second* is that nuclear weapons have so multiplied the potential for violence that even the defeated side may, before defeat, wreak destruction incommensurate with any political gains the eventual winner may hope to gain from victory. That this possibility is by no means certain has been made clear by Wohlstetter in his article, "The Delicate Balance of Terror," and by others. Nevertheless, the very enormity of violence implied by nuclear war has had the effect of liberating other tools of diplomacy and foreign policy from their former subservience to the military tool.

Today it would appear that the most important tool of foreign policy is prestige. Prestige is a complex concept. It has a number of elements. Like the economic tool, it is a mixture of immemorial principle and new scope. One component of a nation's prestige is the belief of others that the nation has the will and the capability to bring about whatever it indicates as its serious intentions. From this standpoint the brutal Soviet suppression of the Hungarian uprising contributed to the growth of Soviet prestige. The failure of the British and French to press their intervention in Suez with speed and effectiveness was a blow to England and France in this component of prestige.

A second component of prestige is the respect and agreement which the other nations and peoples hold for what they understand to underly a nation's policy. In this component of prestige, the United States has had, and in my opinion still has, a decided edge over the Soviet Union. The fact that we have had no territorial ambitions, that we do not seek world hegemony, that we have been understanding of diverse viewpoints, that we have been on the side of self-determination by important national groups, that we have attempted actively to assist others in making the transition to the modern technological, economic, and political world have all contributed to the strength of this component of prestige. Whether our assets here can long outweigh a growing debit in the other component is doubtful.

With respect to both of these components of prestige, the precision with which we indicate our serious purposes and intentions is important. If we give the impression that we intend to support the liberation of the satellites and then do not do so, our prestige suffers. If on one day we say that U-2 flights are vital to our security, and a week later cancel them, we damage our prestige.

The same principle applies to many of the terms which today provide the framework within which peoples judge our purposes. If we permit "peace" and "peaceful coexistence" to become associated in people's minds with a cessation or mitigation of resistance to Soviet intentions and do not ourselves intend any such one-sided abandonment of the struggle, we do ourselves a disservice. If we permit "relaxation of tensions" and "ending of the cold war" to be understood as good things to be obtained, by a modification not of Soviet purposes, but largely of ours, we put ourselves in a box the moment it is found that Soviet purposes have not changed and that we must continue to oppose them and thus continue tensions and the cold war or else give up the struggle.

The point about prestige is that it provides a multiplier to all other elements of national power. If people respect and agree with our purposes, they will wish to do what we wish to do; they will add their strength to ours. If they believe we will be able to do, and will in fact do, what we indicate our intention of doing, they will accommodate themselves to our intention (even if they disagree with it) without forcing us in most instances to prove our point by doing it. Obviously the same holds for Soviet prestige.

This brings us to a consideration of the tool of negotiation. The ancient principles of negotiation still seem to apply, although sometimes apparently forgotten.

It still is true that negotiations between two or more parties having a large measure of common interests, in relationship to which the matter under negotiation is of minor significance, generally place greater value upon agreement than upon victory for their particular viewpoint. Our negotiations with the British, French, and Germans may not have produced dramatic or startling results, but they have produced agreement.

It also seems still to be true that in negotiations between hostile powers, the stronger power may seek victory for its side and be unwilling to agree unless he secures advantages commensurate with what he considers the strength of his position. Success is more important to him than agreement. In such negotiation among hostile powers, the limits of the negotiating possibilities are set by the alternatives available to the two sides in the event of non-agreement.

In today's world of mass communication and mass opinion the public-opinion effect of negotiations may be more important to the participants than the agreements arrived at. The Soviet Communists have always made a clear distinction in their theoretical papers between negotiations primarily for support of their propaganda positions and negotiations entered into to produce agreement. Generally they try to exploit all the possibilities of the first type before they get down to wringing the last possible drop out of the second.

Many on the Western side believe that there is virtue in negotiation as such, that to continue to talk is in some way to avoid action other than talk. Certainly keeping the lines of communication open with the adversary is important; and negotiation is one way of so doing. Furthermore, it is important that we always have a clear view of our negotiating position versus our adversaries on every important point at issue between us. But the proposition suggested by some, that the tool of negotiation provides an escape from the necessity of developing the other tools that support policy, seems dubious in the extreme.

Managing the Contest with the Soviet Union

Having briefly surveyed the evolution of the Secretary's task and of the tools with which he must deal, we can examine some of the parts of his problem in greater detail. No portion of the Secretary's task can be wholly isolated from the other portions. For convenience, however, it is useful to take one focus and then another. In this section we shall focus on the Secretary's role in managing the free world's contest with the Soviet Union, its bloc, and its apparatus.

A pre-condition to the intelligent management of our side is knowledge and understanding of what is going on on the other side. We should know what assets and liabilities the other side has and is likely to have at given times in the future; and we should have a judgment as to the probable strategy and tactics of the other side and as to their probable reaction to moves that we on our side may plan. Obviously the Office of the Secretary cannot do all this itself. But if the show is to stay on the road, the Office of the Secretary must see to it that this job gets done and that the Secretary himself and the President have available and understand the results of the work done. A major portion of the effort of our diplomatic missions and of the departmental service is devoted to political reporting and to analysis of reports received.

The scope and magnitude of CIA (Central Intelligence Agency) activities are decided directly by the President in his capacity as Chairman of the National Security Council (NSC). But when a conflict arises between the conduct of our foreign policy and what appears to be desirable from the standpoint of gathering information, the President must rely heavily on the judgment of the Secretary of State. The Office of the Secretary must, therefore, be concerned with the manner in which such information is obtained.

Another pre-condition to the intelligent management of our side of the contest is a judgment of the evolving politico-military relationships between the two blocs. Here again, the Secretary and his Office cannot, and should not, attempt to do the job single-handed; but they must see to it that the job gets done and that the Secretary and the President know and understand the results. It should be pointed out that the CIA is restricted to gathering and analyzing intelligence about others. It is not its job to strike a balance between our capabilities and those of any potential enemy. Furthermore, it is the job of the military services to concentrate on military relationships and not on politico-military relationships. And it is the politico-military relationships which are crucial, particularly during a period of peace, or rather of cold war. A continuing appraisal of these politico-military relationships is therefore a function of the Secretary's Office.

A third pre-condition to the intelligent management of the conflict with the USSR is a decision as to the broad outlines of our own purposes, our strategy, our preferred tactics, and the terms in which we propose to make the overt portions of that strategy and tactics understandable to our own people, our allies, and those hostile to us. That this pre-condition is fulfilled is assumed to be a responsibility of the President and his principal advisors in the NSC. But the Office of the Secretary of State cannot sit idly by if it is not fulfilled; in fact the Secretary should always be the President's principal advisor in this field.

But if we assume that these three pre-conditions have been met, what is it that the Secretary can do in the way of action directly related to the Soviet Union to modify Soviet behavior? The military tool he can use, at least as a threat. This was one of the principal tools in Mr. Dulles' kit bag. Some of the present day limitations of this tool were discussed in the preceding section. Furthermore, that tool loses its efficacy unless we build and maintain a truly superior military instrument. Today it is Mr. Khrushchev, not Mr. Herter, who is making the military threats. Nevertheless, the intelligent management of the political aspects of the free world's military confrontation with the Soviet bloc is one of the principal tools with which the Secretary can hope to influence Soviet actions.

Direct action vis-a-vis the Soviet Union in the economic field is possible but does not promise substantial results. The Russians have made their ideas on a trade deal clear. They would want a substantially one-sided arrangement under which they could have access to all our latest industrial technology, receive substantial credits, and repay us eventually with raw materials or cheap consumer goods. It is difficult to conceive of negotiable economic inducements to the Russians which would not be so one-sided as to be humiliating to us and thus to decrease our prestige rather than to increase it. The opposite possibility, that of bringing direct economic pressure against the Soviet Union, also offers little room for maneuver. The potential of the Soviet system for autarky is so great that there are few points of external vulnerability. But the problem of relating the economics of the free world to the growing impact of Soviet bloc trade cannot be ignored. Some bridge to, or protection against, Soviet bloc trade should be worked out; otherwise effects seriously disruptive to the free world economics are likely to develop.

Somewhat more hopful is the prospect that we can influence the minds of the Russian people by going over the heads of the Soviet government through overt information and exchange programs. The Secretary, as he has been doing, can foster the exchange of cultural missions, of teachers, of scientists, of students, travellers, and others. If, however, Mr. Joseph Novack's reports of conversations with Russians in *The Future Is Ours, Comrade* are even approximately representative, the prospects are not good that early results of strategic significance can be expected from such exchanges.

If one accepts the analysis in the preceding section, it is unlikely that specific agreements can be expected from negotiations with the Soviet Union which do not fully reflect what the Soviets desire and think themselves entitled to on the basis of what they deem to be a presently favorable correlation of forces. Nevertheless, the conduct of direct negotiations with the Soviet Union is one of the principal concerns of the Secretary and his Office.

In sum, it would appear that the principal forums in which the contest between Soviet purposes and our own is to be fought are the forum of the Western alliance, and the forum of the new states of Asia, of Africa and of the politically uncommitted groups in Latin America. It is always possible that the situation may again become more symmetrical through the development of troubles in or with the European satellites or between the Soviet Union and Communist China. The ideological debate between the Chinese Communists and Moscow now seems to have grown in intensity. Great subtlety of policy is required, however, if the Secretary is to foster the growth of such divisions rather than push the communist bloc closer together again.

The fact that the contest with the Soviet Union does not appear to be soluble through direct action upon, or negotiation with, the Soviet Union and its bloc does not at all diminish the care and skill with which these operations must be conducted. If they are imprudently or unskillfully conducted, they greatly impair our prestige in other parts of the world and even with our enemies, where it is almost as important to maintain our prestige as it is with those who wish us well. The prudent and imaginative conduct of these direct relationships is a pre-condition to the hopeful and successful conduct of other aspects of our policy.

Management of the Coalition

If our analysis of the evolution of the Secretary's task is accepted, it is hardly necessary to argue the importance to us and our policy of the Western coalition. It is enough to point out that, if alone, we would be in a position of inferiority to the Sino-Soviet bloc in most indices of power. With the other NATO powers we exceed them in most of the significant indices other than raw manpower; in the manpower index the West is inferior only because of the inclusion of the vast Chinese population, much of which cannot be effectively brought to bear on matters external to China.

A principal task of the Secretary of the State in the execution of policy is then the management of the Western coalition. What are the major elements of that task?

The first and most important, if our leadership is to be accepted, is to assure that our policy is responsive not merely to the narrow interests of the United States but also to the needs and interests of the coalition as a whole. We cannot force our leadership or buy the adherence of other members. If the coalition is to maintain its effectiveness, the policies pursued in its behalf must be designed to promote the interests of the whole coalition. The task of the Secretary of State in this regard is two-fold. On the one hand he must carry this point of view in the debates within the policy-making organs at home, which is the subject of other papers in this volume. On the other hand he must make sure that the responsible leaders of other member governments of the alliance know this to be the spirt in which we approach the problem. Furthermore the policies followed must be explicable in these terms to the majority of the people in the member nations.

A closely related element is to assure that the other members of the coalition have confidence that we know what we are doing in the contest with the Soviet Union. It is not necessary that we always be successful; sometimes an unexpected check will rally the alliance. But persistent incompetence, persistent failure to explain to our allies what we are about, persistent imprecision in indicating our policy or our intentions can seriously undermine the alliance. The revelation of truly significant failure correctly to gauge the situation, or of imprudence or cowardice in action, could shatter it.

It was Mr. Dulles' view that only he could handle the job of holding the alliance together by making sure that (a) each member of the alliance was confident we would use our military strength in defense of the alliance when necessary, and (b) we would be prudent in so handling it as not to let matters get out of hand and bring on an unintended war. In his estimation these tasks could not be delegated; confidence in his personal will and prudence was essential, and only he could instill that confidence.

As brinkmanship has come to play a lesser role in our policy, this aspect of the management of the coalition can to a greater extent be carried by the Secretary in collaboration with his ambassadors and the departmental staff. The task, however, becomes more complex and requires continuous consultation and collaboration.

A further element involves the differential in the closeness of our collaboration with the various members of the coalition and the direction in which we throw our weight in influencing the relations among them. In the immediate postwar years it was possible to maintain a uniquely close relationship with the United Kingdom and bring in the French, Canadians, Germans, and others primarily on matters of direct and immediate concern to them. With the recovery of Germany and now with the drive of Mr. de Gaulle for tripartite direction of the coalition, the problem has become more complex. Closely related to this problem is that of our attitude toward the relation of the Six[1] and the Seven.[2]

Two other areas with which the members of the Western coalition are much concerned are their economic relationships with each other, and their relations with the new states of Asia and Africa. As a result of the success of our postwar economic assistance programs, none of the industrialized countries of the free world now has economic problems beyond those which should be within its own competence and power to surmount. Nevertheless economic matters come close to home and the Secretary must be sure that these do not get out of hand. In large measure they can, however, be delegated to the Under Secretary.

Relations with the new states or emerging states of Asia and Africa is a much more ticklish problem. Those of our allies who once governed some of these states as colonies naturally feel a particular interest in them, similar to that which we feel for the Philippines, and are concerned lest we handle them incompetently or selfishly to promote largely United States interests. Luckily most of the former colonial relationships which plagued our dealings with England, France, and Belgium for so long have been or are now being liquidated. As a result the main task facing the Secretary in this connection is to see to it that we handle ourselves competently with respect to the new and uncommitted nations. That is the subject of the next section.

---

[1] The European Economic Community (France, West Germany, Italy, Belgium, The Netherlands, Luxembourg).

[2] The European Free Trade Association (Great Britain, Denmark, Norway, Sweden, Austria, Switzerland, Portugal).

Relations with the New States

Though the core of basic power necessary to balance the Sino-Soviet bloc must be found in the Western alliance, primarily in NATO, the arena which offers the greatest challenge to policy is that of the newly emerging or uncommitted states. It is there that the situation is most fluid, that a more diverse set of tools is available both to the Sino-Soviet leaders and to our own, and that the effect of growing or declining United States prestige is apt to show up most clearly in results favorable or hurtful to our cause. It is here that the executive, general manager functions of the Office of Secretary of State are in greatest need of development.

The most notable circumstance about the new and emerging nations is that many of them are hardly nations in the full sense of the term. They are of recent origin. Their boundaries may have been arbitrarily drawn. Nationality, in the sense that loyalties to the nation are stronger than those to clan, family, sect, or political party, is an objective and not a fact. A civil service or other government apparatus having a sense of public responsibility is often non-existent or rudimentary. Even a police force able to insure public order and control conspiracies subversive of or treasonable to the state is often lacking. Under the circumstances power is apt to gravitate to the army, the only institution having both force and discipline.

In such situations the primary need is for political leadership which can bring the force and discipline of the army under the control of state policy and insure a degree of public order. For such leadership to survive and strengthen its position to a point where more representative political organs can have some prospect of functioning, leadership must also achieve a substantial measure of mass support.

Soviet strategy in recent years has concentrated upon the elimination of both European and United States influence from these areas. To achieve this objective it has called for the use of all the tools of policy—propaganda, economic and technical assistance without overt strings, and diplomacy. It has sought the support of all nationalist forces. It has soft-pedalled its former emphasis upon the development of communist cadres aiming at the eventual seizure of power. In its propaganda it has emphasized the themes of nationalism, peaceful coexistence, lack of racial discrimination, and rapid industrialization and social progress.

Most of the leadership groups in these new nations would like to remain independent of either Western or Sino-Soviet control while accepting benefits from both sides. Even though it has become obvious to most of them that the danger today is greater from the Sino-Soviet side than from the Western side, the growth of anti-Western sentiment at the mass level in many instances limits the resistance they feel it expedient to put up to Soviet penetration.

Under the circumstances United States policy is called upon to act vigorously on a number of fronts. If our economic and technical assistance programs are allowed to become halting and ineffective, we leave that field uncontested to the communists, as has happened in Guinea. If we concentrate solely upon economic growth, we leave untouched the field of political development which is a pre-condition, in most of these countries, to economic growth. If we ignore the ideological and propaganda fronts we permit the growth of a climate of popular opinion in which forceful and active policies become impossible for any but communist-oriented leaders. Furthermore, a number of these countries are on the periphery of the mainland of China and are threatened by direct military pressure.

The complexity of the problems makes it difficult, if not impossible, for the Secretary of State to have expert judgment on all of them. It is part of his general manager function, however, to see to it that none of them is uncovered and that timely steps are taken to recruit, train, and organize the talents and mobilize the resources required to cope with them.

From time to time, situations in this arena are bound to arise as key and crucial problems, as Korea, Iran, Vietnam, Quemoy, Suez, and Cuba have in the past. At such times it is the function of the Secretary to take direct command of our side of the operation. No one else is in a position to pull together the pertinent aspects of Presidential and Congressional policy, those of defense and economic policy, together with the interests of our Western allies, and the effects of the crisis upon our continuing conflict with the USSR.

The United Nations and the Problem of World Order

The problem of the United Nations presents itself to the Secretary of State and his Office under several related aspects. On the one hand, the Security Council and the General Assembly provide forums in which certain aspects of those problems discussed in previous sections—the conflict with the Soviet bloc, the management of the coalition, and the relations with the new states—can, or have to, be dealt with. Secondly, the United Nations Organization itself, primarily the Secretary General of the United Nations and his staff, has a measure of influence and power in its own right which the Secretary of State can encourage or check but must at least deal with. In the third place, the specialized agencies present forums for debate and discussion in their particular fields, as well as instruments of action.

These aspects of the United Nations share certain common qualities. The member nations have all taken a formal commitment to uphold the principles stated in the Charter. Even the Soviet delegates and their representatives have never overtly challenged those agreed basic principles, much as they may have twisted and perverted their interpretation and application. The atmosphere of the United Nations is therefore a special atmosphere. There is a presumption that the general interests of mankind as a whole should have priority, in particular circumstances, over the interests of individual nations or groups of nations. Obviously every nation, or group of nations with common interests, attempts to identify its interests with those of mankind and its proposed course of action with the principles of the Charter. This combination of overt commitment to the general interest and necessary concern with political conflict reflects itself in the prevailing United Nations atmosphere, an atmosphere compounded of idealistic phrase-making, of a tendency toward minimal action, but also of latent real power.

Most of the formal debate and discussion in the principal United Nations organs is not only public, but highly public before masses of radio pickups and under klieg lights. The debate and discussion tend, therefore, to be directed to the molding of world public opinion rather than toward agreement on specific action on specific problems. Nevertheless if the Office of the Secretary does not exercise the greatest care and foresight, positions will evolve hampering our future freedom of action. The fact that the General Assembly set disarmament, not the control and regulation of armaments, as the objective of the Disarmament Commission seriously hampered our negotiators at Geneva in their endeavor to get away from the sterile debate over ultimate objectives and on to a discussion of practical measures designed to mitigate and contain the dangers and risk of the present unstable and dangerous weapons confrontation.

The significance of the UN Organization as a power in its own right has increased. At the time of the attack into South Korea the UN observer teams gave credence to the fact of North Korean aggression. The conduct of the combat operations, however, was under effective United States command, even though as agent for the United Nations. In the Suez crisis the UN police force effectively sealed off the area of potential conflict; the situation, however, had developed to a point where both the Western powers and the Soviet Union saw no interest to themselves in a continuation of hostilities; as a result nothing could be gained either by Nasser or the Israelis in challenging the UN force.

In the tension in Laos the presence of a UN agent had a calming effect. At this writing it appears that forces under direct UN command will be called upon to maintain order in the Congo against native troops, and in spite of conflicting interests of the great powers. It remains to be seen whether the prestige of the UN is sufficient to carry such a direct intervention in an important power struggle.

In any case the Secretary of State must concern himself with the desirability or undesirability of an increase in the autonomous power and prestige of the UN. Such increased UN power may limit the freedom of action of the United States and its allies more than it effectively limits the freedom of action of the USSR. On the other hand, with the decline in American nuclear superiority and a continuing inferiority in conventionally armed forces in most of the areas subject to potential conflict, it may well be to the interest of the United States to promote the maximum restraining effect of which the UN is capable.

Furthermore the tasks of United States policy outlined in the first section, that of fostering a world compatible with United States purposes, a world of tolerable order, probably can be achieved only through a combination of developments. We may require not only a strengthening and growing cohesion of the noncommunist world and a gradual modification of Soviet political strategy and tactics, but also a growth in the power and prestige of principles and organs of action most appropriately associated with the UN.

We have already seen a considerable growth in the activity and prestige of the affiliated agencies such as the International Bank for Reconstruction and Development and the International Monetary Fund. It appears probable that their activity and importance will further increase and that additional affiliated agencies will gain maturity and stature. During the immediate postwar years it was only the United States itself which had the resources, will, and trained personnel to do most of the things which needed doing on behalf of the general community. It is to be expected that today, with postwar recovery behind us, others should prefer that an organization in which they participate as equals, in theory if not in practice, take over much of the load from us.

As this process proceeds and particularly if it spreads to important instances of maintaining order and containing aggression, the problems of the Secretary of State may become more complex rather than less so. Some of the tools which gave him influence in the political conflict when exercised under his direct control will have become neutralized or apolitical when in the hands of the United Nations. The realities of the developing situation may nevertheless cause him to wish to drive hard in this direction, other courses of action offering less prospects of success for our most basic aims.

Conclusion

At the outset, the general manager function of the Secretary of State in execution of foreign policy was stressed. Having surveyed the evolution of the task and of the tools available, and having briefly examined his role in managing the contest with the Soviet Union, in managing the coalition, in developing relations with the new states, and in dealing with the United Nations, it is evident that overriding these separate functions is the requirement to give cohesion and style to our foreign policy as a whole.

Much of what the Secretary of State does in any one context is immediately known to those interested in other contexts; in time almost everything he does becomes known to the world as a whole. It is not possible for the Secretary to take one position in his speeches before the General Assembly and another in his diplomatic talks without undermining the credibility of both positions. Cohesion and style can be imparted in part by the speeches and press conferences of the President and of the Secretary of State; in larger measure they are reflected in the logical relationship between the decisions and actions taken.

Thus the Secretary must not only manage, he must also conduct. And in the last analysis the success of the production as a whole depends on the star individual performers, the President and his Secretary of State.

These pre-conditions of a successful performance include, however, a smooth working relationship between the President and his Secretary of State, understanding and support on the part of the public and the Congress, effective coordination of policy between the departments and agencies of the Executive Branch, and appropriate organization of the State Department and the Foreign Service. These subjects are dealt with in the other chapters of this volume.

2.

The President and the
Secretary of State

The Selection of a Secretary

♦ DEAN ACHESON

On January 17, 1889, President-elect Benjamin Harrison wrote two letters to Mr. James G. Blaine. The first was short—only two sentences—and presented no difficulty. It offered Mr. Blaine "the position of Secretary of State," and asked for his early and favorable reply. The second letter was much more difficult, and between the first draft and the final letter lay revealing revision.

In the second letter, the President-elect wanted to say "some further and more familiar things." [1] His instinct was right. Mr. Blaine was a distinguished and potent man— on the record to that date, more distinguished

---

[1] This and subsequent quotations from President Harrison, and relating to this correspondence, are taken from *Correspondence Between Harrison and Blaine* (ed. Volwiler), The American Philosophical Society, Philadelphia, 1940.

27

♦ DEAN ACHESON served as Secretary of State from 1949 to 1953. He had previously been an Assistant Secretary and Under Secretary of State, and Under Secretary of the Treasury. He is a member of the law firm of Covington and Burling, Washington, D. C.

and potent than General Harrison. As one Blaine man put it in the very week these letters were written, "Blaine has been the leader of the party for years. H. is a mushroom." Blaine had been Speaker of the House of Representatives, Senator, Republican Presidential nominee, and for a few months under President Garfield, Secretary of State. More than anyone else, he was responsible for the nomination of Harrison. In short, Blaine was a power in the Party, perhaps *the* power, and his reputation in politics was not that of an idealist.

Harrison wanted to make three points: that Blaine should not expect the President to fill diplomatic posts with party hacks (Garfield's death and Arthur's administration were fresh memories); that certain outstanding questions with European countries—the Samoan controversy was one —should be solved and not exacerbated; and that Blaine should discipline his imperious nature in the interest of party harmony. This was no easy assignment as the revisions show. Particularly interesting in the second paragraph is the Presidential pen striking out the self-deprecating phrases of the Indiana lawyer—"the Indiana accident," as Mrs. Blaine called him.

Your familiarity with the origin and progress of these differences [with the European countries], &~~will enable~~ indeed with
would
the whole history of our diplomacy ~~will~~ I am sure give you great advantage in dealing with them ~~& will compensate for~~
foreign
~~my lack of study & experience in Diplomatic affairs. I am a~~
~~conservative by nature, and all the more a lover of peace from~~
feel sure
~~having seen a little of war. But~~ If ~~in my strong & deliberate~~
~~conviction that you can as Secretary of State make a very large~~
~~be very conspicuously useful to the country. As to~~ I am strongly
general
~~impressed with the thought that~~ I have another‸purpose and duty in which I am sure you will cooperate with the greatest

28

cordiality. It is to preserve ~~the~~ harmony ~~of~~ in our party. ~~The conspicuous fidelity Nothing~~ The continuance of Republican control for a series of Presidential terms is I think essential to the right settlement of some very grave questions. I shall be
         promote dissentions
very solicitous to avoid anything that would ~~divide or disrupt.~~
~~You have not allowed any provocation to~~ and very desirous
  civil service   placed & conducted
that the ~~public business~~ shall be ~~so conducted as to establish~~
           recommend
    upon that high plane   which will ∧ the
our party to the confidence of all ~~our~~ people. ~~You have never allowed any provocation to lessen your zeal & effort as a Republican and I am sure your wide acquaintance with our public men will enable you to give me valuable suggestion and very efficient aid in preserving that happy unity which in the recent election brought us success I know you will~~ This purpose is absolutely disassociated with any selfish thought or ~~purpose~~ am-
         proper
bition, ~~and~~ I will be quite as ready to make ∧ concessions as to ask others to do so. ~~I shall give to~~ Each member of my official
  will have   I
family ∧ my full confidence and ∧ shall expect his in return.
~~Mistrust~~. . .

There is no reason to doubt that the offer and the acceptance were both activated, as General Harrison wrote that they should be, by "a spirit of the most perfect cordiality and confidence." Perhaps "perfect" is too strong a word, for there had been a past of which both men were aware. In Mr. Blaine's best seller, *Twenty Years of Congress*, he had written at some length of the relations between another President and another Secretary of State, President Polk and Secretary Buchanan. Among his observations were these:

> Mr. Buchanan was an older man than Mr. Polk, was superior to him intellectually, had seen a longer and more varied public service, and enjoyed a higher personal standing throughout the country.

And again,

> The timidity of Mr. Buchanan's nature made him the servant of the administration when, with boldness, he might have been its master. . . .

> Mr. Buchanan, therefore, held absolute control of the situation had he chosen to assert himself.

If these passages give us some insight into Mr. Blaine's approach to the new relationship, President Harrison has thrown an even clearer light upon his own. After leaving the White House, he wrote in 1893 a private memorandum of his relations with Blaine. Two portions of it are relevant here.

> Mr. Blaine['s] relation to the Convention of 1888 was a singular one. He felt I do not doubt even then such fears as to his health, and such misgivings as to his ability to endure a campaign that at times he spoke strongly and sincerely in declination of the honor which his many friends were urging him to again accept. But that at other times he hoped his declination would not be taken too strictly and toyed with the old ambition is more than probable—especially in view of his course in 1892. . . .
>
> My letter offering the portfolio of State to Mr. Blaine and his answer accepting the offer show the terms upon which our official relations were opened. My purpose was to keep them upon the basis of perfect confidence and friendship—or failing in that to make it plainly appear that the fault was not mine.

Harrison's reference to "his course in 1892" was to the crashing denouement of their relation. The inauguration was hardly over when Blaine asked that his son and close confidant, Walker, be made First Assistant Secretary of State. The President understandably refused. "All first propositions are rejected," wrote Mrs. Blaine. "It is a most uncomfortable twist in the make-up of a man."

Relations between the two became increasingly formal. Blaine's bereavements and stroke in 1891 led to the transfer of his duties to the White House. Irritations grew. On June 4, 1892, when a divided Republican convention was considering the renomination of the President, Mr. Blaine sent to the White House a curt note of resignation. Within the hour the President as curtly accepted it. "Well," he said, "the crisis has come."

Twice in our lifetime Presidents have chosen to be Secretary of State men who believed that the higher office should have been theirs. As Mr. Truman has told us in his *Memoirs:*[1]

> With this [his] impressive record, I felt that Byrnes could make a further major contribution if he were to be appointed Secretary of State. But this was not all. There was still another consideration, though it was mostly personal.
>
> Byrnes had felt that by virtue of his record of service to the party and the country he had been the logical choice to be the

---

[1] Quoted by permission. MEMOIRS BY HARRY S. TRUMAN, Harry S. Truman. Time Inc. Copyright 1955.

running mate of Franklin Roosevelt in the 1944 election. In fact, he had asked me to nominate him and give him my support before that convention.

As it turned out, Roosevelt and the convention willed otherwise, and Byrnes, undoubtedly, was deeply disappointed and hurt. I thought that my calling on him at this time might help balance things up.

Here, as in the case of Wilson and Bryan thirty years before, the relationship did not work. In a still earlier instance—with the same factors involved—it did work; but only because the President was our most magnanimous and patient one, and because the Secretary of State had the good fortune and ability to see the light in time. This was the relation between President Lincoln and Secretary Seward.

Lincoln's unexpected victory in the Republican Convention of 1860 was Seward's unexpected loss. Seward was the pre-eminent Republican Senator, and Lincoln, in his estimate, an upstart. The general view, as Rhode's *History* of the 1850-1877 period put it, was that the nomination was a case of "the sacrifice of commanding ability in favor of respectable mediocrity." Seward was the Republican spokesman in Congress during the short session intervening between the election and the inauguration. He became deeply involved in the frantic interim efforts to stave off collapse of the Union. "Once for all," he wrote Mrs. Seward, "I must gain time for the new Administration to organize and for the frenzy of passion to subside." And again: "The revolution grows apace. . . . I have assumed a sort of dictatorship for defense."

And yet later: "It seems to me that if I am absent but three days, this Administration, the Congress, and the District fall into consternation and despair. I am the only hopeful, calm, conciliatory person here." And then "Mad men North and mad men South are working together to produce a dissolution of the Union. The present Administration and the incoming one unite in devolving upon me the responsibility of averting these disasters."

And then after the counting of the electoral vote on February 13, 1861: "We have passed the 13th safely. I am at last out of direct responsibility. I have brought the ship off the sands and am ready to resign the helm into the hands of the captain the people have chosen."

Seward was not ready for anything of the sort. He confided to his New York colleague in the Senate that Lincoln actually wanted him for a Prime Minister, and to a European envoy, that "there is no difference between an elected president of the United States and an hereditary monarch. The latter is called to the throne through the accident of birth, the former through the chances which make his election possible. The actual direction of public affairs belongs to the leader of the ruling

party. . . ." He even tried tentatively to force his own will in the matter
of Cabinet appointments. "The President," he wrote his wife, "is determined that he will have a compound Cabinet. . . . I was at one time on
the point of refusing—nay, I did refuse, to hazard myself in the experi-
ment. But a distracted country appeared before me and I withdrew from
the position. . . . At all events I did not dare to . . . leave the country
to chance."

Seward did his best to prevail. He was one of the Cabinet minority of
two in favor of withdrawing from Fort Sumter when the President in-
sistently polled his advisers anew after a majority had at first favored
capitulation. He turned desperately to the hope of finding in his own
specific field of responsibility—foreign relations—a basis for saving the
Union: the precipitation of external conflict to reunify the riven nation.
This would be coupled with an idea he had been advocating ever since
the December of the interregnum—a complete concession to the South
on slavery.

What led to the climax was Seward's resolve to draw the issue with
a set of policy recommendations entitled "Thoughts for the President's
Consideration." These he took personally to the President. Dr. Temple
tells the story:

> Seward's criticism of the President's delay was severe. He
> had said: "We are at the end of a month's administration and
> yet without a policy, domestic or foreign;" further delay would
> "bring scandal on the administration and danger upon the
> country." But it was his final proposal that was most astound-
> ing. He said: "Whatever policy we adopt, there must be
> energetic prosecution of it . . . it must be somebody's busi-
> ness to pursue it and direct it incessantly. Either the President
> must do it, and be all the while active at it, or devolve it on
> some member of his Cabinet. Once adopted, debates on it
> must end, and all agree and abide. It is not in my special
> province: but I neither seek to evade nor to assume respon-
> sibility."
>
> Seward's offer to assume control was not limited to the for-
> eign policy, but applied, as he said, to matters not in his special
> province. His demand that debates must end when a policy
> was once decided upon was a reference to Lincoln's second
> request for opinions on Fort Sumter after five out of seven
> members of the Cabinet had once given their judgment that
> the fort should be evacuated. The proposal was a very blunt
> expression of Seward's belief, which, it must be admitted,
> was that of many public men of the day, that he and not Lin-
> coln was to be the real head of the Administration. Lincoln's
> reply was in few words of unmistakable meaning: "Upon your

closing proposition . . . I remark that if this must be done, I must do it. When a general line of policy is adopted I apprehend there is no danger of its being changed without good reason, or continuing to be a subject of unnecessary debate; still, upon points arising in its progress I wish, and I suppose I am entitled to have, the advice of all the Cabinet." [1]

That was the end of Seward as putative Prime Minister—the end of the most ambitious scheme yet put forward for establishing a coadjutor for the President. Two months later Seward wrote his wife: "Executive skill and vigor are rare qualities. The President is the best of us; but he needs assiduous co-operation. But I have said too much already. Burn this, and believe that I am doing what man can do." [2]

Now for once he was right. This is what he was doing. He was settling down to the complex tasks of running the foreign office as the President's agent—and beginning that estimable record of public service which earned him distinction and gratitude enough to fill any life.

These experiences are worth pondering. If, as Justice Holmes has said, in the life of the law a page of history is worth a volume of logic, it seems likely that in what is called political science these pages of history may be worth as many volumes of theory. At least it gives us a fairly solid point from which to start our discussion of the desirable relations between the President and his senior Secretary.

That point might be put this way: it is highly desirable that from first to last both parties to the relationship understand which is the President. Without this mutual understanding a successful relationship is most unlikely.

This does not mean subserviency on the part of the Secretary. In a much more hazardous age Lord Burghley saw and did his duty of standing squarely up to the great Queen when her interests and those of the realm required it. Much else, as we shall see, should rest upon this cornerstone of the relationship, the recognition of primacy. It is enough here to mention two mutual obligations. One, of course, is the Secretary's duty to see that the President is kept fully and timely informed so that he may perform his constitutional duty of conducting the nation's foreign relations with all the freedom of decision which each situation permits. The correlative obligation is that the President should perform his function of decision so clearly, and support his decisions so strongly, that action may flow from them.

---

[1] The various quotations above relating to the Seward episode are from Henry W. Temple's "William H. Seward," in *The American Secretaries of State,* edited by Bemis.

[2] Conrad, *The Governor and His Lady* (G. P. Putnam's Sons, New York, 1960), p. 357.

The other obligation, only a bit less important to the success of the relationship than recognizing who is President, though less often achieved, is recognizing who is Secretary of State. A President may, and will, listen to whom he wishes. But his relationship with the Secretary of State will not prosper if the latter is not accepted as his principal adviser and executive agent in foreign affairs, and the trusted confidant of all his thoughts and plans relating to them. We can all recall times when this has not been true. Such times have always called for makeshift arrangements, the cost of which has often been considerable.

So far one can be dogmatic with some confidence. But not much further. The relationship is essentially one of partnership; and here, of course, personalities, experience and training, political exigencies, the nature of the times—all determine what the senior partner seeks in a junior partner to complement him.

One afternoon toward the end of November 1948, I stopped at Blair House at the President's request. The request was not unusual, as I was at that time Vice Chairman of the first Hoover Commission, in the work of which the President was keenly interested. I anticipated nothing unusual. The President greeted me as I came into his minute study in the Blair-Lee House, and without further preliminary said that he wished me to become Secretary of State when his new term began in January. For reasons of sentiment he wanted General Marshall, then in the hospital after severe surgery, to stay in office until the anniversary of his taking office, January 21, 1949. This would coincide with the completion of the first Truman term.

Partly to collect my wits, partly to explore the President's mind, I asked that we discuss the matter for a while. Since some of the conversation which followed bears on the perplexing question of the selection of a Secretary of State, I shall summarize that part of it. Some years of experience in the State Department, I said, made me one of the few persons invited to head it who knew the full extent of what he was asked to do. Moreover, I knew the tower of strength which General Marshall had been, having served under him. As I looked at the problems, I was appalled to measure my capacity beside them.

The President replied that without doubt there were people in the country more capable of being Secretary of State than I was, and more capable of being President than he was. The fact of the matter, however, was that he was the President and he wanted me to be Secretary of State. It seemed a waste of time to talk about that any further.

I made one more try for time. Several people, I said, mentioning them, clearly called for consideration. Might I, with propriety, ask whether the President had given thought to them. He most certainly had, and cheerfully told me exactly why each would be more useful to him in another capacity. After a few minutes more of private talk, I was sent off to sleep on the problem and to answer in the morning.

To list all the qualities and qualifications which a President would do well to seek in a Secretary of State would be to belabor the obvious. It would also be silly, since in each instance specific men, and not abstractions, are involved. I remember a series of board meetings devoted to making a most important appointment upon which the members held strong and conflicting views. It was suggested that we first agree on the qualifications for the position before discussing individuals. I asked my neighbor what he thought of this logical procedure, to which he replied, "Nothing matters till we start to vote."

Enough has been said to suggest the two basic truths in this matter of the selection of a Secretary: one negative, the other positive. *First,* a President will be disappointed if he chooses as Secretary a man of greater political stature than himself, in the belief that the appointment will add to the power of his administration, or will placate a rival's resentment, or that the rival—to quote President Harrison again—will "do less harm inside than outside." *Second,* a President's best guide is a sense of confidence in his appointee and a belief that the man can help him more than others in dealing with the problems he sees ahead. In informing a President's judgment on this point, there are no rules. The experience of having worked together, where this has occurred, is invaluable.

The Nature of Foreign Relations

The nature of an undertaking must obviously have a great bearing on the desirable relations between those who are directing it. Running a battleship is different from running a bank and calls for differences in the relations between the top men. Two factors make the nature of the problems of our foreign relations quite different from those existing, say, in agriculture, finance, or the administration of justice.

First of all, we are dealing with people and with geographical areas which are beyond our jurisdiction and control. Within our borders our government may command. Beyond them it cannot. In the second place, what is occurring in what the Supreme Court has called "that vast external realm," is so complex, so complicated, and so voluminous that we cannot currently comprehend it; nor, until too much time has elapsed, grasp its full significance. This is not wholly, or even principally, because of man-made impediments to knowledge—iron curtains, censorship, etc.—but because of the obscurity and complexity of the molecular changes which combine to bring about the growth or decay of power, will, and purpose in foreign lands. While it was reasonable to suppose that changes in the relative power of European states had occurred in the four or five decades before Sarajevo, not even the First World War wholly revealed how great they were. The façades of vanished power, including our own, still deceive us. Even yet our understanding of this changing world is far behind the fact.

This means that the basic problems of our foreign relations are those of understanding the true nature, dimensions, and immediacy of the problems which confront us from abroad and of putting in train the measures with which to meet them. These problems are particularly hard for Americans to keep in focus. Townsend Hoopes writes: [1]

> Our difficulty is that, as a nation of short-term pragmatists accustomed to dealing with the future only when it has become the present, we find it hard to regard future trends as serious realities. We have not achieved the capacity to treat as real and urgent—as demanding action today—problems which appear in critical dimension only at some future date. Yet failure to achieve this new habit of mind is likely to prove fatal.

Years ago, when I was about to assume sobering responsibilities, an old lady expressed the short-term pragmatic view when she said to me, "Always remember that the future comes one day at a time." This was heartening and wise advice. At times one must live by this faith with thanksgiving. But, like most wise sayings, it is not the totality of wisdom. While it is true that the problems of the voyage come to the mariner day by day, it is essential to his success, and perhaps survival, that he know where he is going, keep on course, and also use all the knowledge at his disposal to learn what forces are building up around him and to prepare, as best he may, for what lies ahead.

Foreign policy is not a book of answers. Our foreign policies—for many are needed—should be inter-connected courses of action adopted and followed to meet external conditions confronting us. The action of others beyond our borders can rarely be exactly predicted, and may take us by surprise. But these actions may be modified greatly in our interest if our courses of action have been founded on correct analyses of conditions and have been vigorously followed. Should we still be surprised by acts hostile to us, we can act more effectively to counter them if our policies have given us the capability of doing so.

At the heart, therefore, of the conduct of our foreign relations, a task confided to the President, lies this primary task of understanding the forces at work abroad, and devising, adopting, and energetically follow-

---

[1] Quoted by permission. *Yale Review,* Spring, 1960. Copyright Yale University Press.

ing courses of action to affect or meet these forces. Important as other essential tasks may be, it is this one which should most color the relations between the two men principally involved with it, and hence the President's judgment in choosing his foreign Secretary.

One can see at a glance that if these two men are going to do their work properly they have got to spend a lot of time together, much of which may not be pleasant. The problems are frustrating. They are sure to provoke controversy in many quarters. Most of the desirable measures are distasteful to accept. All of the decisions are hard. So the Secretary of State has the makings of an unwelcome visitor. But for the President to delegate the functions of understanding and deciding is to delegate his office. The worst of all courses would be for the President to delegate the function of understanding to some super staff officer and retain the function of deciding, or apparently deciding, for himself.

So, to get the job done and to have the relationship successful needs solid mutual respect, based upon conviction by each that the other is wholly straightforward, loyal, and living up to his full obligation. It helps enormously to maintain mutual confidence if there is a strong admixture of affection between them; for in Washington they are working in an environment where some of the methods would have aroused the envy of the Borgias.

The Hierarchical Position of the Secretary

The reader will already begin to gather one bias of the writer which will run through this chapter: that the relationship between the President, our Chief of State and Head of Government, and his Secretary of State, his chief adviser and executive agent in the conduct of our foreign relations, is an intensely personal one. Insofar as this relationship is attenuated or institutionalized—or Parkinsonized—the task on which they should be jointly engaged suffers. We need to rediscover the individual in government, not submerge him. This does not mean that either man should act, as prototypes of both have done, independently of the rest of the government, or in the Secretary's case, independently of the Department of State.

The busy advocates of elaboration in organization are pressing in upon the relationship from both sides. On the President's side, the National Security Council already has a staff of its own. This staff must have some one to report to; but must not bother the President, whom it was supposed to help, since he cannot give the time if he is to be able to think. So—true to Parkinson's law—some of his functions are to be devolved upon two new officials, a First Secretary of Government (a sort of prime minister) and a General Manager of Government (a species of superior managing clerk).[1]

The Secretary is thought to need relief too. One proposal would do this by incorporating the defects of Defense Department organization into the State Department. The Secretary, like the President, is to be relieved of duties so that he, too, can think. Below him his subordinates —or erstwhile subordinates brought home—undergo an inflation of titles. The Secretary is to be elevated into the higher realms of pure policy, with a staff, to keep him from contaminating contact with action. He would preside over three or four service secretaries to whom the bureaucracy would report: A Secretary for External Affairs, who would do all the traveling (Vice President in Charge of Sales); a Foreign Minister, who would run the State Department (Vice President in Charge of Production) a Secretary of Public Affairs, who would head the United States Information Service (Vice President in Charge of Advertising); and a Secretary for International Development (Vice President in Charge of Exports).

The result of this reorganization would give the President and the Secretary plenty of time to think and talk, but not much to think or talk about. It will not be recommended in this paper. Here we shall assume that the persons bearing the titles of President and Secretary of State exercise their familiar powers and perform their familiar functions.

From this point of view, what should be the position of the Secretary in the hierarchy of the President's advisers and executive agents? Obviously, it is going to be determined in large part by the character of the men involved. Secretaries Hughes, Stimson, and Marshall had within them a natural force which Secretaries Lansing and Colby could not equal. Secretary Hull was intimidated by President Roosevelt, who was, in turn, bored by the Secretary. It is idle to press men into types. But we can speculate on the position and influence which we could properly hope that ability, character, and luck would combine to confer upon the Secretary of State.

Protocol assigns the Secretary the senior position in the Cabinet because his office and department were the first created. The nature of the times in which we live should assign him pre-eminent influence because of the paramount importance of foreign policy and the need that domestic and defense policy be shaped in aid of it.

To some this has meant that the Secretary of State should be elevated into a sort of prime minister, coordinating and directing other Cabinet

---

[1] For a somewhat similar suggestion, see Statement by Governor Nelson A. Rockefeller before Subcommittee on National Policy Machinery of the Senate Committee on Government Operations, July 1, 1960.

officers under the President's authority and supervising eye. This will not work. No Cabinet officer can direct other Cabinet officers. Neither can any Presidential assistant, whatever his title; nor should he. In cases where the latter has, for a time, seemed to be doing this, power has become anonymous, and the President, for one reason or another, a *roi faineant*. There can be no more dangerous situation in a constitutional system such as ours, where the President exercises—or there are exercised in his name—vast powers affecting the very survival of the nation and people.

At this point it is essential to differentiate between the proper scope of the Secretary's interest and influence within the government and the proper scope of his legal authority. To give him legal authority over the Defense Department, for instance, as has been suggested, would further weaken and confuse the conduct of military affairs. Nevertheless, he has deep concern in a great variety of matters with which government must deal. He is not merely a department head whose jurisdiction is bounded by the diplomatic field. Foreign policy is the whole of national policy looked at from the point of view of the exigencies created by "the vast external realm" beyond our borders. It is not a "jurisdiction." It is an orientation, a point of view, a measurement of values—today, perhaps, the most important one for national survival. Obviously, our military capability to do or deter certain specific and varied things has an immense bearing on foreign policy. So does our economic capability, that of our friends and adversaries, and their relative growth or stagnation. Since internal fiscal and economic policies, public and private, affect both military and economic affairs, they, too, affect foreign policies or can affect them.

Of course, it can be argued—as, indeed, it has been argued, and successfully, in the past eight years—that fiscal considerations are the paramount ones. When this point of view triumphs, fiscal and budgetary considerations will determine the rate of economic growth and fix the limits and direction of foreign policy. This situation is tolerated only when the dangers from abroad are given a low rating. In time of war or clearly recognizable national emergency, it is not tolerated for a moment. One of the ironies of the present is that its dangers appear to diminish in direct relation to our ignorance of them as a people.

While the security of the country demands that considerations of foreign policy shall dominate the more parochial interests of finance or of military strategy and tactics, the final decision and synthesis lie not in any of them, but in the Presidency.

To give the Secretary legal authority in these farflung fields would be to usurp the Presidential office. But the best, even a good, operation of government requires that the Secretary be able to advise about the most important of these matters from the point of their incidence on our foreign problems and policies. It requires, too, that his advice be given great and respectful consideration. Neither of these requirements can be met unless the Secretary has the personal capacity and the necessary help to think more, and more deeply, than others about the nation's needs and interests, as a state among other states, in a world of change and movement and of unparalleled danger.

The President is the mode by which this can come to pass; and, the only mode. Unless the Secretary has the President's most intimate and abiding confidence and respect, he is only a diplomatic bureaucrat. He must not merely persuade the President but press him with all the means at his command to use the Presidential influence, authority, and where available, command to resolve national policy in accordance with the scale of values just mentioned.

At one point in the Korean war a difference arose bewteen the State and Defense Departments on policy toward defecting Chinese prisoners. The Defense view was that the test of policy should be the military desirability of getting back as soon as possible our own men held prisoner. State insisted that the United States and the United Nations should not compromise in any way the position that prisoners defecting from the communists would not be handed over to them. To hand them over would involve the widest consequences in communist and noncommunist countries and to the integrity of the United States government.

The Secretary of State did not persuade the Defense Department to accept his view. He got the President to order them to do so. If it becomes clear that ninety per cent of the time the Secretary will get the President's backing, it becomes unnecessary to carry the majority of disputes to him. If, on the contrary, it is evident that the views of the Secretary of the Treasury will prevail, then fiscal and budgetary considerations will fix the limits and direction of foreign policy.

The Multiple Nature of the Secretary's Function

Three aspects of the Secretary's function wherein his success or failure will be most immediately determined seem to me to have gone almost unrecognized. We may call these his corporate character, his judicial character, and his diplomatic (in the sense of representational) character within the government of the United States.

I have spoken of the "State Department" and of "it." In fact, of course, the work of the Department is performed by many thousands of trained, intelligent, and devoted men and women in all parts of the world and in Washington. Some Secretaries of State have carried on their work as though these people did not exist. On occasion they have been treated like clerks of whom all that was asked was "positive loyalty" to the administration in power, and that they be neither seen nor heard. This is a mistake. My own view has been expressed before:

> . . . Popular conceptions about government are in large part interesting folklore; and the instinct of the bureaucracy for self-preservation and the egotism of the chiefs [of Departments] perpetuate it. One of these concepts is that "policy" originates at the top and is passed down.
>
> To be sure, *great decisions* are, for the most part, made at the top, when they are not made by events. But, as for policy —the sum total of many decisions—it must be said, as it has been said of sovereignty, that its real sources are undiscoverable. One fact, however, is clear to anyone with experience in government: the springs of policy bubble up; they do not trickle down.
>
> When this upsurgence of information, ideas, and suggestions is vigorous, appreciated, and encouraged, strong, imaginative, and effective policies are most apt to result. When the whole function of determining what is what, and what to do about it, is gathered into one hand, or into a small group at the top, the resulting action may or may not be strong, but it is likely to be ill-adapted to reality and self-defeating.
>
> What has just been said underlines the judicial element in the function of headship and the great importance of interplay between head and staff at all stages in the development of decisions. By this I mean that the chief must from time to time familiarize himself with the whole record; he must consider opposing views, put forward as ably as possible. He must examine the proponents vigorously and convince them that he knows the record, is intolerant of superficiality or of favor-seeking, and not only welcomes but demands criticism.[1]

In other words, the individuals organized under the collective designation, Department of State, are not merely aides or subordinates of the Secretary of State. They are originators, as well as executors, of foreign policy. In the course of his meetings and discussions with them the Secretary can and should guide his colleagues in the Department into an understanding of the purposes and problems of national policy as they appear to the directors of government policy as a whole. The method, manner, and time of actions abroad can in a wide variety of situations be adjusted to a broader plan of campaign.

For converse reasons, as already stated, all the actions of government should harmonize with and support—or, at least, not weaken—its foreign

---

[1] New York *Times*, October 11, 1959.

policy. To accomplish this, the President and some Cabinet officers must be kept continually aware of probable and possible developments looming in the outside world and of the courses which seem to be indicated. This is essential to wise national planning.

It is in this sense that the Secretary of State is, in some important part, an intermediary between two groups, both of which are in a proper sense beyond his control: the government as a whole, for obvious reasons; the State Department, because its duty is to report facts, honest opinion on them, and to make honest recommendations. When in the early 1950's the attempt was made to punish the honest reporting of unpleasant facts and unpopular opinions, the departmental and foreign services were preserved only by the almost indestructible nature of a bureaucracy. The French bureaucracy, for instance, survived the great revolution, two empires, and five republics with little change. The Secretary's role is one in which command is not an important function. It is one of guidance and influence.

This role can be successful only if his colleagues within and without the Department have complete confidence in his integrity and disinterestedness. Then only will the President be willing to accept and rely upon reports and recommendations which must nearly always be troublesome, if not worse. Similarly if the men and women of the Department know that their work is respected and used in the most far-reaching decisions, they will give their best and cheerfully accept ultimate decisions which must weigh factors beyond their responsibility.

A good deal of the education of a Secretary, who will accept it, can come through the work with his colleagues which I have just described. These are not only diplomatic officers. There are also officers trained and working in fields which are not usually thought of as within the purview of a foreign office, although they are vital to foreign policy— economics, trade policy, finance, nuclear energy, etc. The Secretary needs their help and advice. From time to time the Budget Bureau wishes to abolish these positions believing that adequate advice and help could be obtained from the Departments of the Treasury, Commerce, the Atomic Energy Commission, etc. This is quite untrue. The difficulty is like that which arises in translating foreign legal papers. The translator must know not merely the two languages, but the two legal systems. Otherwise he is worse than useless.

Beyond the scope of these nondiplomatic assistants, many problems which must concern the Secretary and his colleagues involve—and will increasingly involve—science and technology and judgments requiring knowledge in these fields. Within the government there are men who have this knowledge and, perhaps, could form these judgments. But these men are already overburdened with pressing tasks which are their primary concern and which, quite naturally and properly, may well impair their objectivity as advisers on some of the problems on which the Secretary may need help. Where help in dealing with these problems, and with what is called long-range thinking, may be sought is discussed in the last section of this chapter.

The Secretary's Working Relations with the President

Here, again, everything depends on the temperament and character of the men involved. But one can note certain recurring circumstances. President-elect Harrison wrote, and then struck out, in his letter to Mr. Blaine a reference to "my lack of study and experience in foreign affairs." He was a perceptive and truthful man; but the presidential instinct prevailed. In 1960 an unusual number of the aspirants to the White House have had some exposure to foreign affairs through study and travel. This will doubtless fortify a conviction of competence in foreign affairs which soon comes to a President and to his personal staff, often outrunning the fact.

This is not peculiar to Presidents. To columnists, correspondents, legislators, some academicians, and most New York lawyers over forty, foreign affairs are an open book, though they often differ on the meaning of the text. Their opinions are available to the President directly, through the press, and through reports of various groups, more or less devoted to the study of our foreign relations. These opinions usually call for a change from conventional, unimaginative, and outmoded policies—i.e., those currently being followed—in favor of flexible, dynamic, and forward-looking policies, governed by faith and hope in the future rather than by fear and distrust.

From these groups comes a great deal of advice which reaches the President through the White House staff. To this staff foreign affairs present the ideal subject for a speech by the President. By "ideal" is meant a speech which will attract not merely national but worldwide attention and comment; a speech which will display "world leadership" on a "high level;" and which will not produce disagreement within the party, such as might come from a speech on tax revision or on the issues presented by school or farm problems. The State Department is apt to be terror-stricken by these suggestions with very considerable justification. But to oppose is a losing gambit.

Since the Secretary cannot, and perhaps should not, stop these initiatives, he had better join them. And he must do it himself. No one down the line—least of all a speech writer—can control the White House composers gathered around the Cabinet table, with a draft of a foreign policy speech before them and the bit in their teeth. The Secretary, if he is wise, will join the fray himself, with his own draft, and try to guide and direct it. He can carry more weight than any of his associates, particularly in the final stages when the President himself, as I knew the procedure, joins the group and makes the final decisions.

It may seem absurd—and doubtless is—for a Secretary of State to be spending his time as a member of a Presidential speech-writing group.[1] But this is often where policy is made, regardless of where it is supposed to be made. The despised speech, often agreed to be made months beforehand without thought of subject, a nuisance to prepare and an annoyance to deliver, has often proved the vehicle for statements of far-reaching effect for good or ill. As both a junior and a senior official, I have fought this guerrilla warfare; sometimes to get things done which would otherwise be stopped, and sometimes to prevent others from doing the same thing. The Point Four proposal contained in the Inaugural Address of January 20, 1949—in which I was not involved—can be used to illustrate many points made here.

While on the subject of the White House staff, it is pertinent to mention a question which is often presented to all Cabinet officers: to what extent does a communication from the staff, or from the Executive Office of the President, represent a Presidential order? The Executive Office is a congeries of agencies housed in that monument of late Victorian architecture adjoining and to the west of the White House—the old State, War and Navy Building.

The most notorious of these, perhaps, is the Budget Bureau. Obviously its vast and pervasive intrusion into the business of diplomacy, conducted under the authority of the President, represents at most only his most general decisions. Armed with these, a host of zealous, able, and, often, uninformed young men inquire, through hearings in which officials must "justify" their appropriation requests, into the innumerable policies and programs of the Department. The attempt is made to assign costs to various activities and to reduce the appropriation requested by striking out moneys thought to be representative of the cost of activities not adequately "justified." This rarely gets at a quite appropriate area of saving, which I shall not betray my old friends by disclosing. The importance of this budgetary process lies in the President's order that no executive agency may ask for more funds than are included for it in the President's budget. Therefore, as the process nears its conclusion, the Secretary, if he believes that some vital activity has been grossly handi-

---

[1] My former colleagues tell me that I exaggerate my participation in Presidential speech-writing. They are doubtless right. Messrs. Philip Jessup, Paul Nitze, Marshall Shulman, and others, all did much of the work which I have described here.

capped, armed with the vigor of his outrage, goes to the President for redress. Rule by the Budget Bureau has often seemed to me aptly described as tyranny tempered by assassination. That of the House Committee on Appropriations is entirely untempered.

In a different form the personal staff in the White House can often pose the same question whether an order or request is what it purports to be. On one occasion a note from a member of the staff informed me that the President had learned that a certain foreign service officer was stationed in an African "hardship post" and wished him transferred to a more healthy spot. I took the note to my next meeting with the President. Before showing it to him, I said that I wanted to know whether he had, indeed, issued this instruction, in which case it would, of course, be obeyed. In doing so, I pointed out, other changes of personnel would become necessary and it might be desirable to refer the whole series of decisions to the White House, although they hardly seemed worthy of the President's time. He read the note, tore it up, and we went on to the next item.

Returning from this digression to the working relations between the Secretary and the President, there were times when I would see the President on business almost every day, and rarely less than four times a week. Every Monday and Thursday we met alone for a half an hour to an hour; or two other days in the Cabinet and in the National Security Council. Special meetings prepared him for foreign visitors, to deal with a variety of emergencies, great and small, to confer with groups of Senators and Congressmen, and so on. Finally, we talked frequently on the White House telephone.

The private meetings began by disposing of his and my agenda of specific matters, such as appointments, troubles (foreign and domestic), legislative goals and obstacles. The great utility and importance of these meetings lay in the opportunity for talk, talk in which I could learn from the President his thoughts of all sorts; what portended in the domestic field or in defense matters and their probable effects on foreign policy; how he was appraising the consequences of various actions of ours abroad; whether our conduct had or lacked Congressional or popular support and what should be done. Then, again, these talks gave me an important opportunity to prepare him for developments which were foreseen by my colleagues and to discuss courses of action before crises burst upon us. In short, over the years these talks enabled us not only to keep one another informed but to see events and choices each from the other's point of view. This, I venture to suggest, can play a more effective part in developing a coherent national policy than the multiplication of staff and what is called "coordination."

President Truman, as his memoirs tell us, believed that he was not kept currently and adequately informed of Secretary Byrnes's negotiations when the latter was attending international conferences abroad. Having observed the consequences of this opinion on the President's part and the reporting procedures which General Marshall inaugurated, I determined to carry these procedures a bit further. The result worked well from all points of view, the President's, the Department's, and the delegation's.

Accompanying the delegation was a small secretariat whose sole duty, other than keeping me informed of the cables on developments elsewhere in the world, was the preparation and communication of reports of three types. Each evening a detailed descriptive account of the day's negotiations, prepared by a secretariat officer in attendance at the meeting, and checked by a senior officer, to which any significant memoranda of private discussions were added by my secretary, was sent to the Department with a copy for the President. This report contained the bulk of information on factual developments and chronology, and provided detail on the various national positions presented. It was widely analysed in Washington by the various agencies concerned and was available as a basic reference for the President.

Also each day a condensed summary of the longer report was sent to the President through the Department. In this document we gave our opinions on the course which the negotiations were taking, the principal difficulties anticipated, and ways of meeting them. If instruction or guidance was needed on any point, it was asked for. Drafts of important statements, such as the Control of Armaments Proposals of 1951, were discussed in this section. The President, through the Department, and often the Department alone, commented and instructed. (The Under Secretary, as General Marshall had insisted, was in fact as well as in title *Acting* Secretary.)

Finally, about twice a week, or more often when things moved swiftly, I sent a personal, "Eyes Only," message (which is not so restricted as it sounds) to the President, giving him my own opinions on how things were going, whether toward a successful conclusion as in the NATO meeting of February, 1952, or toward failure, as in those of September and December, 1951. I also sent in this form highly confidential information imparted to me, as for instance, in May, 1950, when Mr. Robert Schuman informed me of his coming proposals on the European Coal and Steel Community.

As a result of this systematic flow of information, the President was kept as familiar with what was going on as though he were present himself. He was always able to give, and frequently gave, direction, encouragement, and suggestion to the United States delegation. In consequence the delegation was assured that its course continuously had the full support of its government.

The Central Task: to Recognize Emerging Problems in Time

In the section above on the nature of foreign affairs, I stressed the vast complexity of the myriad daily actions all over the globe which, like the combination of simple organisms into larger and more complex ones, form and shape the emerging future. The central task of a foreign office should be to understand what these forces are, to do what can be done to shape them favorably to our interests, and to prepare to deal with them.

This should be the task, but it is not. The principal effort goes into dealing with the overpowering present, the present, which, like the Mississippi in full flood, absorbs the whole energy and thought of those who man the levees.

Those who have never stood watch are impatient about this. "Act," they demand, "Don't always *react*. Seize the initiative. The best defense is an offensive." And so the clichés go. Most of those who utter them are not expressing an idea, rather an exasperation. But underneath the exasperation there is an idea—and, what is more, a truth. It is a truth which makes mincemeat of most of the plans for reorganization of the conduct of foreign affairs.

The truth is that in foreign affairs manhours spent in thinking and planning on future action are by far the most profitable investment. The thundering present becomes so soon the unchangeable past that seizing it at any moment of its acceleration is as dangerous as mounting a train gathering speed. To change the metaphor, every bird-shooter knows that you must lead your bird and swing with its flight. This requires, in Mr. Hoopes's phrase already quoted, treating future trends as serious realities. To treat them in any way one has first to recognize them. Preoccupation with the so-called "machinery" for the execution of foreign policy misses this point. The true problem lies in determining the emerging future and the policy appropriate to it. It has been said of the late, unhappy Summit meeting that, once President Eisenhower had arrived at Paris, he dealt with the situation as well as one could. Undoubtedly so; but then it was too late for any action to have any effect. He could only emulate St. Sebastian by suffering the arrows of his martyrdom with dignity and Christian fortitude.

In an article in the *Bulletin of the Atomic Scientists* (March, 1960), Mr. Roger Hilsman has gone to the heart of the matter:

> It is almost traditional in America to view foreign affairs as a problem in public administration. When our minds turn to the business of relating ourselves to the outside world, we tend to think of reorganization, of rearranging the parts of the government. Yet all this organizational tinkering hardly seems rewarding. Many of our failures in foreign policy are probably not failures at all, but lack of power to shape the events we deplore. No nation is so strong that it can dictate the course of history, and much of what happens in the world is simply beyond our reach. What is more, one suspects that even our true failures in foreign policy would not have yielded to better organization. Good organization seems to imply efficiency in implementing policy, yet few of our true failures are attributable to bad administration in carrying policy out. Our true failures probably lie more often in failing to recognize emerging problems in time to evolve effective policies or in meeting big, bold, demanding problems with half measures, timorous and cramped.

It was the recognition of this source of our true failure which led General Marshall to establish the Policy Planning Staff when he became Secretary of State in January, 1947. This staff made a notable contribution for some years. There were, however, inherent limitations upon its ability wholly to meet the need of recognizing and focusing attention on emerging problems. These can be laid only in part at the door of the Policy Planning Staff and its members.

The temptation to involve the staff in current operating problems has been too great on both sides. The staff members sorely want to have a hand in action rather than remain more remote from it, as planning, criticism, and analysis require. Then, too, the staff has often had on it some of the ablest men in the Department whom the high command cannot resist drafting, from time to time, for the more puzzling problems of the day.

Other limitations lie, partly, in the fact that the training and life of a foreign service officer are not apt to produce men well fitted for the task we are discussing; and, partly, because the staff needed for the purpose should be larger and of more diversified professional training than the State Department will be permitted to, or probably could, obtain. The bureaucratic routine through which foreign service officers must go produces capable men, knowledgeable about specific parts of the world, and excellent diplomatic operators. But it makes men cautious rather than imaginative, and more guided by an intuitive hunch than by a judgment in which quantitative appraisal of voluminous data has played a part.

In the conception and development of the Marshall Plan the leading parts were, with few exceptions, played by men whose training and experience were broader than the State Department mill provided. The Fulbright educational exchange program was not of State Department origin; and the Point Four Program was vigorously opposed in the Department before its enunciation.

To peer into the yet unfolded future as it bears upon the relations of states in the latter half of this century is more likely to yield results if done by a group well staffed with scientists and technical people from many fields, including the military and economic, as well as with people experienced in all the world's areas and with its peoples. Such a group might discern in the detail of daily events patterns of emerging events, and be able to suggest courses of action to deal with them.

To accomplish this on a more elaborate scale than either the Rand organization or the Institute of Defense Analyses is now able to provide, Mr. Hilsman proposes, in the article cited above, a National Research Organization, with a Congressional charter financed partly by an endowment, partly by contract work, and, perhaps on occasion by special appropriation. Its chief client would be the State Department, though other agencies in the Executive Branch and the Congress could contract for studies if they were willing to pay for them. The ideas of an outside organization and of the contract relationship are to keep the group independent of administration fashions in thought and to keep it efficient and competent.

Either Mr. Hilsman's proposed organization or Rand or the Institute of Defense Analyses could be of immense help to the State Department or the Secretary. Whether they would avail themselves of this help only experience can tell. Undoubtedly the apparent admission of insufficiency by acceptance of outside help would cause initial resistance. But this would be a mistaken view, and, if one is inclined to be hopeful, might be overcome in time. The very removal of this research and analysis from operations would give important reassurance against usurpation. The breadth of view, the infusion of military knowledge, which the military are too busy or too cautious or too circumscribed to give, and of technological knowledge and judgments, which are readily available elsewhere, would make this help invaluable, particularly to the Secretary, who would be alerted to developments not ordinarily uncovered by Departmental procedures.

One final observation upon the current plethora of reorganization plans may be appropriate. The passion for reorganizing the executive is

a passion of Congress. Singularly unsuccessful in reorganizing itself—
the last spectacular failure being the LaFollette-Monroney effort in 1946
—the Congress delights to turn its attention to the State Department
which has the least defense against it. What it has done with foreign
aid and propaganda, beginning with the Vandenberg-Brookings scheme of
1948, to date has both boxed the compass and demonstrated a strictly
limited capacity to deal with the problem. It fairly raises the question
of the extent to which the Executive should submit to the vagaries of
Congress as to how it should conduct its consultations and the procedures
for reaching its conclusions.

To be sure, the Congress obviously has power to prescribe the organization and procedures for expending the appropriations made for, say,
the Marshall Plan; and the Comptroller General would disallow expenditures not made in accordance with law. But the Congress should not be
encouraged to believe that it should determine the manner of Executive
consultation and decision. Should the President believe that elaboration
of the NSC organization, or other procedures provided by Congress, are
of no use to him, he can and should disregard them and establish others
more agreeable to him.

From the very beginning of our federal government we have acted
upon the constitutional theory that, especially in the field of foreign
relations, the processes of consultation and decision among the highest
officers of the Executive branch are essentially political processes within
the responsibility and prerogative of the President. In this field the
Legislative and Judicial branches have been admonished of the unwisdom
of attempts to narrow the President's responsibility or scope of action.
(See *United States* v. *Curtiss-Wright Export Corp.*, 299 U.S. 304, 321.)
This theory has happily accorded with political reality. Top policy
councils work best when the President assumes responsibility for determining their form and procedures, for mastering their content, and for
making the ultimate decisions. The Secretary of State can make his, and
his department's, greatest contribution to wise and timely decision when
he is accepted and used by the President as his chief adviser and executive agent in the field of foreign affairs. The President does not improve
the conduct of business, peculiarly his, by inviting the Congress to
organize it for him.

3.

The Secretary and the development and coordination of policy

♦ Robert R. Bowie

What is the role of the Secretary of State in policy-making? The short answer is that it depends entirely on the wishes and methods of the President. The office of Secretary of State, as such, confers on the incumbent little authority and few specific functions. The organic act of 1789 which established the office (quoted in the Introduction) is premised on the ultimate authority of the President in foreign affairs. In their conduct, the Secretary and his Department were to serve as an arm of the President as he saw fit.

That concept applies to the office as much today as it did when Jefferson, as its first holder, was able to discharge its duties with five clerks as the entire staff of the Depart-

51

◆ ROBERT R. BOWIE left the position of Assistant Secretary of State in 1957 to become Director of the Center for International Affairs and Dillon Professor of International Relations at Harvard University. For four years he had been the Director of the Policy Planning Staff of the Department, and its representative on the Planning Board of the National Security Council.

ment. The President may treat the Secretary as his chief advisor and delegate for foreign affairs or he may by-pass and disregard him. The last fifty years have seen notable examples of both situations. Wilson and Franklin Roosevelt depended less on their Secretaries than on others for advice and assistance; Trumen and Eisenhower relied heavily on their respective Secretaries.

Even so, this short answer, while strictly true, is misleading. Indeed, for our purposes, the question should be rephrased: In the interest of effective policy-making, how *should* the Secretary of State assist the President? So stated the issue is quite different. It can be answered only in the light of the requisites for adequate policy-making. Accordingly, the following discussion seeks to analyze, first, the nature of the task and its requirements; second, how the Secretary can contribute to their fulfilment; and third, how his Department must assist him to do so.

Demands on Policy Making

The key fact about foreign policy is the most obvious one: that it deals with the environment beyond the national domain. The fate of the nation may depend on its relation to that environment, but its capacity to control it is subject to serious limits. With the stakes so high, the nation must use its resources and influence to maximum effect to shape this environment.

The necessity exists in any period. But never has it been more compelling or more difficult to meet than under modern conditions.

THE COMPLEX ENVIRONMENT

In our era, the international order is being radically transformed at a pace and on a scale without parallel. A world in transition clearly makes it much harder to appraise the unfolding conditions, to identify the various forces, and to anticipate how they will interact. On the most crucial issues, history offers little guidance.

The very number and diversity of states complicate international relations as compared to the period when a few European states, with shared or familiar cultures and history, were dominant, with the Western Hemisphere peripheral, Asia and Africa colonies, and China disorganized. Today, all that is changed. The Sino-Soviet bloc espouses a hostile and alien ideology. The twenty-five or more new nations which have emerged since World War II and the fifteen or twenty soon to follow, the new states of Asia and Africa, and the evolving nations in Latin America, differ widely from Europe and North America, and from each other, in culture, experience, attitudes, and conditions of life.

Both old and new nations are undergoing change. The drive of the newer countries to modernize their economies is bound to remake the structure of their societies and the attitudes of their people. The effort of Western Europe to transcend ancient rivalries and to draw together, if it succeeds, must greatly enhance its power and influence. The Soviet Union continues its rapid growth in power and prestige; no one can say how social evolution there may modify its external purposes and aims. Finally, the revolution in military technology, in nuclear weapons, missiles and space, creates wholly new questions about the role and control of force in international affairs.

The world also continues to grow more interdependent. The security and welfare of even the strongest nations is enmeshed with that of many others. To survive and prosper, they must identify common interests and pursue common actions in many fields. International relations penetrate far more deeply into domestic affairs; the line between the two domains becomes continually more fuzzy or irrelevant. Domestic events and decisions have far-reaching repercussions outside the borders and are themselves influenced by external forces. Thus, the economic and political progress within the new countries may profoundly affect the situation of the developed nations and in turn may depend heavily on their assistance and support. And collective defense has entailed an extensive range of such interactions.

Our generation is engaged in a struggle to determine what kind of world will emerge from this transitional era. This struggle has two aspects. One is the contest with the Sino-Soviet bloc. Those powers, confident of the ultimate triumph of communism, have developed effective techniques of pressure, infiltration, and subversion for assuring communist successes. Convinced that they understand how to manage the forces of change and revolution, they have shown great skill in exploiting the conditions of turmoil and instability in many parts of the world. In its other aspect, the struggle is an effort to create a viable international order which will take account of the mutual dependence among the nations of the world today.

IMPACT ON POLICY-MAKING

This struggle makes heavy demands on policy-making by the United States and other noncommunist states. Given the nature of the challenge, they must use their influence and resources as effectively as possible, if they are to succeed in countering the Sino-Soviet threat and creating a viable order.

As the basic forces—political, economic, and military—are long-term, their own actions must inevitably be geared to long-term objectives. The major problems will not yield to short-run measures; they will be resolved only by the cumulative effect of many separate steps, spread over a long time. Each nation must be able to mobilize domestic support for costly measures for an extended period, and to concert its policies with other nations over a wide front. This support and cooperation requires general consensus regarding the objectives and direction of policy.

An accepted framework of purposes is also vitally necessary as a guide to assure that specific policies and measures do form a coherent pattern. The grist of foreign affairs consists largely of a host of concrete issues calling for decision and action. Should an alliance be made with State A? Should State B be recognized? How should a vote be cast on a resolution in the United Nations? Should a proposed irrigation project in State C be assisted? Should a specific form of inspection be accepted as a basis for test suspension? Each issue presents its own particular setting and considerations. But to decide them in isolation "on their merits" could easily fritter away the influence and resources of the nation.

In practice, therefore, policy-making has to be performed in several stages or levels. The primary task is to create a strategic framework which integrates basic interests, objectives and means. Such a strategy can define the general direction of policy and establish priorities among conflicting purposes or interests. It can define the kinds of instruments needed to carry out its purposes. It can identify fields of common interest and bases of cooperation with other nations. It can provide a basis for rallying and organizing the requisite common action at home and abroad.

No strategic framework can furnish automatic answers to all the day-to-day practical problems of foreign relations. They will still need to be analyzed and decided on the basis of concrete situations and alternatives, but the decisions must be made in the light of the strategic priorities and objectives. Nor can any strategic plan be definitive in a world of uncertainty and change. It must be based on the best predictions and analyses feasible at the time, but its premises and analysis must be constantly reviewed in the light of new evidence or understanding, or of changing conditions. Only in this way can the broader objectives and priorities be kept in step with emerging realities.

In short, effective policy-making depends on (1) developing a long-term strategic concept; (2) creating and shaping instruments for carrying it out; (3) coordinating specific actions with the strategy; (4) constant review and revision as necessary.

THE PROCESS OF POLICY ANALYSIS

The analysis underlying strategic policy must relate three variables which interact:

1. *Appraisal of External Conditions and How They Are Likely to Develop*—The policy-maker views the outside environment not as a bystander but as one of the actors. His purpose is to identify those forces and events most likely to be harmful or beneficial and to judge how far they may be malleable and by what means. What will be the interests, purposes, and future actions of other states? How will their interplay affect the interests of his nation? How may they be modified by its actions and policies and by those of friendly or hostile powers?

2. *The Practical Objectives Which Should Govern the Foreign Policy* —The broad aim of foreign policy is to create and maintain external conditions favorable to our way of life and values. To provide a basis for action, however, this general goal must be converted into specific objectives related to security, economic activity, etc., and relative priorities must be established among them. These practical objectives must be chosen in the light of external conditions facing the nation and the means for influence available to it.

3. *The Choice of Means for Influencing the Outside World*—The resources and skills available to the nation impose limits but still allow for a wide spectrum of activities. What is the best way to use military, political, economic, propaganda, and other means? In deciding which instruments to create and utilize, the policy-maker must consider what he wishes to accomplish and what methods will be most suitable and effective for obtaining specific purposes.

The analysis does not, of course, start with a clean slate. The nation's outlook and aims, especially in a democracy, grow out of its history and traditions. Experience influences the appraisal of the situation and the choice of objectives and means. Under changing conditions, intelligent and forceful leaders are needed to keep national purposes and policies in step with emerging needs. At times only the shock of events can change the outlook and response. It took the threat to Greece and Turkey, the Berlin blockade, and Korea to alert the United States and its allies to the full scope of the Soviet military danger and to provoke them into collective defense in NATO and other alliances and the creation of more adequate military strength. Where an interest is long-term and not dramatic (as in aid to the less-developed countries) democracies tend to be slow to adopt and carry out adequate programs.

ROLES IN POLICY-MAKING

In the United States the creation of an effective strategic plan and coordinated policy is complicated by the separation of powers between the Executive and Congress and the structure of the Executive itself. Under our system there is no substitute for leadership by the President. The full use of his position is indispensable for obtaining the support of Congress and public opinion for requisite financing, instruments, and legislation. And within the Executive Branch only his authority can assure that the Departments conform their policies and actions to a basic policy framework. Since many Departments have special partisans and interest groups in Congress and the country, the President's power may often be needed to offset pressures or divergent tendencies.

The President must, however, have assistance in focusing his own efforts and the use of his authority. Devising the necessary framework of purposes and priorities demands full-time attention with expert participation of many kinds. The working out of specific policies also requires coordination of the hierarchy of decision-making. The President must decide the most crucial or basic issues but cannot possibly cope with a vast range of lesser matters. These must be resolved at the level of the Department heads or their subordinates. There must be some way of sorting out those matters which justify his attention.

These needs of the President could, of course, be met in various ways. The Secretary of State, however, seems to be best situated to assist him in meeting them in foreign policy. Tradition gives his office a certain primacy within the Executive Branch. Among Cabinet officers he alone can devote his full time and attention to foreign affairs. As head of the Department of State, he can command the assistance of a large corps of experts specializing in this field. Since his Department represents no special interest, his position should facilitate an over-all view integrating the various components of policy.

The Secretary should, therefore, play a central role both in developing the basic framework of foreign policy and in coordinating policy-making by the Departments. This concept of the Secretary has in fact been adopted both by President Truman and President Eisenhower. As

Secretaries of State, General Marshall and Mr. Acheson clearly enjoyed the full support of President Truman and were also looked to as his principal advisors for the making and coordinating of foreign policy. President Eisenhower has repeatedly expressed a similar conception. On June 1, 1953, early in his first term, he said:

> I personally wish to emphasize that I shall regard the Secretary of State as the Cabinet officer responsible for advising and assisting me in the formulation and control of foreign policy. It will be my practice to employ the Secretary of State as my channel of authority within the Executive Branch on foreign policy. Other officials of the Executive Branch will work with and through the Secretary of State on matters of foreign policy.

This role is surely a demanding one. Its success depends ultimately on the relations of the Secretary with the President; the Secretary can fulfill it only if he can count on the support of the President when necessary. But in addition he must have the personal qualities essential to carry it out, and the effective support of his Department.

The Secretary of State and Strategic Planning

The National Security Council is the crucible for strategic policy. Created in 1947 the Council was designed to advise the President on integration of domestic, foreign, and military policies relating to national security and to facilitate cooperation among the interested Departments and agencies. Composed of the heads of these Departments and agencies, the Council is solely advisory to the President. Under it are the Council's Planning Board and the Operations Coordinating Board (OCB). The statutory members, in addition to the President and Vice-President, are the Secretaries of State and Defense, and the Director, Office of Civil and Defense Mobilization; the Secretary of the Treasury, and Director, Bureau of the Budget, attend regularly by invitation of the President, and others for specific topics. The Chairman, Joint Chiefs of Staff, and Director of Central Intelligence are statutory advisors. The distinction between statutory and invited members has little or no practical significance.

The statute creating the Council also set up the Central Intelligence Agency (CIA) to correlate and evaluate intelligence relating to national security, the Defense Department to unify (but not to merge) the three military services under a Secretary of Defense, and the Joint Chiefs of Staff to foster more orderly strategic planning and allocation of resources in the military field.

The primary reason for creating the National Security Council was the urgent need for better integration of political and military aspects of policy. The idea was that the Council would keep in balance political commitments, military capabilities, and economic resources. This objective is, of course, essential, but foreign relations today are much more complex and subtle than the initial concept suggests. With systems of collective defense, the stationing of forces overseas, allocating military assistance, and the choosing of strategies involve political, military, economic, and psychological factors. In applying the concept of deterrence, these factors must also be taken fully into account, in deciding on strategies, weapons, and forces. And the same is true in preparing or analyzing any proposals for arms control.

But an adequate framework for policy today must go far beyond military means. It must embrace the whole range of purposes and instruments involved in foreign affairs. Indeed, military strength, if it succeeds in deterring aggression, merely buys the time and opportunity to use political, economic, and other means for facilitating constructive evolution toward a more viable world order.

OPERATION OF THE NATIONAL SECURITY COUNCIL

The main function of the National Security Council should be to consider the broad framework of our policy and the instruments and resources necessary to carry it out. By custom this has taken the form of papers analyzing the general policies or specific segments of policy. Normally these include an annual paper specifically addressed to national strategy. For this and other papers, the preparatory work is done by the Planning Board, composed of Assistant Secretaries or similar officials from each Department or Agency represented on the Council. Under the direction of a Special Assistant to the President, the Board analyzes the issues and proposes policies for dealing with them. The Board may submit an agreed paper or, if its members disagree, they may present alternatives to the Council. In their work the Planning Board and the Council have available the national intelligence estimates prepared through the Central Intelligence Agency, which provide a common appraisal of future conditions for a period of two to five years.

In essence the National Security Council and its Planning Board are forums for pooling analyses and judgments and for posing issues for decision by the President. In the Council, the Secretaries of State, Defense, and the Treasury, with the Chairman of the Joint Chiefs of Staff, the Director of Central Intelligence, and others, can discuss with the President the critical issues and examine the alternatives for dealing with them. In this way the President can consider the opinions and divergences of his principal advisors before making up his mind on central policy issues.

Neither the Council nor the Planning Board has a separate staff for original planning or analysis. The small staff of the Executive Assistant to the President helps in managing the work of the Planning Board and the Council.

The output of the Council and the Planning Board depend, therefore, primarily on the contributions of the Executive Departments charged with national security and foreign affairs. Each member of the Council and the Board has behind him the resources of his own Department or agency. Within his Department, the Planning Board member is normally tied into the planning machinery. The State member, for instance, is the Director of the Policy Planning Staff. The Defense member is the Assistant Secretary in charge of political military matters for his Department. These men can draw on a wide range of experience and analysis within their respective Departments to bring it to bear on the preparation of a unified strategy. Ordinarily, the work of the Planning Board and Council will reflect the quality of the thinking and planning done in the Departments separately or jointly.

On occasion, however, special committees, composed entirely or partly of private citizens, are created to study designated fields or problems and to recommend measures for dealing with them. Recent examples include the Killian[1] and Gaither[2] Committee reports on defense and the Draper Commission[3] on military and economic assistance. Such committees can provide a fresh approach to a persistent issue, or an independent judgment when Departmental positions conflict, or an analysis of novel problems by qualified outsiders. Such studies must be used sparingly and with care. Preparing materials for such committees and briefing their members can be time-consuming and disruptive. Moreover, in focusing on the assigned problem, such studies entail the risk of divorcing it from the larger context of policy and distorting the alternatives or choices.

The Secretary of State and his Department are crucial to successful operation of the NSC procedure. Other Departments and agencies, especially Defense, Treasury, and CIA, have important parts to play; they must contribute expert knowledge and advise on important segments of the national strategy. But the Secretary of State must provide the synthesis of the political, military, economic, and other elements to produce a coherent strategy. In meeting this need the Secretary must be assisted by an expert staff in his Department, as will be discussed later.

---

[1] President's Board of Consultants on Foreign Intelligence Activities.
[2] Security Resources Panel of the President's Science Advisory Committee.
[3] President's Committee to Study the Military Assistance Program.

But that staff, while essential, cannot replace the contribution of the Secretary himself as chief advisor to the President.

SHORTCOMINGS AND IMPROVEMENTS

One weakness of the NSC machinery has been in relating instruments to policy. The basic decisions on national strategy inevitably involve the broad allocation of resources, yet the National Security Council has tended to be too much divorced from the budget process. The Budget Bureau has insisted on its prerogatives, and the Council and the Planning Board have either stayed out or been kept out. Obviously the Council should not attempt to make the budget. It could not. But it could exercise more influence on the allocation of resources among the types of military forces, between military and economic purposes, and so on. If it did so, the Secretary of State, for example, might have a better chance to influence these decisions than when they are made within the framework of the regular budget procedure.

Decisions regarding the size and type of military forces are normally discussed in the Council. But the form of the military budget poses a serious obstacle to their consideration in relation to foreign policy objectives. Since the breakdown of funds is normally based on the three services, it is extremely difficult to determine how various budget levels or fund allocations would affect military capability for specific tasks relevant to foreign policy. On the basis of the submission, the Secretary of State can hardly reach judgments about the adequacy of planned forces. Moreover, it has not been customary to channel through the Planning Board where these aspects could be analyzed more systematically. The result has been to impede efforts to relate military needs to political requirements.

The requisite integration could not be achieved, however, merely by discussion at the level of the Planning Board, or the National Security Council. That could not overcome whatever difficulties arise from the structure and missions of the military services. Moreover, for proper results the staffs of the various departments will have to work together intimately at much lower levels in order to mesh thinking and analysis. The extent to which these officials do consult with each other has varied in different periods and with different officials. Top officers in the Pentagon have sometimes been reluctant to see too much exchange, and the State Department has not been active enough in this field. One obstacle, of course, is the shortage of people on both sides able to carry on integrated analysis of this kind. The military services have probably done better in training such people, as in the war colleges. While Foreign

Service Officers attend these courses, there is still a serious lack of officials with the necessary competence.

The existing system has been criticized in other ways. Some have objected that the National Security Council papers are too general. In some cases they may fail to sharpen the issues or pose conflicts and alternatives with sufficient clarity. But this criticism is often based on unsound conceptions of what the machinery can and should do. The NSC papers cannot provide detailed prescriptions for future crises, nor the specific measures to be taken over the next several years in each area. Those specific policies and actions must be worked out by other procedures within and between Departments. Indeed, the more valid criticism might be that too many papers are submitted to the Council with too much detail.

Others have objected that the machinery does not assure creative or original analysis and policies. Often this criticism reflects disagreement or discontent with the policies or decisions of the Executive and tends to blame the machinery for the result. It is not necessarily valid, however, to assume that the planning process failed to pose alternative policies or analyses. In the end, the President has the authority and duty to decide among the alternative appraisals and measures.

Some of these critics have urged the creation of a White House staff for policy planning. This proposal has been commented on by Averell Harriman, whose service as Secretary of Commerce, as Special Assistant to the President, and as Ambassador, allowed him to see the process at first-hand. In his testimony before the Subcommittee on National Policy Machinery (June 2, 1960) Mr. Harriman said:

> But such a move, in my opinion, would be a mistake. Insofar as possible, the place for policy-making should be concentrated within the departments. The departments are on the firing line of planning and policy-making; they include specialized skills; they have the invaluable advantage of intimate day-to-day contact with operating problems. In contrast, those working in the White House have largely second-hand information. Any effort to do detailed planning in the White House therefore inevitably runs the danger of resulting in ivory tower policies.

Others have suggested creating a semi-autonomous policy-research agency analogous to RAND but responsible to the White House or NSC. Its members would have much of the freedom of an academic research center, though presumably a continuous access to classified data. It is hard to estimate how much value the reports and studies of such an agency would have. Perhaps it could go beyond the existing agencies in foreseeing emerging problems and in suggesting means for preparing for them. Except in the military field, however, classified data are seldom required for such long-range analysis or prescription. In the military, several such agencies have been operating for some years, but it is by no means apparent that their output (whatever its intrinsic worth) has resulted in superior military planning. Some think that such a group might achieve some of the benefits of the public committee on a continu-in basis. It should be recognized, however, that such committees derive their influence in part from the public standing of their members and in part from the fact that the study was specially commissioned. Such a permanent agency could hardly duplicate these claims to attention for its output.

No doubt strategic planning could and should be strengthened. The various proposals for doing so should be sympathetically considered. But the main hope for improving it appears to lie in better staff work within the Departments themselves, and receptivity to its results within the Executive Branch.

Even so, the President needs expert help in the White House in posing issues for decision, especially where conflicts between the Departments are deep and involve highly technical issues. The field of arms control illustrates the problem. In the Defense Department and especially in the State Department the relevant staffs should be greatly strengthened. But their approaches may well be so different as to involve basic conflicts which are highly technical in nature. The Secretary of State is hardly likely to have the special competence or the time to master the scientific intricacies. And the fact that the subject matter falls so directly within the fields of Defense and State further complicates the problem. In such cases the President may well need an expert on the White House staff to sort out the issues and to advise him regarding conflicts. On less technical subjects, a similar function should be performed by the Executive Assistant for National Security Affairs or other special assistants.

The Secretary and Policy Coordination

The fact that policy-making takes place by stages and at several levels has already been mentioned. The President has final authority but can make only a limited number of decisions. He must settle the broad strategy, the priorities among interests and purposes, and the allocation of resources and effort among the possible alternatives. He can also handle specific decisions of critical importance. But the great mass of policy issues within the Executive Branch must perforce be settled by the appropriate Secretaries or their subordinates. And the same is true of the coordination of policy with allies and other friendly nations.

Both within the Executive Branch and with allies, the Secretary of State plays a vital part in concerting policy.

INTERDEPARTMENTAL COORDINATION

Today, the State Department, while the only Department dealing solely with foreign affairs, has no exclusive franchise in this field. (Strictly speaking, the Department of State has a few domestic functions, like custody of the Great Seal, but these are of negligible importance.) Many other Departments and Agencies are now concerned with foreign affairs. With our network of alliances, the Defense Department and military services have become deeply involved with overseas bases and units, large-scale training, and military assistance missions in many countries. In the economic field, the Export-Import Bank, the International Co-operation Administration (ICA), the Development Loan Fund, and the Agriculture Department are all engaged in supporting economic development in much of the world. USIA (United States Information Agency) has a far-flung program of information. And foreign activities now occupy many other agencies such as the Treasury, Interior, and Commerce Departments and the Atomic Energy Commission, Civil Aeronautics Board, and Federal Communications Commission. In relations with a specific country, these manifold activities may either conflict or cancel the influence of the United States, or if used in a coordinated fashion, may reinforce one another in achieving its policy objectives.

In general, three principal methods are used to coordinate policy: (1) direct policy guidance by the State Department for a few agencies; (2) a large network of intergovernmental committees and informal contacts; (3) the ambassadors in the field.

DIRECT POLICY GUIDANCE

USIA and ICA, which are solely instruments of foreign policy, should clearly operate under the policy direction of the State Department. Two methods have been used to accomplish this. USIA operates under a separate Director, appointed by the President, but receives its guidance on policy matters from the Secretary of State. ICA, which has had a similar status when outside the State Department, is currently assigned to the Department of State as a semi-autonomous unit.

In practice, autonomy with policy guidance can succeed only if the Director and his staff genuinely accept this relationship to the Secretary and the subject matter lends itself to this treatment. The President, however, can encourage the proper relation by consulting the Secretary of State on appointments and making the tenure of incumbents depend on satisfactory relations with the Secretary. If it works, this system has real advantages from the point of view of the Secretary of State. By relieving him of their administration, it conserves his time and energy for other matters more germane to his primary responsibilities. It may also be easier to obtain more senior or experienced men to head such agencies when they have a separate status.

Where the Director or his staff seeks to pursue an independent course, or the subject matter does not lend itself to generalized guidance, the friction resulting from an autonomous status can consume undue time and energy and seriously impede the use of the instruments. And even when the agency is within the Department, the Secretary can avoid the administrative burden, if the Congress will recognize the responsibility of an appropriate Under Secretary.

INTERDEPARTMENTAL COMMITTEES

The usual technique for coordinating policy among interested Departments is the interdepartmental committee. Some of these are statutory like the National Advisory Council, headed by the Treasury, which prescribes policy for the United States representatives to the International Bank and the Monetary Fund. Usually, however, they are created by Executive Order or more informal action. The most recent tabulation shows well over one hundred such interdepartmental committees on which the Department of State is represented. Some of them should probably not be treated as policy committees, but a large proportion clearly are.

Of these, the most important is the Operations Coordinating Board which was created by Executive Order in 1953 to improve the carrying out of NSC policy decisions. On it are Under Secretaries and other senior officials from the agencies engaged in foreign activities. Under their direction, working groups from these agencies develop more specific plans for various countries and regions to coordinate the activities of the operating agencies and to insure that they will reinforce each other, especially in the field. These subordinate committees now number more than forty. At regular intervals the Board submits to the NSC progress reports on each area, drawing on the experience of missions in the field. The comments and suggestions in these reports provide material for policy revision.

The Departments also create *ad hoc* committees to develop policy on specific topics, such as for a meeting of the NATO Council or a Foreign

Ministers meeting. By joint staff work, proposals or positions take account of the knowledge and views of the several interested Departments.

AMBASSADOR AS COORDINATOR

Each United States mission abroad, under its ambassador, is today an inter-departmental group, with representatives from Defense, ICA, USIA, and other agencies, as well as State. Their primary functions are to execute decisions made in Washington. But the ambassador also submits recommendations on policies which are often the result of collaboration among the officials from several agencies. Moreover, the ambassador has an explicit responsibility to coordinate the activities of the several agencies in his area. Where policy divergences appear, he must either iron them out on the spot or report them to Washington through the State Department. This procedure provides an important check on whether the policies of the various agencies are in fact consistent with one another and with the general guiding policy framework. Through it, the Secretary of State can be kept informed of differences requiring his attention.

CRITICISMS AND PROPOSALS FOR REFORM

The existing procedures have been strongly criticized as inadequate.

It is true that the use of committees is subject to weaknesses. Where they are expected to produce agreed reports and all members enjoy equal status, the members may tend to compromise unduly or water down proposals to achieve agreement. If carried to excess this can destroy the chances of new proposals or original analysis; it may also prevent real issues from being brought to the surface for discussion. The end result may be divergent policies or actions by the several departments or agencies.

This danger can be greatly reduced if the Secretary of State and his subordinates assume a primary role in this process. They should normally serve as chairmen and should be considered as having special responsibility for insuring that policies are consistent with the national strategy. The Secretary should be ready to submit to the President for decision significant issues where differing views appear to run counter to that strategy. If the Secretary enjoys his full confidence, the President should normally support the views of the Secretary in such cases. If that is in fact the practice, the hand of the Secretary will be greatly strengthened in coordinating policy with other Departments.

More radical reforms have been proposed. Some have recommended that the Secretary of State be elevated to a position above other Cabinet officers with explicit authority to direct them on policy matters. In effect, his relation to other Departments would be similar to that to USIA. This does not seem a practical proposal under our system. The heads of major Departments like Defense, the Treasury, or Agriculture have a position which cannot be defined merely by charts. Each Department has its own supporters in the Congress and its clients among the electorate. In case of serious disputes regarding policy, only the authority of the President will be adequate to resolve them finally, and even his authority may have to be exercised with vigor. Whatever the nominal status of the Secretary of State, his capacity to resolve such disputes depends on his ability to invoke the authority and prestige of the President. When the President normally upholds the Secretary of State on such policy issues, the heads of other Departments are likely to accept the *de facto* primacy of the Secretary of State. This relation seems more valuable in achieving real coordination than a formal change in his status.

Another proposal has been for a First Secretary or Minister under the President to coordinate the various Cabinet officers concerned with national security affairs. Assistants to the President can help in sorting out issues and in preparing materials for decision by the President. They can act as his eyes and ears in observing the execution of his decisions and in keeping him informed. But the idea of a First Minister with power to direct the heads of Departments raises serious doubts. In large measure it is subject to the same infirmities as elevating the Secretary of State which has already been discussed. There is, however, an additional objection. This proposal would tend to insulate the President from day-to-day contact with key Cabinet officers. It might thereby deprive him of the benefits of much of the analysis and discussion with the Secretary of State which goes on today. Since the ultimate authority would continue to rest with the President, it seems unwise to reduce this give and take. The price would be too high for the amount of time and effort saved. It would seem better to curtail other drains on the energy and time of the President before adopting this proposed remedy.

POLICY COORDINATION WITH ALLIES

Many matters today require joint policies with allies or other friendly nations. Various methods have been developed for concerting such policies:

(1) In a few cases permanent bodies have been created for this purpose. The NATO Council is one such body. Its members meet regularly to

discuss matters of common interest and where necessary to concert policy. The crucial decisions regarding the strategy for the defense of Europe, the kinds of forces required, the sharing of burdens in providing them, and related matters have been settled through this channel. The primary burden for relations with the NATO Council falls on the Secretary of State and his Department. The Secretary instructs the United States' member of the NATO Council, coordinating with other Departments if appropriate, and he himself regularly attends Ministerial meetings once or twice a year.

The Security Council and General Assembly of the United Nations also provide permanent facilities for consultation and discussion, but not on so intimate or continuous a basis as in the NATO Council.

(2) *Ad hoc* working groups are frequently created to concert allied policy on specific matters. Such working groups have become a regular method of preparing for meetings with the Soviet Union. They enable the Western nations to work out joint proposals and policies on issues such as German unity, arms control, exchange, and similar matters. The initiative for such *ad hoc* groups ordinarily rests with the Secretary of State, but it is not unusual for officials from other Departments to be members of such working parties.

(3) Foreign Ministers meet for the specific purpose of concerting policy and action on pressing matters. Such meetings, among two, three, or four Western powers have become common. Larger meetings are also held in some cases. After the French defeat of EDC, for example, the Western nations met in London on the policy for ending the German occupation and rearming Germany. Similarly after the Suez seizure by Egypt some 22 of the interested nations of Europe and Asia met to consider what regime would be acceptable for the future operation of the Canal.

In general the Secretary of State is responsible for carrying on all these forms of policy coordination with other nations. Where appropriate he consults with other Departments and if necessary obtains their approval of proposed courses of action. And, of course, he acts at all times under the general direction of the President and will take up important issues with him in detail. However, the burden of this consultation with allies falls mainly on the Secretary and the Department of State.

One result has been a great increase in the amount of travel by the Secretary. On major policy decisions the Foreign Ministers often prefer to discuss the issues in person. Knowing the key position of the Secretary of State they naturally desire to hear his analysis and reasoning for themselves. Moreover, where the stakes are large, they wish to have the chance to present their views directly for his consideration. His attendance at such meetings serves a very real function in insuring common policies and action with allies on critical matters.

Even so, it might well be feasible to send an alternate for some types of negotiations. It has been proposed that a Secretary of Foreign Affairs, of cabinet rank but subordinate to the Secretary, might be established for this purpose. It would seem, however, that most of the benefits could be achieved more simply by wider use of ambassadors-at-large, with real authority to speak and act on behalf of the government.

The Secretary and the Department

In fulfilling his policy-making functions, the Secretary of State requires a staff to assist him (1) in the analysis and planning for the strategic concept and for instruments for carrying it into effect; (2) in coordinating policy-making by and among the Departments.

OPERATIONS AND PLANNING

To supply such staff assistance is one of the responsibilities of the Department of State and the Foreign Service. But the Department is also an agency for executing policy as well. It must furnish much of the staffing and back-up for the 288 missions maintained by the United States in 88 countries, and for the nearly four hundred international conferences in which the United States participates each year. It must administer a Foreign Service of some 8,300 officers of whom 2,000 are normally on duty in Washington and 6,300 overseas. Other chapters in this volume deal with the Secretary's functions in the execution of policy and in administering the Department. Here we are concerned with such activities only as they compete with and complicate those relating to more basic policy formation and coordination.

The Department is organized on both regional and functional bases. Five Bureaus are devoted to areas: Europe, including the Soviet Union; the Middle East; Africa; the Far East; and Latin America. Each Bureau is headed by an Assistant Secretary with a Deputy, and contains Desk Officers specializing in matters relating to each of the countries within the region.

Other specialists are organized into functional divisions also headed by Assistant Secretaries. These include Bureaus for UN Affairs, for legal matters, for Public Affairs, for Economics, for Congressional relations, and for Intelligence and Research. There is also the Policy Planning Staff. Finally, Special Assistants to the Secretary are available for certain specialized activities such as Atomic Affairs, and Mutual Security Affairs.

In providing policy assistance, two problems arise: *First,* the regional and even the functional Bureaus are charged with a heavy load of day-to-day activities in the execution of policies. Each day they must answer a thick stack of cables from the missions asking for advice, assistance, instructions on a wide range of issues. The Assistant Secretary and his staff must deal with the press, and must often appear before Committees of Congress to explain or defend particular actions or policies. Each regional bureau must receive the members of embassies from countries in their region and keep them informed of American actions of interest to their countries. Finally, as part of their duties, these officials must take part in a substantial round of social activities.

The heavy pressure on their time has a tendency to cause them to focus on the immediate or short-range problems constantly on their doorstep. Yet longer-term issues may be the most fundamental of all. The military balance is likely to be affected only gradually by factors working over periods of months or years; the problems of economic and political growth require actions planned and carried out over a long period. These more basic aspects of policy are not likely to seem quite so pressing or urgent in competing for the time and attention of the bureaus.

Second, the officers in bureaus may see problems from the limited view of the region or function for which they are responsible. In a sense, it is their duty to do so. Of course, there are offsetting tendencies. Many officers are rotated among different bureaus and gain wider perspective. Also, the functional bureaus, while still having a partial view of their own, do tend to transcend the regional perspective. And the regional views tend to compensate for each other. In the final analysis, the Secretary must weigh the various partial points of view and try to strike a balance or make a choice between conflicting opinions and advice. In doing so, he has the help of certain officers such as the Under Secretaries and the Deputy Under Secretaries, whose responsibilities are also worldwide.

POLICY PLANNING STAFF

In addition, the Secretary has the assistance of the Policy Planning Staff, created by General Marshall in 1947, to compensate for some of these shortcomings in the policy-making processes of the Department. One purpose of the Policy Planning Staff is to assist the Secretary in integrating the different viewpoints and considerations transcending the regional approach. The Staff is expected to examine policies from a global point of view and in relation to the broad strategy of our foreign policy. It is also expected to try to look somewhat further ahead in terms of longer-range problems and forces which tend to be slighted. To allow time and opportunity to devote to this sort of consideration, the Staff has been relieved of many of the duties carried by the regional bureaus. In general, it does not deal with the press, with Congress, or with foreign representatives. It has no operating responsibilities, no obligation to instruct or service field missions.

Even so, the Policy Planning Staff has been criticized frequently for becoming too deeply involved in current actions. This criticism is partly valid. In large part, however, it reflects a misconception of what is useful and possible in long-term planning. The concept of long-term thinking and planning poses a basic dilemma. A group of people set off in an ivory tower to think about the future can write learned papers, but their work will bear little fruit in the effect on what takes place. The purpose of a policy planning staff is not merely to produce literature, but to produce results. For better or for worse, foreign policy becomes operative largely in specific decisions. A decision this week or this month about actions in the Middle East, or disarmament, or economic assistance, may determine the course of policy over a period of years. If insights and thinking on long-term factors are to be effective they must be brought to bear on such decisions as they are made.

It is true, however, that the Policy Planning Staff will have no special contribution to make if it becomes unduly bound up in current activities. This is the dilemma of the Staff; it must find the time to devote itself to analysis of long-range factors and, at the same time, must be able to take part in selected decisions which are likely to be significant for the future. Undoubtedly, there is a constant tendency to pull the Staff into operations to an undue degree. This must always be resisted. But many critics, in objecting to this tendency, disregard the question of how to mesh thinking with action.

What contribution, then, should the Planning Staff try to make? Some have suggested that its main activity should be contingency planning, such as military staffs frequently do. To my mind, this is a misguided view. It would not be fruitful for the Staff to devote itself to developing a wide catalogue of solutions for possible crises which might arise over a period of years. Experience suggests that such crises are not likely to occur in the manner which can be foreseen concretely enough to make the planning very helpful. In addition, the potential number would be much too extensive to manage if they were really expected to cover the possible contingencies.

The purposes of such a staff should be quite different. Its first concern should be with identifying the long-range or basic forces at work in the world, and then examining what they imply for the premises of

American policy and for our interests and purposes. It should be a focal point for the analysis and planning for basic strategic policy.

A second duty of a planning staff is to direct attention to instruments of policy or types of actions which may not pay off in the short run, but which may be quite vital in shaping the long-run environment.

Third, the Staff has a vital role as critic of existing policies. It should continually review them in the light of experience and new analysis to determine when they no longer fit the situation. In a world changing as rapidly as ours, this reappraisal of premises and actions is essential to overcome the inherent momentum of existing views and policies. Finally, the Staff should seek to stimulate similar analysis, review, and planning in the regional and functional bureaus.

COORDINATION

The Secretary, as has been said, must be able to bring to the President a point of view which integrates military, economic, and other factors which may be primarily the responsibility of other Departments. Those Departments, of course, submit their views to the President. But the President is entitled to obtain from the Secretary of State a synthesis which gives due weight to all the relevant factors. For this purpose, the Secretary needs on his staff experts in various fields who can relate these fields to the larger framework of foreign policy. Though the detailed data may come largely from the other Departments, the specialists in the State Department should assist the Secretary in analyzing and interpreting the data and in appraising any policy proposals based on them. Only in this way will he be able to play his proper role where conflicts arise with other Departments.

The Department has not always been strong in this type of staff. By tradition, Foreign Service Officers have tended to consider diplomacy their special province and to look askance at some of these other specialties. Gradually, however, the staff of the Department has been strengthened in these respects. In the military field, the practice of sending Foreign Service Officers to the National War College and the other service colleges has been important in developing a corps of officers better able to advise on this range of problems. The transfer of part of the Office of Strategic Services to the Department after the War brought in a group of analysts with a wide range of background who provided the core of the intelligence and research staff. Similarly, economists have been drawn into the Department in larger numbers. Still more could be done to improve the capacity of the Department in these and other respects. In the field of arms control, for example, the Department has not had a large enough staff with the requisite special skills to develop and defend its own proposals. Too often, proposals have had to be based on inadequate preparation or inadequate technical knowledge.

USE OF THE STAFF

The Department and its officers constitute a reservoir of knowledge and skill. How far these talents are used and in what manner depends primarily on the Secretary, for he controls the valve, so to speak, which determines to what extent their views and knowledge flow into the blood stream of policy within the Executive Branch and flow outward to the field in the form of instructions and messages.

But the Secretary is far more than a conduit. If he performs his role properly, he contributes major ingredients of his own to the output of the Department. In relation to the President, the Secretary of State is a staff advisor. He cannot be content merely to transmit to the President views formulated by his subordinates within the Department. He owes an obligation to the President to reach his own conclusions and synthesis as a basis for his advice to the President. He must use the members of the Department to inform him, to stimulate him, to guide him; but, in the final analysis, he must put the pieces together and reach his own conclusions.

The occasions for policy discussions and decisions are extremely varied. A telegram from an ambassador may raise a policy issue which requires an answer. Instructions may be required for a delegation to some international conference or may have to be supplemented during the course of the conference. A proposed speech by the President or the Secretary of State may be the occasion for some new statement of policy or review. One of the bureaus, or the Policy Planning Staff, may present some issue or proposal to anticipate a problem. A paper on the agenda for an NSC meeting may pose some issue on which the Secretary will be required to make a recommendation.

The precise method which the Secretary uses to take advantage of the resources of the Department depends greatly on his personal methods of work and style. In the postwar period, two different methods have been used.

One style was exemplified by Secretary Marshall. In effect, he made Under Secretary Acheson his Chief of Staff and delegated to him authority over policy formulation, operations, administration. He expected Mr. Acheson, as his deputy, to work with the staff and collate the issues, and to put the problem before him for decision with a written analysis and recommendations. He would then approve, reject, or modify the proposal.

The second method was used by Messrs. Acheson and Dulles as Secretaries. Their practice was to meet, themselves, with the senior members of the Department for discussion regarding issues and proposals. Mr. Acheson often used the method of designating specific working groups on particular problems and might have four or five such groups working at one time. He would meet with the groups at various stages of their work in order to give general direction to the discussions. With Mr. Dulles, the normal practice was to circulate a proposal before meeting on it with the interested Assistant Secretaries and other officers. In both cases, the meeting enabled each participant to express his views on the proposal or any alternatives. It might end with the decision by the Secretary or with a request for further work on some aspect to be discussed at a later meeting.

The Secretary will be properly served only by forthright expressions of views by his associates. He should have the benefit of frank statements of dissent or disagreement or criticism. Clashes of opinion serve to bring out and illuminate the real issues. The habits of a career service do not always foster this type of sharp criticism. There is some tendency to moderate dissent or unduly forceful conflicts of opinion. The cause is not necessarily lack of courage, but partly the necessity of serving with one another over a period of twenty or thirty years. This tendency justifies the use of some appointees outside the career service in the upper levels of the Department. A limited number of qualified Assistant Secretaries from other backgrounds can inject a somewhat more critical atmosphere.

There is another obstacle to the full discussion and analysis of all policy issues within the Department. The time of the Secretary is not unlimited. He cannot, and should not, personally decide many issues which arise from day to day. Yet he must insure that policy is clear and forceful. Consequently, much depends on the process by which particular issues are selected for his consideration and decision.

Too great a premium on resolving questions at lower levels to save the time and energy of the Secretary can have the effect of blurring the direction of policy. The practise of "coordinating" papers before submission to the Secretary for approval can have this same effect, if abused. Officers who disagree may cover over the disputed issue by compromise language which leaves it unresolved. If the document goes forward in that form to the Secretary for his approval, he may not be aware that any difference of opinion exists. Where the dispute is not vital, no harm is done; but sometimes the result may simply postpone real differences which should be brought up for decision.

The same thing may happen in the work of committees. Where the committee is under undue pressure to reach an agreed report, the members may have the same tendency to compromise and thereby conceal, by ambiguous language, real differences of opinion.

The morale of the Department created by the Secretary will have much to do with whether such practices do defeat proper discussion and decision of policies. They are less likely to do so if it is understood that he wishes to have brought before him real issues which should be debated and decided, but that he expects decisions once made to be loyally carried out and applied. If, on the other hand, it is difficult for subordinates to obtain prompt and effective decisions through the Office of the Secretary, then compromise and clouding of issues is more likely to take place.

Conclusion

The role of the Secretary of State in policy-making, as outlined above, is clearly a demanding one. For him to fulfill the role, four conditions must be met.

First, the Secretary himself must have personal capacities and qualities of unusually high order. He must have the intellectual capacity to understand and analyze complex and technical matters involving many disciplines and specialties. He must have the ability to appraise evidence of many kinds, and the courage to reach decisions, despite uncertainties, on fragmentary data. He must be able to work with his associates and to inspire their interest in order to extract the maximum benefits from their advice. He must be able to enlist the confidence of the President and other officials in the Executive Branch as well as allied nations. These qualities of character and intellect are needed for his role in policy-making. Still other capacities are required for executing policy and administering the Department and for his share in relations with the Congress and the public. Given these many demands, it is obvious that the Secretary also requires enormous energy and stamina.

Second, the staff of the Department must effectively assist the Secretary in policy planning to integrate the political, military, economic, diplomatic, and other factors and in coordinating policy in all its aspects. The members of the staff must understand these responsibilities and be equipped to perform them.

Third, the heads of other Departments and their staffs must accept the primacy of the Secretary of State in the field of foreign affairs in the sense described. No system of coordination can substitute for active and genuine cooperation in so intricate and far-flung activities. Coordination can assist officials in understanding what must be done for effective action, but it can enforce concerted effort to only a limited extent. The staffs of the various departments must be able to combine two kinds of support. They must be ready to carry out faithfully the decisions and policies adopted by their responsible superiors, as long as they stand. But they must have the energy and courage to struggle for revisions or changes in policy which appear to be necessary or desirable.

Fourth, the Secretary of State must have the complete confidence and support of the President. The role of the Secretary, while staggering, is no substitute for that of the President. At best, the Secretary can assist the President to use the authority of his office wisely and constructively in foreign affairs. With the leverage of Presidential support, the Secretary can do much to produce coherent policies and actions. But only the President can provide the leadership essential to make them fully effective.

4.

The Secretary and the management of the department

♦ HENRY M. WRISTON

To the public, the Department of State seems a vast, mysterious bureaucracy. I recall leaning out a window of "Old State" overlooking Executive Avenue one hot day in 1920. A "rubberneck wagon" was passing and the guide was addressing his captives through a megaphone: "On your right is the State, War, and Navy building. It has eight miles of marble corridors. Here Uncle Sam supports thousands of people in ease, idleness, and luxury. On your left. . . ." I have never since heard so graphic a description of the popular image of the Department.

The numbers of persons in its service are large: about 23,000 officers and employees, of whom nearly 10,000 are foreign nationals. The American citizens are divided about

♦ HENRY M. WRISTON, President of The American Assembly, served in 1954 as Chairman of the Secretary of State's Public Committee on Personnel. Since 1951 he has been President of the Council on Foreign Relations. In 1960 he was appointed chairman of the Presidential Commission on National Goals.

equally between service in the United States and in foreign countries, and between those of officer rank and employees without it.

This would be a huge number for the Secretary to manage, even with unlimited discretion. However, almost endless legal complexities restrict him. After the second World War, there were at least four separate personnel categories with different terms of pay, tenure, and retirement: the Foreign Service, the Foreign Service Reserve, the Foreign Service Staff, and the Civil Service, besides the political appointments. This tangle of personnel systems greatly impaired flexibility of management. Moreover, the Secretary's management is always likely to be second-guessed by any one of several Congressional committees, almost certainly by the Controller General, and, so far as the next year is concerned, inevitably by the Bureau of the Budget.

In the light of such obstacles, perhaps we should not be surprised if some Secretaries give little thought to administration in order to concentrate upon "more important" responsibilities—the formulation and execution of policy. The impulse to eschew administration is understandable; it is also disastrous.

Administration and Its Effect on Policy

Every Secretary confronts a myriad of problems. During an average day, he must approve, disapprove, or modify approximately twenty proposals for urgent action. Literally none is simple; the timing of each may be as vital as its substance; and the most innocuous may suddenly explode by touching some hidden sensibility, some concealed or secondary interest. Most affect more than one nation; many transcend an entire geographical area. They are compounded in varying degrees of political, economic, strategic, cultural, and scientific components. They are simultaneously foreign and domestic: most foreign policies have domestic repercussions, and vice versa.

The tempo, swift almost beyond belief, adds difficulties. Foresight is desirable and can clear the way for quick, yet wise, decision. But it is often ruled out, for it involves reading minds half a world away, and judging the transient tempers of peoples whose mood can never be measured. What starts as a student riot may blossom, unpredictably, into a full-fledged revolution.

THE USES OF EXPERTS

Even if the Secretary has long experience and extraordinary intellect, he can be an expert in only a trifling fraction of the issues. Of many he will not even have heard. Much less will he have had opportunity to study their backgrounds or ways to keep them under control, to ameliorate them, or—if possible—to find solutions. Even when he delegates the actual decision, as he has done increasingly in recent years, he must accept the risks in whatever action is taken—and literally none is without risk.

Fundamental to his job, therefore, is the effective use of a great company of experts. Some are in Washington, others scattered in embassies, legations, and consulates around the earth. They must propose not only policies for meeting the instant necessities but also measures to prevent issues not yet acute from maturing into crises. The public never hears of success; it is not "news." The failures are conspicuous, and supply a built-in adverse bias to public estimates of the Secretary's performance.

The only means by which these vast resources of knowledge and judgment can be made available to him is through sound administration. One would therefore expect great effort to be expended upon it. Yet deep concern and earnest efforts to that end have too often been lacking.

RIGIDITIES IN THE LAWS

The deficiency begins with Congress, which has been more concerned with the negative side—with preventing the Secretary from abusing power. As early as 1884 Woodrow Wilson wrote that Cabinet officers "are in the leading-strings of statutes, and all their duties look towards a strict obedience to Congress." Since that passage was written the laws have become longer, more detailed, and more explicit.

The laws governing the Civil Service, the Foreign Service, and the Department of State are the most complex of their kind in the world, so that the Secretary now requires a large legal staff to tell him what he may and may not do. It therefore takes far more administrative energy than it should to achieve a relatively modest change in the organization.

A needed reform is legislation that deals with principles and leaves details to departmental regulation. To this end, the Hoover commissions and others have made good recommendations, but all too many have been disregarded or only half-heartedly implemented for lack of public support.

PROFESSIONAL AND AMATEUR DEPUTIES

Few Secretaries of State, before taking office, have managed large organizations. Most have been lawyers whose administrative experience has been negligible and who do not have enough time in office to develop administrative skill. The Secretary should therefore take great care in the selection of his administrative deputy. With some notable exceptions, however, the record has been one of carelessness in making this choice, and often the Secretary has had no effective role in it. Sometimes the post has been a patronage plum for a party stalwart, second degree, bestowed at the behest of the party chairman; sometimes a businessman has been selected to put administration on a "businesslike basis," with no awareness of the vital differences between government and industry. When the assignment has been given to well-equipped men, they have usually been loaded with other responsibilities to the detriment of their administrative function.

Worst of all, in a period of ten years, the Department had nine administrators. Even an experienced man requires a considerable period merely to grasp the rudiments of his job. None—literally none—of those who held administrative office during that decade served long enough to master its subtleties. Until the second World War continuity in administrative management had been a fundamental tradition of the Department. William Hunter, Alvey A. Adee, and Wilbur J. Carr had served without a break from 1829 to 1937—well over a hundred years. They were professionals in the truest sense, able to work with successive Secretaries of whatever party or policy. The administrative deputy of the Secretary should always be that sort of man. That office is no place for a political appointee, or for a businessman without government experience.

Over-all Departmental direction must remain in the hands of a political Secretary. It is so much the more necessary that the infinite complexities of government management be delegated to a seasoned professional. This will assure the Secretary not less control, but greater. It is far too easy for recalcitrants—as the last two decades have shown—to confuse or "wait out" one who is not expert in Departmental procedure.

CLOGGING THE PIPELINES

The consequence of poor administration has often been clogged pipe-lines between the Secretary and the experts. The result was to curb the effectiveness of the Secretary. There are frequent demands for "bold, fresh, imaginative" approaches to foreign policy. In plain terms, stripped of oratorical sonorities, that is a call for ideas. Ideas come only from individuals, and the experts in the Department and abroad generate many of them. Poor administration can enmesh them in bureaucratic snarls and keep them from ever getting to the Secretary. Others have reached him, but so curtailed and compromised by successive revisions that their authors would scarcely recognize them; or so slowly that their utility has been destroyed. These frustrating things happen not by design, but as a consequence of inadequate administration. The result goes beyond mere inefficiency. In the words of a Department report:

> Individuals, denied the machinery to have their views consid-
> ered and, if logically sound, incorporated into foreign policy,
> have taken their case outside of the Department and have inter-
> ested columnists, Senators and Representatives to plead their
> case for them. This results in the washing of 'dirty linen' in
> public with a consequent loss of confidence within the Depart-
> ment and further deterioration of the Department's prestige.

It should be evident that, if the Secretary of State is to develop more realistic, more forward-looking, and more intelligent policies, he first needs an administrative organization which would keep clear the chan-nels to his host of experts.

It is sometimes assumed that in the "good old days" access to the Secretary was much easier. Perhaps it was if one goes back far enough—but it would have to be a long time back. In 1915-1916 the United States occupied Haiti and the Dominican Republic. A friend of mine de-nounced that occupation in a lecture in the early '20's. I remarked that his criticism seemed to me unfair, since as head of the Latin-American division he must have drafted the instructions to the occupying forces. He conceded as much, but said he was governed by a fixed policy. To every preliminary paper, as well as to the final instructions, he had at-tached a memorandum dissenting from the official policy and urging a different one. So far as he could learn, his dissent in no case reached the Secretary.

I inquired why he did not see the Secretary to explain his view. He told me that in his entire period in the Department he had been able to see the Secretary only once—for a period of fifteen minutes, at the

Secretary's order, about another matter. When he sought to raise this issue, the Secretary cut him off without allowing him an opportunity to express his opinion. He left the Department.

Incidentally, that episode illustrates another point also. It is often suggested that there should be a *current policy line* for each nation—a codified written statement—to guide subordinate officers, so that they might take action on "ordinary matters" without imposing upon the harassed Secretary. This would reserve the vital function of determining policy to the Secretary; it would assign the execution of that policy to subordinates. The device has been tried. A general policy manual was inaugurated fifteen years ago. It was supposed to be revised quarterly, but revision fell behind and the project was dropped, to be succeeded for a time by a policy statement for each country.

Unless such a manual is not only well done but constantly revised with great skill there are dangers, as the illustration regarding Haiti and the Dominican Republic makes clear. The policy statement may easily be too rigid; a policy may be carried forward routinely, no occasion sufficiently dramatic arising to warrant "bothering" the Secretary. Protection of his time may lead the Secretary up a blind alley. In a world of rapid changes, fixed or established policies can become fully as dangerous as the practice of making policy "on the cables"—that is, by reacting to specific episodes.

There is another danger in over-dependence upon settled policy statements. They are altogether too neat and tidy; they assume a distinction between policy making and execution which is deceptive. The timing, the deftness, the mode of execution are integral parts of policy. Clever execution can make a defective policy suffice; ineptitude can destroy the utility of a sound basic decision.

As will be stressed later, a good deal of progress has been made in clearing the channels by the institution of the Executive Secretariat. It ensures that appropriate comments, including dissents and suggestions for alterations in policy, get through to the Secretary. Yet such dissents and suggestions may not really come to his attention; they may only reach his desk. In many instances the dossier, as it arrives in his office, has a cover sheet. On a single page is a statement of the facts, an outline of alternatives, a recommendation. If he wants—and has time for—further study, there is a *précis* of several pages beneath the cover sheet; beneath the *précis,* in turn, is the file. If the Secretary reads deeply enough into the dossier, he will find many opinions. At the rate he must act, that cannot be as often as he could wish.

It is not only the officers in the Department who have administrative problems in communicating with a Secretary. He has advisers scattered in embassies and consulates all around the globe—men in direct contact with events, as neither he nor his Departmental colleagues can be. It requires great effort to keep lines of communication open with these men and women and to prevent those who serve abroad from coming to think of themselves as virtual exiles.

It is particularly important not to think of this problem as peculiarly American. The research of Professor Gordon Craig on *The Diplomats: 1919-1939* led him to conclude:

> One of the recurring themes in those books on the diplomatic prehistory of the second world war which have come to us from the former enemy countries is the plight of the professional diplomat, whose training and knowledge convinced him that the policy of his government was leading straight to disaster but whose advice was seldom solicited and never followed.

The same difficulty afflicted allied nations, especially Great Britain and France.

In the United States we have always been defensive about our Foreign Service, feeling that other nations do a great deal better. The more we review the habits of other nations, the more American experience with the status of the professional diplomat fits into a general pattern. We should take no satisfaction from the troubles of other nations, but it should make us more patient and understanding of our own difficulties.

The Integration of the Services

One of the clearest evidences of administrative neglect was the failure to expand the Foreign Service to meet the enlarged responsibilities of the United States, and to staff new embassies in the nations created after the two world wars.

THE SHORTAGE OF CAREER TALENT

Two figures dramatize this lack of foresight: when the Rogers Act of 1924 became effective, the new Foreign Service Officer Corps, uniting the diplomatic and consular services, consisted of 633 men. Twenty-one years later, at the end of the Second World War, it had only 792, despite the fact that in 1939 the Foreign Service had absorbed 114 men from the foreign services of the Commerce and Agriculture departments. In 1953, the number of officers had risen to only 1400. No wonder Mr. George Kennan has spoken bitterly of "the complete suspension of admissions for periods of years on end, a procedure which starved the Service at the bottom and sharply disbalanced its age structure."

Since it takes from ten to twenty years for an officer to gain the experience and maturity for large responsibility, such disastrous mistakes in personnel recruitment are not evident until years after the error. The failure properly to enlist members of the Foreign Service ten and twenty years ago and false assumptions with regard to its desirable size are now startlingly clear. There is an acute shortage of trained and seasoned personnel to staff all the embassies that the current world now demands; all of the new nations are sensitive areas; none may safely be taken for granted.

The grave shortage of personnel has had serious secondary effects. For example, the process of "selection out"—dropping those whose records proved that they were not equal to their growing responsibilities—was virtually abandoned for a considerable period of time. The Department had to make use of every available man; it retained in service men who had not shown capacity for growth, and who, under the provisions of law, should have been dropped.

The Congress has made provision for both inflow and outflow in the armed services. It has never given the Foreign Service authorizations regarding its numbers which would give like assurance of stable recruitment and retirement. When travellers or Congressmen scold the Secretary of State for the "grave deficiencies" in our representation abroad, they are complaining of the wrong man. The Secretary inherited the Service; the Congress helped create the difficulty by refusing authorizations for a larger service years ago.

THE EVILS OF SEPARATISM

A continuous inflow of new members of the Foreign Service was particularly essential after the war because Civil Service officers, who were permitted but not required to serve abroad, did not do so; in eight years, fewer than fifty accepted such assignments. As demands for service abroad increased, therefore, there was no alternative but to fill the overseas posts with Foreign Service Officers. Those demands became so urgent that most Foreign Service Officers were required to spend nearly all their working lives abroad. Few remained available for service in the Department of State, and positions in Washington were staffed by persons drawn from the Civil Service. This proved to have five main disadvantages.

1. The Secretary lost much of his control of the Department. Before the Second World War, Civil Service employees in the Department were primarily clerical. Substantive and administrative officers, who were not members of the Foreign Service, served at the discretion of the Secretary, and his administrative authority over them was complete.

During the middle forties, however, most of those were "covered into" the Civil Service and thus gained permanence of tenure. Under the laws and rules governing the Civil Service it became exceedingly difficult to displace a departmental officer who had not committed any gross offense but who was simply not imaginative, or not cooperative, or not efficient. Having attained permanence, members of the Civil Service naturally looked forward to a career in the Department, and as the Foreign Service Officers left the Department to go abroad, Civil Service officers took the vacant places. Thenceforward they were virtually immovable—except to progress upward. Step by step key positions in the Department were frozen in the hands of permanent officers.

That development involved a sharp curtailment of the opportunity for flexible administration. The Secretary was forced to accept responsibility for the acts of persons he could not effectively control. This situation contrasted sharply with an earlier time when most of the important policy posts had been held by Foreign Service Officers who were under the direct supervision of the Secretary and could be moved out at his discretion.

A typical case was the failure of a diplomatic officer in the Department to draft responses to League of Nations communications. He let them pile up, and did not notify the Secretary. After more than twenty had gone unanswered, League officials let newspapers know of the discourtesy. Within twenty-four hours the Secretary dispatched the delinquent officer to a post of such hardship as to lead to his resignation. In the new circumstances no such prompt or drastic action could be taken; a report in July 1946 spoke bitterly of the "absence of internal discipline."

2. The second result was even more disastrous: members of the Foreign Service were more and more deprived of experience in the Department of State. In order to become an effective officer abroad, service in the Department is essential. A Departmental report remarked that after "too many consecutive years of service in small, out-of-the-way foreign posts," Foreign Service Officers proved to be "industrious but poor organizers and executives."

Fourteen years after that report, another (to a Congressional committee) stressed the point that

> service in the Department gives a Foreign Service Officer a better grasp of the basis of our various foreign policies. It helps him to understand the kind of information which is most useful to the Department and the type of action in given circumstances which the Department would expect of him. It may also provide rigorous training in the art of drafting documents used in international exchanges and in the prepara-

tion of reports to the Department. Furthermore, the knowledge of the organization and operation, not only of the Department but also of other agencies of the government dealing with foreign affairs, which an officer derives from a tour of duty in the Department enables him when serving abroad to be more responsive to the needs of the Department and other interested agencies.

So many Foreign Service Officers were held abroad, and so many Departmental posts were filled by civil servants, that by 1954 only 119 (a tiny fraction) of the officer positions in the Department of State were occupied by Foreign Service Officers. Among Foreign Service Officers (above the entering class) over 40 per cent had less than one year of experience in the Department, and one fourth of those with twenty years of service had had not more than two years in Washington.

3. This situation, moreover, led some parts of the Foreign Service Officer Corps to continue their mistaken resistance to specialization. The dogma that all Foreign Service Officers must be "generalists" could be preserved because the Civil Service supplied specialists.

Administrators, economists, agricultural and commercial experts, and other specialists had not been welcome in the Foreign Service. Promotion panels were dominated by Foreign Service Officers, and those seeking advancement could see that the path to promotion was not smoothed for specialists, except a few of a "diplomatic" kind. It had been hoped that after the war "lateral entry" would bring the needed infusion of specialists into the Foreign Service. During five years 228 applied for such admission, but only 26 got through the meshes of the net. In 1951 the Secretary made a new effort; this time over two thousand Departmental and staff officers applied for lateral entry. Three years later less than a quarter of the applicants had been examined. Only 179 had passed; of these only 25 had actually been commissioned as Foreign Service Officers. The blockage of lateral entry was almost complete. Yet specialists within the Foreign Service there must be. The only method available was to force a lateral infusion through integration—strong medicine, indeed.

4. Another disadvantage was a feeling of tension between Foreign Service Officers in the field and the staff of the Department. Foreign Service Officers asserted that policy was shaped by men who did not know the foreign situation, and that the advice of those in the field was often entirely neglected. There were instances where a man was for many years in charge of a "country desk"—the point of immediate responsibility—who had never been abroad, did not read or speak the language of the country, and had no intention of doing any of those things. It needs

no elaborate argument to stress the grave effects upon both morale and policy arising from such a permanent separation of function.

A report to the Secretary said explicitly that the Foreign Service

> complains that the Department keeps it inadequately informed on purposes and policies, and often fails to provide it with vitally needed information; it complains that the Department is intolerably slow to act in many urgent matters; it complains that when the Department does act, it often acts without a clear sense of direction and arrives at decisions which to the field are unrealistic.

This rift between the home office and the foreign agents was by no means unique to the United States. Britain became so sharply aware of it thirty-five years ago that the Foreign Office and the Foreign Service were united. Professor Craig cites a report of a French parliamentary commission which reviewed the relation of French diplomatic service to the Quai d'Orsay: the ambassador's reports, it was found, were read by "a departmental staff composed largely of men who had never served in the field." This "tended to raise an 'impassable barrier' between France's agents abroad and those charged with the formulation of her policy." [1] The parallel is obvious.

5. Finally, the virtual exile of Foreign Service Officers made compliance with an explicit provision of the Foreign Service Act of 1946 impracticable. That law stipulated that every Foreign Service Officer must be assigned to duty within the United States for not less than three years during his first fifteen as an officer. Sometimes this provision was described as providing a period of "re-Americanization." Experience has shown that long absence from the United States lets a man get out of touch with American public opinion. Calling men home frequently was discussed and ardently defended by Thomas Jefferson when he was Secretary of State for Washington. Many an ambassador could—and some did— testify from first-hand experience that the need for this provision had not become obsolete. Yet for eight years no significant effort was made to obey the law. By that time Departmental openings were so few that practically it was most difficult to conform to the intent of Congress.

PROPOSALS FOR INTEGRATION

Clearly the disadvantages of the separation between the Department and the Foreign Service were increasing to the point of becoming intolerable. Other nations, facing similar problems, had united their for-

---

[1] Gordon A. Craig, "The Professional Diplomat, 1919-1939," *World Politics*, January 1952.

eign offices with their foreign services. That union had long been proposed for the United States. As early as 1909 Wilbur J. Carr advocated interchangeability between service at home and abroad, and when the Rogers Act of 1924 was under consideration, former Secretary Robert Lansing urged that, in the merger of the diplomatic and consular services, Departmental officers should also be included. His counsel went unheeded. In 1945 Secretary Byrnes asked the Bureau of the Budget to prepare a report on the organization of the Department. It proposed prompt steps "to bring about a substantial degree of unification" in order to "remove the barriers that now prevent the Secretary of State from assigning qualified personnel wherever they are needed, whether in Washington or abroad." As an alternative, the Office of the Foreign Service suggested a gradual merger, extending over ten or twelve years. The Assistant Secretary for Administration shelved both proposals.

The President came close to vetoing the Foreign Service Act of 1946 because the Bureau of the Budget observed: "The provisions that tended to build up the separatist character of the career officer corps and to impede administrative control by the Secretary of State were considered objectionable."

The Hoover Commission referred the problem to two former Assistant Secretaries of State. On the basis of their report, the Commission in February 1949 recommended "amalgamation" of the Departmental personnel and the Foreign Service. In 1950, a new advisory committee repeated the recommendation with some modifications. Thereupon the Secretary took preliminary steps. Passive resistance by both sets of officers, lack of administrative energy, and want of continuity combined to defeat his instructions. The fact that explicit orders of the Secretary could be disregarded with impunity was sufficient evidence of the disastrous erosion of his administrative control.

By 1954 it had become clear that only an emergency operation could restore the Secretary's effective authority. After another committee study, integration was undertaken, though on a less complete and sweeping scale than had been earlier contemplated.

RESISTANCE AND DIFFICULTIES

The program of integration when finally adopted was both incomplete and hasty. It was incomplete because the split had continued so long that the situation had lost much of its malleability. For one good reason or another some experienced and valuable civil servants could not reasonably be expected to join the Foreign Service. To force them to do so after their careers had been founded upon a different expectation would have been grossly unfair. To have dropped them from the Department forthwith would have had a seriously disrupting effect, and would have diluted Departmental experience intolerably. Thus under no fair plan could full flexibility be attained in a short period of time.

Many civil servants, moreover, had hoped to rise still further in the Departmental hierarchy. Integration virtually put an end to such prospects for those who did not enter the Foreign Service. Under the Civil Service rules, the change meant also that there would be no significant increases in salary. Salary and rank in the Civil Service derive from the post the individual occupies; they are not attached to a personal rank. In the Foreign Service, on the other hand, salary depends upon rank, and rank is a status independent, for the most part, of the particular post to which the officer is assigned. Thus a Civil Servant not only saw his advancement in the Department blocked, he might work side by side with a Foreign Service Officer who received more pay. Such adverse effects on individual careers led to resistance.

To defeat the program, some chiefs of bureau allowed vacancies to remain unfilled rather than accept a Foreign Service Officer. In fields in which few Foreign Service Officers had specialized, particularly in Economic Affairs and in Intelligence, the color of reason could be given the reluctance. In other instances, the resistance was no less firm though with less justification.

Civil Servants were not alone in resisting integration. Some old line Foreign Service Officers asserted that the admission of specialists—particularly those with administrative skills—was a "dilution of an elite corps." The same cry had been raised several times before. In 1924 it was a common complaint among the diplomats after the Rogers Act integrated the consular and diplomatic branches. Indeed, it led to efforts to defeat the will of Congress by maintaining two separate sets of service records. After a Congressional investigation, a subcommittee of the Senate Committee on Foreign Relations reported unanimously in May 1928 that the Rogers Act had been applied "in a manner far at variance from the purpose of the legislation." The legal officer of the Department held that the procedures seeking to perpetuate separation were improper. Resistance collapsed and forty-four consuls were given promotions by way of "reparation" for mistreatment. The fears so vocally expressed in 1924 are now almost forgotten.

The same cry of "dilution" was raised in 1939 when the Foreign Services of Commerce and Agriculture were assimilated; this, too, proved to be an error in prediction. It was also this resistance to "dilution" that crippled lateral entry as a means of strengthening the corps. It was only natural that with integration the heavy infusion of outsiders, particularly specialists, should reawaken fears in the old guard. Time has softened resistance from this group, but it will not completely disappear until retirement overtakes the last recalcitrant.

To the opponents of integration, the way in which earlier directives by the Secretary had been effectively ignored seemed a good omen for the failure of the new effort. Many felt that if they dragged their feet the effort at reform would be abandoned outright, or lose its energy and die. It was because of this danger that emphasis was put upon rapid, limited integration rather than a gradual merger, which would otherwise have been preferable. This led, of course, to genuine difficulties.

The integration program required that the newly admitted former Civil Servants go abroad as promptly as possible, and to staff their posts, Foreign Service Officers had to be reassigned to the Department. Both types of transfers led to the assignment of men to unfamiliar tasks, on which their work might seem unsatisfactory to a superior who had perhaps been reluctant to have them. Efforts to obey in seven years a requirement of law all but neglected for eight (the requirement that Foreign Service Officers serve specified periods in the United States) did not arise from integration, but occurred simultaneously and were easily confused with it. So many shifts in so short a period, particularly soon after the famous Reducation in Force (RIF) and the uproar over security regulations, gave a temporary feeling of great instability.

Inevitably amid these swift changes some were integrated into the Foreign Service whom experience will reveal as not adaptable to their new environment. The restored process of "selection out" will eliminate such officers. It may be remarked that the shortcomings of some members of the Civil Service were not easily detected during the selection process because they had not been subjected to frequent inspection, and their fitness reports had been virtually worthless.

CONSOLIDATION BECOMES EFFECTIVE

By no means all the early experience under the program was bad. On the contrary, from the first there were promising aspects of the reform.

The design for its implementation was put in the hands of one of the members of the committee which had recommended it. He had had previous experience in the Department and a great deal of administrative work in government. Under his vigorous and thorough direction, an admirable step-by-step plan of action was developed.

Even more important was the re-establishment of stable administration. The execution of the program was committed to a Deputy Undersecretary for Administration. He was a Foreign Service Officer who had risen through the grades to the highest rank—Career Ambassador. He had seen long service both in the Department and in many posts abroad. He had been a member of the consular branch before the Rogers Act of 1924 and had first-hand remembrances of the tensions during that earlier integration. In short, he was familiar with every aspect of the problem and had earned the confidence of both Departmental and Foreign Service personnel and, no less important, of the Congress. Moreover, he showed none of the rigidity of a martinet; on the contrary, he was as acutely sensitive to humane considerations as he was faithful to the intent of the program. Finally, he was kept in office for several years, more than any predecessor in more than two decades, so that the program had continuity and consistency in its direction.

In six years there has been no flagging in the pursuit of the long-range objective of full integration. Already the phase of acute dislocation is passing. Experience and competence have been gained in new duties; the era of rapid transfers is drawing to a close; periods of service in a given post are being stretched out toward a normal schedule. For the most part, the program has now been accepted, though some opponents still hope that when there is a change in the administration, there will be a fresh opportunity to obstruct fulfilment of the goal.

The success of such a complex operation cannot finally be judged until at least a decade has passed. A drastic reorganization is somewhat like an emergency surgical operation. It is more severe if too long delayed. It removes difficulties but is a shock to the system, and time is required to permit recovery from the side effects. Moreover, there is always a tendency to expect too much of any drastic treatment. But the difficulties arising from the split personality of our officers concerned with foreign affairs, while serious, were by no means the only administrative weaknesses in the Department of State. The integration program was not designed as a cure-all; it was a specific for certain shortcomings in the management of personnel. It should be judged in those terms, rather than as a panacea.

From this episode arises one painful reflection upon the Foreign Service. The inflexible insistence upon traditional concepts by Foreign Service Officers was not a good augury for the type of flexible diplomacy required by a revolutionary world in an era of dramatic change. It is devoutly to be hoped that, with the infusion of new blood, the old rigidities will give way. The changes made in the first few years have laid the groundwork.

The Reform of the Foreign Service

THE DIRECTOR GENERAL

The distinctive character of the Foreign Service, together with administrative weakness in the Department, produced a special difficulty. The Service, lacking adequate official recognition, developed a notable internal *esprit de corps*. The consequence was an undesirable sense of self-sufficiency.

As a result, the Secretary had, for a time, almost as little control of the Foreign Service as of the civil servants. The Foreign Service Act of 1946 provided that "the Service shall be administered by a Director General, who shall be appointed by the Secretary from among Foreign Service officers in the class of career minister or in class 1." He was to coordinate its activities with the needs of the Department and other government agencies and direct the performance of the duties imposed upon officers. The Act was drafted by an influential group of Foreign Service Officers, and this provision can fairly be described as a deliberate attempt to curtail the administrative control of the Secretary.

To some extent this was a defensive measure. Mr. George Kennan has spoken of "Mr. Roosevelt's dislike of the Service and unconcern for its future." And there is evidence that some Secretaries, and more particularly their administrative deputies, shared that feeling. In those circumstances it was natural that the Service should attempt to protect its own future, in the interests of the United States.

Nevertheless, setting up its own Director-General with such broad powers severely curbed the Secretary. It was an intolerable limitation. Later, as a result of a report from the Hoover Commission, of which Secretary Acheson was vice-chairman, the Secretary was once more given full control.

PERSONNEL TECHNIQUES

Another serious deficiency in the administration of the Foreign Service was the total lack of modern personnel techniques. For a long time the number of officers was so small that everybody knew everyone else, and could estimate his capabilities with a fair degree of accuracy. When such intimate methods of judgment were no longer adequate, more formal methods were not adopted. It is hardly too much to say that they were not seriously considered.

As the first reason for poor personnel technique was historical, the second reason was philosophical. Every Foreign Service officer was supposed to be a "generalist," able to serve in any post and in any capacity. Under that dogma there was some, though slight, justification for the "slots and bodies" method of assignment. Men were sent hither and thither with little regard for special skills or training. There were some conspicuous exceptions where men who had specialized—in Russian affairs, for example—were given the opportunity to exploit their *expertise*. But there was no system for so doing.

Personnel data were stored in folders which grew more and more bulky, increasingly miscellaneous, less and less usable. This concealed the serious—and growing—deficiencies in linguistic competence. When an analysis was ordered by Mr. Dulles the humiliating reality was revealed.

By order of the Secretary a comprehensive analysis of the skills in the officer corps was undertaken. At the start it was based largely upon self appraisal. Now, however, the analysis is more and more based upon tests, as of linguistic competence, upon inspections, reports of chiefs of mission, and comments of promotion panels.

A study of the scope of the new "functional assignment categories" shows it to be thoroughgoing. Over three hundred "position requirements and officer-employee skills" are listed. For the first time it is possible to compare available officer skills with manpower needs, and to make reasonably accurate plans for the future. It will require some time before the inventory can be complete; thereafter it must be continually maintained and revised. Nevertheless, the Secretary already has available data of great utility in his administrative task, and a new Career Development and Counselling Staff uses these data in guiding officers to those aspects of the Department's work most suited to their talents.

ADVANCED TRAINING

Another project undertaken after 1954 was the reactivation of the Foreign Service Institute. In 1946 the House Foreign Affairs Committee called for a "continuous program of in-service training . . . directed by a strong central authority drawing on the best educational resources of the country." The Foreign Service Institute was designed to be the equal of the National War College.

Those were high aims and for a time very good work was done. But for reasons which are obscure, the whole program of in-service training came to a virtual halt. The Report of the Committee on Foreign Affairs had said that the Director should be "an educational leader of distinction in his field." Instead, the acting director was a civil servant of low classification who, being asked his duties, made explicit reply: "To keep this chair warm." The staff was slender, and with some exceptions, without distinction. Few Foreign Service Officers were assigned to take work beyond routine indoctrination.

That trend has been reversed. A strenuous effort has been made to cure linguistic shortcomings. Junior Foreign Service Officers can be promoted only if they prove competence in at least one of the "world languages." The more difficult languages are being taught intensely, and to more officers than ever before. If this dramatic progress continues, the Service will have no inexcusable shortcomings in linguistic competence. That day will be speeded on July 1, 1963, when the Department makes competence in at least one foreign language an absolute requirement for admission to the Foreign Service.

Mid-career courses in the Foreign Service Institute give specialist training. Unfortunately, shortages of personnel and of funds limit the length of these courses to a deplorable degree.

Officers are now assigned in greater numbers to universities for graduate work, and are chosen for the National War College and the colleges of the Armed Forces with careful discrimination.

Finally, the Foreign Service Institute has established a Senior Officer Course—at last fulfilling the mandate of Congress to make the work comparable to the colleges of the armed services. For the career development of a man long immersed in exacting routines, nothing is more necessary than a period of study and review before undertaking broader responsibilities as deputy chief of mission or consul-general in some important post.

THE SPECIALISTS

Finally, the need for specialists has been given strong emphasis. The Deputy Undersecretary for Administration put it bluntly:

> I should like to emphasize the fact that in view of the multiplicity of functions which members of the Service are now called upon to perform, it is no longer possible for any officer to be considered 'an all-around officer' qualified to hold any position in the Service.

The Department has done more than offer training and admonition. The precepts for the Selection Boards state explicitly: "An able officer who is skilled in a single specialized function is usually no less valuable to the Service than an able generalist." In the light of most of the history of the Foreign Service, this doctrine is no less than revolutionary.

At one point, however, there is, as yet, no recognition of the new trend. Examinations for admission to the Service still emphasize the generalist, and the generalist only. They make no provision for men and women with special interests, training, or capacity. It is a shortcoming in current procedures that calls for speedy redress.

While applauding progress, one may enter a word of caution. There is always danger that any reform will go too far in the opposite direction. The Senate Foreign Relations Committee shows some indications of making language the primary requirement, rather than one appropriate consideration among others. There is need, also, in the midst of this new enthusiasm for specialists to remind ourselves that it is dangerous to go to extremes in that direction. The danger ever present is that the inevitable narrowing of experience may hamper the development of adequate perspective, and impair capacity to cooperate effectively with other persons of equally specialized, but different, skills. Other nations have found that men who serve in a particular region too long and specialize in its languages during their whole professional lives tend to underestimate the significance of other regions and other problems. They also fail to see how many issues local in form have influence far beyond their region.

THE BLIGHT OF PATRONAGE

In one other area, although some progress has been made, further reform is urgently needed. The time has come to cease treating ambassadorships as patronage.

While foreign affairs were marginal, all the posts of minister or ambassador were political plums. William Jennings Bryan's insistence upon positions for "deserving Democrats" is classic. There were some disastrous appointments, a preponderance of mediocre ones, and, fortunately, some distinguished, such as that of Charles Francis Adams to London during the Civil War. When the first World War broke out, however, the situation was tragic. The diplomatic experience of all our ambassadors averaged less than one year. They were far more badly prepared for the great crisis than were the armed services. The United States had some competent professional diplomats; they were kept in subordinate posts to make top positions available for political appointees.

As foreign affairs moved toward the center of national attention, more and more chiefs of mission became professionals, chosen on merit. Today this group includes somewhat more than two-thirds of our ambassadors.

Unfortunately, the statistical figure conceals almost as much as it reveals. All the "hardship" posts go to professionals; such assignments could not be regarded as party rewards! At the other end of the scale the great embassies in London, Paris, and Rome are not open to professionals—unless they happen to be independently wealthy and no "deserving contributor" wants the job.

This treatment of embassies as patronage is an unalloyed evil. First of all, it is dangerous. There are no longer any "safe" posts for the party faithful. Small, weak nations are often sensitive areas—as the names of Laos, Nepal, Ghana, and Cuba remind us. Our difficulties in Latin America were made more acute by amateurs who, in dealing with dictators, did not know the difference between *correct* and *cordial*.

Second, if we are to have a professional service of the highest caliber, it must not only be assured of all the unpleasant posts, but of eligibility for the best. To deny a professional any chance for the premier assignments is to strike a blow at the basic concept of a professional corps—progress through merit.

The work of the Foreign Service Officer is arduous; his family must grow up under unsettled conditions, changing climates, many schools, different languages. These disadvantages are part of the job, and no one should enter the service who is not ready to accept them. Moreover, the rewards will never be financial; no matter what the salary, it will never equal what like service would warrant in business.

The rewards must be professional. There is not the slightest excuse for the United States to be the last great nation to recognize this simple, but essential, fact. This democracy stands absolutely alone in making private wealth the primary consideration for ambassadorial appointments to our greatest allies.

The third reason why political patronage in embassies is evil is this: the man who holds his post as a political reward does not bear the same relationship to the Secretary as does a professional officer. He owes his appointment—and sometimes his loyalty—to the party chairman, or some Senator or other political power. An attempt by the Secretary to discipline him may be met with hostility in influential quarters "on the Hill." Secretaries have been forced to withdraw a demand for a resignation under just these circumstances, or have been embarrassed because a political ambassador confided his confidential views to his sponsor rather than the Secretary.

Two steps are necessary to correct this patent evil. The first is to appreciate in operative fact that the diplomat stands on our first line of defense. An enormous amount of nonsense has been written to the effect that the modern ambassador is merely a puppet on a string, that he is controlled from Washington and merely does as he is told. It is true that he is in closer touch with Washington than his predecessor of an earlier generation, but it is equally true—and vastly more significant—that the matters he handles are infinitely more explosive. Sir Harold Nicolson in *The Evolution of Diplomatic Method* comments in terms which aptly describe American experience:

> Most ambassadors during the period of slow communications
> were so terrified of exceeding their instructions or of assuming
> an initiative that might embarrass their home government,
> that they adopted a purely passive attitude, missed oppor-
> tunity after opportunity, and spent their time writing . . .
> reports on situations that had entirely altered by the time their
> despatches arrived.

Moreover, nothing is plainer upon the record than that good policies can be wrecked by bad negotiation. Clumsy, inept, ill-timed approaches are fatal, however sound the concept. An ambassador may "do as he is told," but his manner and method can make or break a policy.

We have learned that in our second line of defense—the military— it is folly to have political generals. It was not until the first World War that that obvious truth was accepted. No one would now appoint a man colonel because "he raised a regiment." It is high time the same conclusion should be reached regarding the generals of peace—the ambassadors.

The second remedy is so simple as to be almost laughable; it is an increase of two million dollars in appropriations for "representation allowances." Such allowances to the diplomatic officers of the United States are shockingly less than those of other nations. In some cases they amount to only one-fifth or even one-tenth the allowances of their opposite numbers.

This slender fiscal margin blocks the use of professionals in London, Paris, and Rome. It also has led deputy chiefs of mission to request transfers because they could not reciprocate the social amenities of their opposite numbers in Foreign Offices and embassies of other powers. Such instances do not make headlines in the newspapers, but their adverse effect upon the interests of the United States are serious.

To a scandalous extent, the appropriation for representation allowances has been made a political football. It has been caricatured as "whisky money." Congress, as I write, has added over a half billion dollars more than was requested for the military, and (over a veto) three-quarters of a billion for Civil Servants; simultaneously, it has cut heavily into the Department of State funds for waging peace. Until this perspective is altered the protestations of politicians that the Foreign Service is the first line of defense ring hollow.

There is another reason for the proposed reform. Some of the wealthy tenants of the great embassies have been able and industrious. But because it is said they "bought the post by gifts to the party" there is an unfair aspersion upon them.

However, to lay stress upon ending patronage in embassies is not to say that all ambassadors should be professionals. All great nations make use of distinguished persons who are not members of the regular diplomatic corps. Such appointments do not constitute a trespass upon the authority and responsibility of the Secretary as do patronage appointments, nor do they carry the taint of financial influence. They will never monopolize the great posts and bar all professionals.

Departmental Structure

Thus far the principal administrative problems discussed have related to personnel and its management. Those problems are complicated, but not intractable. With reasonable stress on continuity and skill in administration, progress can be continuous.

Vastly more difficult has been the problem of structure. It is more complicated than that of any industrial organization, regardless of size. No private corporation has to operate in *every* country in the whole world. Nor does it have to take a position on such an infinite variety of issues, each of which touches the emotions of exceedingly sensitive people, and a tender sovereignty heightened by ardent nationalism. Nor does any economic organization have to deal with many groups of nations with overlapping memberships. It is often necessary to negotiate with the same nation on the same topic as a member of two or more different groups, the component nations of which have competitive, not to say contradictory, interests.

(*See Charts I and II, pp. 98-100. Chart I,* Organization of the Department of State, *is a bloc listing of departmental offices and activities in accordance with customary practice. Chart II,* Conceptual Structure of the Department of State, *is intended to illustrate the interpenetration—and complexity—of the organization of these activities.*)

Realization of the complexity and magnitude of the problem would eliminate many false starts and deceptively simple solutions which leave matters worse than they were before. Many of the reorganizations of the past vividly illustrate that danger.

The roots of the structural difficulty lie, to some extent, in history. From the very beginning, and up to this moment, Congress has never understood how vital foreign relations really are. When the new government under the Constitution was organized, the Department of Foreign Affairs was the first for which there was legislative provision. Having established it, doubts set in. What would the Secretary do when foreign relations withered away, as Congress hoped and expected? On the basis of these second thoughts, which now seem incredibly naïve, the name was changed and the Department of State was assigned domestic duties; it handled patents, copyrights, registration of laws, pardons, and the

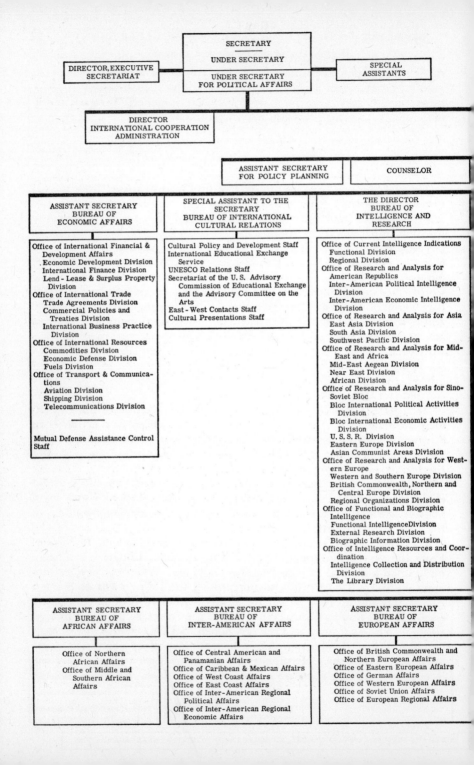

SECRETARY

UNDER SECRETARY

UNDER SECRETARY
FOR POLITICAL AFFAIRS

DIRECTOR, EXECUTIVE
SECRETARIAT

SPECIAL
ASSISTANTS

DIRECTOR
INTERNATIONAL COOPERATION
ADMINISTRATION

ASSISTANT SECRETARY
FOR POLICY PLANNING

COUNSELOR

ASSISTANT SECRETARY
BUREAU OF
ECONOMIC AFFAIRS

Office of International Financial &
  Development Affairs
  Economic Development Division
  International Finance Division
  Lend - Lease & Surplus Property
    Division
Office of International Trade
  Trade Agreements Division
  Commercial Policies and
    Treaties Division
  International Business Practice
    Division
Office of International Resources
  Commodities Division
  Economic Defense Division
  Fuels Division
Office of Transport & Communica-
  tions
  Aviation Division
  Shipping Division
  Telecommunications Division

Mutual Defense Assistance Control
Staff

SPECIAL ASSISTANT TO THE
SECRETARY
BUREAU OF INTERNATIONAL
CULTURAL RELATIONS

Cultural Policy and Development Staff
International Educational Exchange
  Service
UNESCO Relations Staff
Secretariat of the U. S. Advisory
  Commission of Educational Exchange
  and the Advisory Committee on the
  Arts
East - West Contacts Staff
Cultural Presentations Staff

THE DIRECTOR
BUREAU OF
INTELLIGENCE AND
RESEARCH

Office of Current Intelligence Indications
  Functional Division
  Regional Division
Office of Research and Analysis for
  American Republics
  Inter-American Political Intelligence
    Division
  Inter-American Economic Intelligence
    Division
Office of Research and Analysis for Asia
  East Asia Division
  South Asia Division
  Southwest Pacific Division
Office of Research and Analysis for Mid-
  East and Africa
  Mid-East Aegean Division
  Near East Division
  African Division
Office of Research and Analysis for Sino-
  Soviet Bloc
  Bloc International Political Activities
    Division
  Bloc International Economic Activities
    Division
  U. S. S. R. Division
  Eastern Europe Division
  Asian Communist Areas Division
Office of Research and Analysis for West-
  ern Europe
  Western and Southern Europe Division
  British Commonwealth, Northern and
    Central Europe Division
  Regional Organizations Division
Office of Functional and Biographic
  Intelligence
  Functional Intelligence Division
  External Research Division
  Biographic Information Division
Office of Intelligence Resources and Coor-
  dination
  Intelligence Collection and Distribution
    Division
  The Library Division

ASSISTANT SECRETARY
BUREAU OF
AFRICAN AFFAIRS

Office of Northern
  African Affairs
Office of Middle and
  Southern African
  Affairs

ASSISTANT SECRETARY
BUREAU OF
INTER-AMERICAN AFFAIRS

Office of Central American and
  Panamanian Affairs
Office of Caribbean & Mexican Affairs
Office of West Coast Affairs
Office of East Coast Affairs
Office of Inter-American Regional
  Political Affairs
Office of Inter-American Regional
  Economic Affairs

ASSISTANT SECRETARY
BUREAU OF
EUROPEAN AFFAIRS

Office of British Commonwealth and
  Northern European Affairs
Office of Eastern European Affairs
Office of German Affairs
Office of Western European Affairs
Office of Soviet Union Affairs
Office of European Regional Affairs

CHART I

Organization of the Department of State

		DIRECTOR GENERAL FOREIGN SERVICE

DEPUTY UNDER SECRETARY FOR POLITICAL AFFAIRS | **DEPUTY UNDER SECRETARY FOR ADMINISTRATION** | **FOREIGN SERVICE INSPECTION CORPS**

FOREIGN SERVICE INSTITUTE

ASSISTANT SECRETARY CONGRESSIONAL RELATIONS | **LEGAL ADVISER**

ASSISTANT SECRETARY BUREAU OF PUBLIC AFFAIRS

Policy Guidance and Coordination Staff
News Division
Public Services Division
Historical Division
Public Studies Division
Mutual Security Information Staff

ASSISTANT SECRETARY BUREAU OF ADMINISTRATION

Budget and Finance
Office of Budget
  Div. of Diplomatic and Consular
    Activities Review
  Div. of Special International
    Activities Review
  Div. of Financial Management
Office of Finance
  Division of Audit
  Division of Accounts

Personnel
Office of Personnel
  Employment Division
  Personnel Operations Division
  Allowances Division
  Classification and Wage
    Administration Division
  Medical Division

Operations
Office of Operations
  Div. of Communication Services
  Div. of Records Management
  Div. of Publishing Services
  Div. of Buildings Management
  Div. of Reproduction and Distribu-
    tion Services
  Div. of Supply Management
  Div. of Visual Services
  Div. of Language Services
  Div. of Transportation Management
Foreign Reporting Staff
Cryptography Staff

Foreign Buildings
Office of Foreign Buildings
———
Management Staff
Regulations and Procedures Staff

ADMINISTRATOR BUREAU OF SECURITY AND CONSULAR AFFAIRS

Passport Office
Visa Office
Office of Special Consular Services
Office of Security
  Div.. of Physical Security
  Div. of Evaluations
  Div. of Investigations
Office of Munitions Control
Office of Refugee and Migration
  Affairs

ASSISTANT SECRETARY BUREAU OF FAR EASTERN AFFAIRS

Office of Chinese Affairs
Office of Northeast Asian Affairs
Office of Southeast Asian Affairs
Office of Southwest Pacific Affairs

ASSISTANT SECRETARY BUREAU OF NEAR EASTERN AND SOUTH ASIAN AFFAIRS

Office of Near Eastern
  Affairs
Office of Greek, Turkish
  and Iranian Affairs
Office of South Asian
  Affairs
Office of Near Eastern
  and South Asian Regional
  Affairs

ASSISTANT SECRETARY BUREAU OF INTERNATIONAL ORGANIZATION AFFAIRS

Office of Dependent Area Affairs
Office of International Economic &
  Social Affairs
Office of UN Political & Security
  Affairs
Office of International Administra-
  tion
Office of International Conferences

DIPLOMATIC MISSIONS, CONSULAR OFFICES, AND DELEGATIONS TO INTERNATIONAL ORGANIZATIONS

CHART II

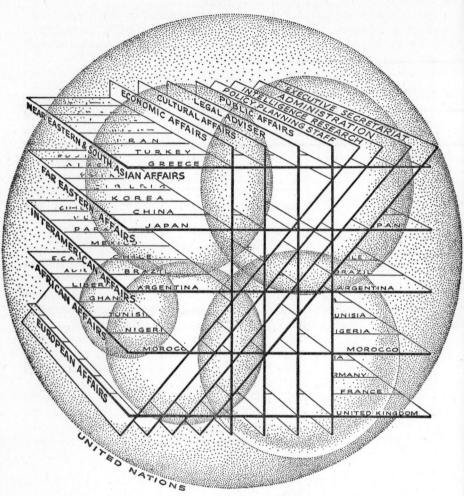

Conceptual Structure of the Department of State
The spheres represent multilateral organizations such as the UN, NATO, SEATO.

Great Seal. With all these duties the Department in Washington consisted of eight men, only two of whom were concerned with foreign affairs. Even so, Secretary Jefferson was seeking to reduce our commitments—and our personnel—abroad.

GROWING PAINS

Partly because of this mental fixation, growth of the Department in Washington was slow; 22 persons in 1833, 52 in 1870, only 209 as late as 1909, and at the outbreak of World War II, there were still fewer than 1,000 officers and employees. From time to time domestic duties—patents, pardons, for example—were sloughed off, and the Department concentrated upon foreign relations. When growth came it was sudden. The Department virtually trebled in size between 1938 and 1943, and more than doubled again the next three years.

Historically, therefore, the administrative problem never became acute until recently. The structure grew by accretion; settled habits were formed which left the Department unprepared for the reorganization its new size and expanded responsibilities required.

Even the mechanical side of administration, such as the handling of messages, broke down. An alert administrator followed the "processing" of a message from its receipt to its arrival on the Secretary's desk; it took 72 hours. What had been an efficient organization and satisfactory equipment only a few years before had become hopelessly inadequate. The same number of persons, with virtually no new equipment, were trying to handle twice as many messages as three years before.

Matters were made more difficult to reform because the Department was scattered in 33 office buildings, and six warehouses. Since that time new methods and new equipment have been installed, and when the new building is completed in the fall of 1960, many of those problems will disappear.

GEOGRAPHIC ORGANIZATION

From the very first there was one basic distinction of function: diplomatic and consular. This differentiation was common to all nations and well established in international practice.

When further differentiation took place, it was by geography. Relations, both diplomatic and consular, were on a country by country basis. As early as 1833, when Louis McLane was Secretary, the fundamental geographical structure began to take form. With each successive reorganization this basic structure became clearer and ever more firmly entrenched. When Philander C. Knox was Secretary in 1909, the geographic areas were organized into separate bureaus. Already, however, in that era of "dollar diplomacy," a functional distinction was beginning to cut across geographic lines. There was a Bureau of Trade Relations, and the number of economic officers was growing.

In 1922, when Charles Evans Hughes was Secretary, the areas were identified as Far East, Near East, Eastern Europe, Western Europe, Latin America, and Mexico. There were now also functional offices—an Economic Adviser, and a commercial office. There were nearly half as many economic as political officers in the Department.

Just before the second World War, when Cordell Hull was Secretary, the functional problem came into still sharper relief. For the first time cultural affairs appeared formally in the Departmental structure; there was not only an Adviser on Economic Affairs, but one on International Economic Affairs also, and a Trade Agreements section. For the first time there were more economic than political officers.

After the war, Secretary James Byrnes planned a "reorganization to end all reorganizations." An historical and analytical study was made, and in 1946 an elaborate report was prepared, with a recommendation that it "be circulated widely." It never was. The outstanding fact, in the words of the report, was that "the geographic or political offices have been established as the pivotal points of coordination, although the functional offices are the pivots in certain areas of action." The general reorganization failed to materialize.

The inner structure of the geographic divisions was built around "country desks." The word *desk* had a historical background; it once meant one man. In modern times, the desk could consist of many individuals, several of them with specialized duties—an internal structure relatively as complicated as the overall departmental fabric. The primary inner construction of the Department, in short, was set up to deal with day to day relations with individual nations.

FUNCTIONAL AND MULTILATERAL ORGANIZATION

Difficulties increased as functional offices—the secondary type of structure—grew in number. Indeed, so wide had become the sweep of foreign policy that there was a special assistant to the Secretary for fisheries and wild life.

Organization by area and organization by function came into such conflict that geographic divisions began to establish functional subdivisions. In parallel fashion, the functional divisions set up geographic sub-divisions. In the struggle for control of policy, the geographic had the prestige of historical position, but the functional were riding a modern trend and seemed less hide-bound and possessed more vitality. Moreover, the functional offices were able to deal with world-wide and regional questions more effectively—and those were gaining in frequency and importance.

The weight of business was shifting. Instead of bilateral relationships, multilateral diplomacy began to have a dominant place in international affairs. As a consequence, it was necessary to set up a bureau of international organization affairs under its own Assistant Secretary. It was obviously not geographic. Equally obviously, it did not have a functional basis. Just as obviously, it further complicated the whole problem of the coordination and correlation of policy. Moreover, it supplied no place for some of our most important and exigent problems.

SPECIAL PROBLEMS

Take, for example, disarmament. It is infinitely more complex than it once was because technology has made concealment of armament so subtle a process that enforcement is exceedingly difficult. In any case, there is no logical place in the whole structure of the Department of State where such a problem can be studied. It is far too technical to locate in the already overburdened planning staff; it does not fit into any geographic or functional category. It was located, therefore, in the hands of a Special Assistant to the Secretary with inadequate staff, inadequate status, and inadequate access to all of the people within the State Department and the other agencies whose work is relevant.

Disarmament supplies only one convenient illustration of issues of vast importance which do not fit into any of the established categories. Sooner or later—and the sooner the better—room must be made for special task force groups, on a long-term basis, adequate in numbers and quality of personnel. They must deal continuously with problems that technology changes too rapidly to be mastered by occasional *ad hoc* studies.

The Managerial Aspects of Policy

Despite all the handicaps of size and complex structure, it would still be relatively simple to coordinate policy and agree upon action but for two dominant facts—volume and speed. There is so much to be correlated and so little time to do it that the adverse effects of structural difficulties are multiplied.

TIME FOR THOUGHT

The first effect of volume and speed is shortage of time to think—to ruminate and reflect. It is an old complaint that has been getting more and more strident. It applies not only to the Secretary and his top staff; it affects the organization clear to the country desk, and below.

Fifteen years ago a sample was taken of a single day's activities of a desk officer responsible for one of the smaller European nations. He received 81 incoming messages of various sorts, and despatched 61, including 20 "action" messages. In addition, he attended five conferences or committee meetings, which occupied about four hours of his day. Since that time the pressure has increased. This situation accounts for the multiplication of proposals and experiments designed to provide thinking time.

For a considerable period, the Assistant Secretaries did not have heavy administrative loads or assignments to specific areas. They were supposed to act as advisers to the Secretary. The net effect was that too many operative officers reported directly to the Secretary and grossly overloaded his desk. Later Assistant Secretaries were assigned to supervise specific areas and often bogged down in the routine. They had no opportunity to think consecutively, and their advice tended to be limited to problems within their own areas. They had less capacity to counsel the Secretary on matters of broadest interest and importance.

POLICY ADVISERS

For a time there was a dual organization—an operating bureau officer with a political adviser beside him. The political adviser, supposedly freed from the rushing routine, could put his energies into the consideration of the broader aspects of problems, and their long-range significance. The idea of separating staff and line has many attractions. In this instance it did not survive.

It has even been proposed to set up a kind of separate service of thinkers—an elite group, recruited by new methods and especially trained. They would give full time to study, thought, and the formulation of policy. Some of these suggestions are obvious reactions away from "making policy on the cables," that is, reacting specifically to particular situations. But policy made in a vacuum is not likely to be any better than policy made under pressure.

The State Department has no Rand Corporation to which it can assign tasks, and it has not entered into research contracts with outside organizations as have the Armed Forces and the Senate Committee on Foreign Relations. What is valuable in the idea of research and policy suggestions out of contact with the daily cables could best be attained by making contracts with universities and other appropriate organizations for special studies.

Since 1947 there has been a policy planning staff; its chief is now an Assistant Secretary. Administratively the staff is, more than almost any other part of the Department, a reflection of the Secretary's own view of his office. In this group he has absolute power and discretion, as near perfect flexibility as could be wished. He may gather a strong group, or a weak one; he may work closely with them or ignore them.

It is small, about a dozen persons; all serve at the pleasure of the Secretary. Members of the staff may be drawn from any source whatever, with an eye single to their ability to be of service to the Secretary. They may be Foreign Service Officers, though none of the positions in the Staff is designated as a Foreign Service Officer position. In practice, roughly half of the Policy Planning Staff have been members of the Foreign Service.

The function of the Policy Planning Staff is to complement bureau policy planning by looking at problems from the point of view of the Secretary's world-wide responsibilities. It is directed to assist the Secretary "in evaluating the adequacy of current foreign policy, in the formulation of long-range policy, and in the coordination of planning activities within the Department." It has had some extraordinarily able and perceptive members; others have lacked imagination and insight. On the whole, the standard has been high, considerably higher than the average in the Department generally. The Foreign Service Officers named to this group have usually been men of high standing in the classes from which they were drawn.

There has been complaint that the turn-over in staff membership is too rapid. But the record and experience show two related things: a good deal of continuity, supplied primarily by those brought in from outside the Foreign Service; so much for the record. Experience has shown that there can be too much continuity; some turn-over is essential. One of the most experienced officers, who has observed the Staff almost from its inception, has been impressed with the necessity for a periodic influx of men with different backgrounds and fresh points of view. "In fact," he wrote, "some of the most valuable contributions from members of the Staff have been made by Foreign Service Officers during their first year of assignment."

The final complaint is that there is not enough long-range planning. Some criticism on this point misses the mark. What the critics really object to is inadequate planning for remote contingencies. Some of that sort of planning is possible and desirable. But the amount is limited because the direction, and more particularly the pace and the circumstances of change are far less predictable than is often thought. Comparisons with situations where the direction and pace of scientific and technological change are observable in advance are invalid. Even economic trends, and other phenomena available for statistical study—such as population—do not offer parallels. It is essential to remember that there are no precision techniques to assist in reaching the kind of judgment the Staff must make.

Establishment of the Staff was a sound idea and indicates that better administration will come step by step. Estimates of its success or failure in discharging its responsibilities will be as various as the critics and commentators, and the time at which the judgment is passed.

TECHNIQUES OF COORDINATION

At best, the Policy Planning Staff can make only a beginning on the vast range of activities which must be fitted into over-all policy. The upshot is that coordination of policy tends to be achieved by committees and informal conferences.

Three things need to be said on this point. As an administrative device, the committee system is vicious. It is an omnivorous time-consumer. Second, it tends to the kind of compromise that takes all the shine off what once may have been a bright idea, and turns it into a drab bureaucratic shadow of a thought. The third observation is that when committees proliferate, as they tend to do, it becomes impossible for members to attend them all; so deputies, and deputy's alternates, and alternate's substitutes act for the member until futility ensues. A review of committee activity some years ago showed a very low average attendance on the part of the official members; it revealed many committees completely inoperative, and still others showing only occasional—and feeble—signs of life.

In practice a great deal of coordination is achieved by informal sessions of the officers principally involved. As one Departmental report expressed the situation:

> Because of the habitual use of *ad hoc* committees set up informally to handle specific questions, the formal organization chart presents a misleading version of how the Department operates. The Department operates largely through a vast network of transitory committees. These committees are of great value in securing coordination.

EXECUTIVE SECRETARIAT

By far the most successful administrative innovation has been the establishment of the Executive Secretariat. It was initiated by General Marshall and carried forward by his staff. Men who had handled that sort of problem in the General Staff were brought in to start the operation. It was a major effort to assure the Secretary that the material coming before him for decision had been fully coordinated. The first two mandates of the Executive Secretariat, as set forth in the Department's Manual of Operations, cover this function. The Director of the Executive Secretariat "directs and controls the orderly and prompt flow of official action and information documents to and from the Secretary . . . assuring full correlation of relevant responsibilities in the preparation of policy recommendations." In the other direction, the officer "assures the proper implementation of decisions and fulfillment of requests made by the Secretary . . . and referred elsewhere for action."

The office has many other duties as well, but these lie at the heart of its task. Since its inception it has had able professional direction and has greatly improved the flow of work to and from the Secretary. It is no mean task. Before its establishment a sample period of 48 hours was chosen to see how much formal coordination was necessary. In that period over 2,500 communications were cleared, about half telegrams and half letters. Nearly half the number had to be cleared by two or more divisions, and many had to have clearance from five or more divisions. To make sure that no responsible office is skipped is a formidable assignment. The Executive Secretariat is one of the best illustrations of a fresh emphasis upon competent, continuous administration. It has done more than any other administrative device to resolve conflict between the geographic, the functional, and the international divisions.

Moreover, it is much more than an efficient mechanical operation. The Executive Secretariat is given a good deal of initiative in "the identification of policy problems that require coordination and advises top officials on the ways in which the Department's resources can best be utilized to handle particular problems." As the staff arm of the Secretary, it performs vital functions.

THE SECRETARY'S PRINCIPAL OFFICERS

There are now two Undersecretaries, one for political and one for economic matters. The economic Undersecretary is, for the first time,

The Undersecretary, second in command. Present recognition of the need to have two immediate deputies to the Secretary is a reversion to an earlier trial of the same idea which was abandoned when a change in personnel occurred. The creation and suppression and re-creation of so important an office as that of Undersecretary is one manifestation of instability in the fundamental administrative concepts that too long governed the Department. This time the office should remain as a permanent position.

Tentative steps were taken toward another administrative reform. When Congress authorized the post of Undersecretary for Administration, it did so for only two years. From any point of view the transiency of this device was incredibly foolish, and a further illustration of the persistent underestimation of the importance and difficulty of the task of administration. To make matters worse, the office was assumed—on a still shorter term basis—by a businessman without experience in governmental bureaucracy. Then management consultants came in to do elaborate studies. A more precise design for futility would be difficult to imagine. At the end of the two-year period, the post was downgraded to Deputy Undersecretary.

Such fitful spasms of redirection are futile. Since that episode there has been only one deputy undersecretary in charge—experienced, able, possessing the confidence of all elements. Moreover, Secretary Dulles supplied firm, unwavering backing during the difficult period of integration, and steadily expanded the powers delegated to the deputy undersecretary. Secretary Herter has followed a like policy. As a result very few administrative matters have to be appealed to the Secretary. Nevertheless, it would be wise to restore the post to the grade Undersecretary for Administration, and make the position permanent. Until that is done, there will not be the outward and visible evidence that the administrative problem is being regarded with adequate seriousness.

PROPOSALS FOR NEW OFFICERS

One proposal for change has been advanced with great force: the creation of a new office, a kind of super Secretary of State. The reasons offered are many. First among them is the fact that the Secretary of State is the principal adviser to the President not only in those aspects of foreign policy handled by the Department of State, but on all phases of foreign policy in which over two score agencies play important roles. Fifteen agencies of the United States government maintain their own overseas representatives. There are approximately fifty major "programs" abroad. These are scattered among a number of prerogative conscious agencies in different parts of the government.

A study of the Brookings Institution proposed to "concentrate under a new executive, in the line of command subordinate to the President, responsibility for and authority over important foreign affairs functions," specifically "the Department of State, the bulk of the economic aid program, and overseas information operations." The new executive should be "close to the President, sharing his breadth of interest, and acting for him, a Secretary in the sense that Washington regarded Jefferson and Hamilton."

Another proposal, much discussed, is the appointment of a negotiating Secretary of Foreign Relations in order to relieve the Secretary of State of the inordinate amount of travel—and consequent absence from Washington—which has been the lot of Secretaries since the second World War. Secretary Acheson sought to attain this end, to the fullest extent possible, by the appointment of an ambassador-at-large. Partly as a consequence, he achieved the lowest percent of time absent from his desk of any Secretary since Cordell Hull.

Whether a change in title would have any better effect is doubtful. If the travels of our Secretary of State were unique, such a change might be useful. But excessive travel is now an occupational disease with ministers of foreign affairs around the world. Until Secretary Herter's expressed desire for a new Congress of Vienna and revised rules of international protocol is realized, it is doubtful that a new title would serve to do more to relieve the Secretary than an ambassador-at-large could do. In this instance, it might set up a rivalry between two high officers. It would impair the standing of the Undersecretaries. In short, it would cause as many difficulties as it might cure.

Some of the proposed changes, in some form, might do some good, but they all have a common defect. They all add another layer to the structure and validate one of Parkinson's more acid observations about bureaucracy. Moreover, they tend to make the administrative problem seem too simple, and promise—or imply—too much. The problems involved in the administration of so vast and complex an enterprise cannot be met by simple solutions, nor by one-shot treatment.

RETURN TO THE AMBASSADORS

One of the most persistent demands is to decentralize much more by "restoring" the position of the ambassador and making him into an executive responsible for all United States activities in the country of his assignment.

Much of what is urged has been done. Some years ago the President issued an executive order making the ambassador head of the "country team," and giving him supervision over practically all the representatives of all the agencies of the government. Thus, the ICA mission reports to the ambassador, the USIS officers report to the ambassador. The Army, Navy, and Air Force attachés are also technically under him.

The order is not perfect and should be strengthened. But there is much that cannot be achieved by such an order. Many supposedly under the ambassador's supervision who report "through" him are under the direction of departments in Washington other than State. Few ambassadors have the staff and other resources to provide them the time—not to speak of the energy—effectively to control all those who report to different agencies. The business of a large embassy today is greater than that of the Department of State before the second World War. The business of being an ambassador is quite different—in an administrative sense—from the old-time emissary.

The inescapable fact is that we have not yet had time to train enough chiefs of mission for the administrative load which a modern ambassador must carry. Readiness for the new scope of performance was retarded by the resistance of Foreign Service Officers (with notable exceptions) to accept administrative training. As for political ambassadors, many have had so naïve an approach to this vast problem as to make a painful record.

The cure for administrative deficiencies cannot be swift, but it is proceeding. If career training and good personnel practices are continued and further developed the future can be brighter. Nevertheless, until the whole coordination of policy among the Washington agencies whose representatives are in the embassy is greatly improved, the ambassador, whatever his talents and training, will be in difficulties.

In any event, the ambassador can do no more than head a "country team." But, as has been pointed out, emphasis has shifted to regions, to functional groups of nations (NATO, the Common Market, the Colombo Plan, etc.) with which the head of a country team cannot cope.

To meet this situation there are separate sets of ambassadors to the United Nations and to NATO, and a representative with the personal rank of ambassador to the Coal and Steel Community and other European structures. The ambassador to the United Nations has been given Cabinet rank. The status of the ambassadors to other groups depends not so much upon administrative decision as upon policy regarding the organizations themselves and the role the United States decides to play within them and with those groups of which it is not a member.

In any event, there cannot be ambassadors to all the regional and functional organizations. That would lead to proliferation beyond the bounds of reason. From all these considerations, the conclusion must be that we can no more give international relations back to the ambassadors, who never had them, than we can give Manhattan back to the Indians, who did have it.

Conclusion

A great deal of headway has been made through improvement in personnel structure and methods. It is now possible for the Secretary to deal flexibly with an able, well-trained, well-disciplined and increasingly well-balanced corps of officers. Steady, unremitting attention to such matters will pay greater dividends with passing years. Already there are signs that the cleavages between those devoted to political matters and those concerned with economic interests, and those occupied with cultural relationships are being reduced. Time and the exchange of professional personnel between the several divisions—and the field— will continue to mitigate feelings of separateness, and antipathy.

Two Undersecretaries and two Deputy Undersecretaries have facilitated the delegation of responsibility. The load of papers paraded to the Secretary's desk and demanding his immediate personal attention has been significantly reduced. Creating an administrative Undersecretary with fullest control of recruitment and training of personnel and their deployment, with sweeping powers in the construction and management of the Departmental budget, would manifest real awareness of the significance of administration.

If the Congress and the President will give the Secretary of State the opportunity to manage the Department and the Foreign Service in a flexible manner, with adequate and consistent financial support, and free from party patronage, we can look forward to steady progress.

5.

The Secretary and Congress

◆ WILLIAM Y. ELLIOTT

The relations of any Secretary of State with Congress so condition the effectiveness of his diplomatic role that full faith and credit for his main policies, steadily given by Congress, is well understood to be almost a prerequisite. Since the rise of the totalitarian threat, when the military position of the United States and its economic support for other systems became controlling elements in the weight of our foreign policy, Congressional relations have become crucial for the Secretary of State.

The corresponding shift in the nature of the world position of the United States, further accentuated by the elimination, to date, of all the great powers except the United States and the Soviet Union as determining the real bal-

112

◆ WILLIAM Y. ELLIOTT, Leroy B. Williams Professor of History
and Political Science at Harvard University, served as a Vice-
Chairman of the War Production Board and on the Combined Boards during World War II. During 1945 he was consultant to the House Special Committee on Postwar Economic
Policy and Planning, and in 1947 and 1948, staff director of the
House Select Committee on Foreign Aid and the House Committee on Foreign Affairs. From 1953 to 1957 he was the
member for the Office of Defense Mobilization of the Planning
Board of the National Security Council, and since 1957 has
been a Consultant to the Secretary of State.

ance of power in a nuclear period, accented at the same time the need for
strong Executive leadership. Programs of all sorts required steady support and assured authorizations of funds for years ahead, both in weapons
and in economic support—a radical change from the normal Congressional pattern, a change introduced by World War II, and continued by
the "cold war." At the same time, since this leadership had to be exerted
through programs on the most massive scale, the shift in content of our
international activities very greatly extended the range of control over
foreign affairs and international activities in both houses of Congress.

The problem posed in this chapter is: How can the Secretary of State,
whose foreign policy is now inextricably meshed with national security
programs and domestic political programs, and the Congress of the
United States, still organized without strong party or programmatic
policy leadership and acting principally through committees, often with
special focus on economic areas affecting the election of their members,
mutually adjust to this new relationship in a manner adequate to our
international responsibilities and supportable by domestic politics?

Basic Political Approach

Several points may be stated as assumptions which are well-nigh axiom-
atic, under these circumstances: The effectiveness of the Secretary of
State with Congress can be no greater than the strength of his support in
the nation. That depends on his personal relations, first of all, with the
President. Beyond that, he is generally dependent on the President's own
strength in the country as a political leader. No matter what the Secre-

tary of State's individual position may be with the Congress or with the public, his foreign policy can, like water, not rise higher than its source —the President in his dual role as national spokesman and as party leader.

Of course an outstanding Secretary may strengthen politically an inexperienced though not a weak President, if the latter is capable of profiting by his guidance. But it is the President's strength that ultimately determines the tone of an Administration, in foreign as well as domestic policy. That much of partisanship is inherent in any Cabinet post. The Secretary of State may be the most effective of diplomats, but have a limited position of domestic political strength from which to operate. That strength rests in the most immediate sense on the position of the whole Administration in national confidence and support. It also rests, at a still deeper level, upon the strength of the United States in the world. This strength depends not only on the more obvious willingness and capability to maintain its power position and to use it at need. It also hangs on the economic strength and vigor which support the nation's position, its superiority in a world where basic research in science as well as technology may ultimately be decisive in power, if not matched —and overmatched.

The political dimension of international confidence in the nation's leadership rests, however, on more than military and technological and economic power. The most essential ingredient for all of these aspects of effective national strength is a moral unity of purpose and a clarity and continuity of aims which are skillfully made effective through the foreign policy of the nation. A nation, like an individual, achieves weight in the world community by known character and predictable behavior.

This modern role requires new dimensions of old talent. The Secretary of State must be enough of an administrator to shape and control the vastly expanded instrument of the State Department. But administrative sagacity and skillful organization of the Department and its adjuncts like the ICA, the USIA, etc., are not enough. He needs, too, an understanding of the limitations of policy and a realistic appraisal of foreign programs of every character.

When he approaches Congress his areas of concern are many. No Secretary who is unaware of the basic necessity of having the right balance of weapons systems immediately on hand for his national political strategy, and even for the relevant military tactics as well as strategy, can perform his role as the principal initiator of foreign policy. His influence on defense programs must be effective. He must be as much concerned with the conduct of our military assistance groups, and with the use and behavior of all our legion of representatives abroad from private organizations, as well as public agencies, as he is with the proper allocation of *all* our national resources. The strengthening of our allies and the anticipation and defeat of our enemies, both in the battle for men's minds and the struggle to maintain the strength of alliances, and the development of responsible freedom in the states which are coming into existence from the crumbling of colonialism—all are principal concerns for the Secretary of State. He must impose priorities and change them to fit events. He can be garroted by a too rigid and unselective budget process.

On the domestic front, he finds almost every committee of Congress—not just the Foreign Affairs and the Foreign Relations Committees of the House and the Senate, respectively—concerned not only with basic foreign policy, but setting the programs which give it meaning. Many of these committees are initiating legislation, holding inquiries of a critical character affecting distribution of necessary funds and resources, and creating international problems by enacting laws, by stimulating or reflecting national attitudes, and by building up political pressures. These pressures can and do run contrary to the Secretary of State's own needs for a continuous and integrated foreign policy in the national interest. He cannot fall back on utopian solutions. He must be able to operate through the whole of the Administration's powers to prevent the weakening of his foreign policy by reductions in the effectiveness of the instruments—military, economic, and political—he must mobilize in its support. He must, above all other duties, be able to set a "tone" that keeps the nation aware of the nature of the struggle in which we are engaged and the objectives to which we must unflinchingly adhere, but without practicing the psychological warfare of hysteria on his own people.

Without a strong Secretary of State, politically wise in domestic as well as in international politics, capable of the expansion of imaginative understanding and policy influence that lets him carry the proper share of his responsibility with the Congress and with the country, the work of the President is made doubly difficult, well-nigh impossible. F.D.R. once said, "I must be my own Secretary of State, War, and Navy." This was in a conversation, in the Brownlow Committee period (1936), to me when he was giving me his views on how to "fit in" with his own thinking the six administrative assistants I was suggesting for his personal staff: though I did not coin the phrase "with a passion for anonymity!"

But the price of this "Pooh-Bahism" is sometimes a neglect of the Presidency itself. The Chief Executive's job is already so stupendous in its range of political initiative, as well as administrative control and policy integration, that the Secretary of State's political capabilities are now recognized as perhaps the most crucial of all factors in the success of an administration. The Secretary already has become (what times of foreign crisis forced him to be from the beginning) something of a "First Secretary"—as the term "of State" implies. His strength must depend at least as much on successful dealing with the Congress of the United States as on the outward face the nation must show to allies and antagonists.

In this matter it goes without saying that no Secretary of State can achieve the kind of foreign policy consensus that permits what we have come to call bipartisan approaches to the basic issues of national security policy—military and diplomatic—without in some ways transcending the role of a political partisan. Yet, at the same time, he cannot fail to be loyal to his chief, the President of the United States, who must perform the same role of national leadership on its highest level, and yet be a responsible leader of a party. It is a mutually difficult assignment, made possible only by a high level of mutual trust. The idea of having a Cabinet Secretary (of any Department) who is "nonpartisan" contradicts the logic of Presidential government.

Foreign Policy and Congressional Powers: Sharing Though Separate

A few examples must suffice here for those areas of domestic policy which make the committees of Congress, particularly the appropriations committees, arenas of political action, and often struggle, for the Secretary of State. The significance of some of them to foreign policy is not obvious at first glance.

There are, of course, the obvious major problems that now depend on Congressional support, where Congressional initiative often makes itself felt in the most direct way: for example, the Lend-Lease legislation clearly showed the need for bipartisan Congressional support during the last war. The continuation of this same approach in the postwar Lend-Lease and loans, in the handling of UNRRA[1] aid and post-UNRRA aid, including the Greek-Turkish programs, and especially in the setting up of the ECA[2] and its successors, involved, in effect, a continuation of massive aid on a global basis, shifted after 1948 outside the Sino-Soviet bloc. Naturally in this process the shaping of the real instruments of foreign policy, including our occupation forces abroad (the period of the proconsulships that we had to set up in Germany and Japan especially), showed the influence of Congress, most dramatically in the Appropriations committees. These committees, especially in the House, became

---

[1] United Nations Relief and Rehabilitation Administration.
[2] Economic Cooperation Administration (predecessor of ICA).

as important for foreign policy operations as the committees of authorization to which one ordinarily looked for the support and control of foreign policy by Congress. Similarly, the Banking and Currency Committees of both houses, not only through their control of the lending instruments but through their criticisms of the economic aspects of policy, assumed a crucial importance. When Hegel said that ideas have to take on hands and feet, he gave the sanction of the greatest modern "idealist" for testing the reality of policies by the effectiveness of programs and actions to implement them. Policies are never self-effecting, and foreign policy is now often carried out by domestic programs.

A sample list of the committees of Congress to which the Secretary of State must pay the closest attention would show that he must be concerned with even committees which seem as domestic as those on agriculture; e.g., the disposal abroad of enormous farm surpluses which today run into several billions of dollars a year—the impact of which on friendly countries who still rely on the disposal of their primary products through the normal processes of foreign trade is of great concern to the State Department. The Secretary must also try to prevent the disruption of his own country's commercial trade policy and the inevitable tendency to undercut normal private channels.

At the same time, he is provided with at least the positive possibility —as yet inadequately mobilized and used—of utilizing local currency funds, both from grants and loans in terms of surplus disposal, particularly from P.L. 480[1] for agriculture, by educating civil servants and professional or technical specialists, helping these young countries better to stand on their own feet, politically and economically. The Agriculture Committees of both houses, therefore, become centers of great power and influence with which the State Department must be most vitally concerned. To subtract agricultural attachés, as was done by Act of Congress, from the ambassador's span of real control weakens foreign policy.

In a similar manner, the Secretary has to exercise whatever constructive influence he can on the whole approach to merchant shipping legislation, and not just in the matter of subsidies for United States flag shipping, given on the alleged grounds of defense or national support. Even more directly, he must try to keep within bounds the tie-in legislation that assured a major percentage of United States foreign aid exports being carried on "American-flag" bottoms.

In a related area, he must protect our communication lines of every character: in telecommunications just as much as in the press and the cultural and information media, such as the export of films. He has to

---

[1] Public Law 480: The Agricultural Trade Development and Assistance Act of 1954.

assure, also, that American airlines are not subject to discriminatory treatment, especially now that the military aspects of air as well as ocean transportation are a part of our reserve for defense purposes, as it obviously is in the days of "air lifts" and modern logistics.

By Congressional action, the Secretary is involved with our most immediate neighbors like Canada and Mexico in the most delicate problems, often highly damaging to international understanding and important defense policies. Well-known examples are pipelines; joint operations of railways or Great Lakes shipping and the St. Lawrence Seaway; development and purchases of strategic materials; and joint planning or use of defense facilities.

In another direction, he has to protect imports, on which the trade with some of our most important neighbors is dependent, from exclusionist or quota policies disruptive of trade. At the same time, he must assure that American exports and the competitive position of our foreign business interests are not crippled. The cross-currents of these two responsibilities put him at the center of a political whirlpool. If that were not enough, he now has to devise countermeasures to a stepped-up tempo of world-wide economic warfare, designed for political control as carried on by Moscow and Peiping, often as allies.

Secretaries of State have differed widely in their methods of handling this range of problems ever since Cordell Hull began what I would call "the modern period" of our foreign policy by bringing the Reciprocal Trade Agreements negotiations and their accompanying pressures within his purview. Yet until the very recent past, one general line has governed the attitude toward Congress of nearly all of the Secretaries from Cordell Hull on: they wish to guide policy without assuming an "impossible" range of operational control. The Department has normally been regarded as a staff arm of the President, whose interests extended only to the control of policy, and not to the taking over of direct responsibility for administering anything abroad. This attitude substantially controlled the Department's attitude in keeping ICA and USIA either outside the Department, or in a relatively autonomous status within it.

Perhaps each Secretary has shown a sound instinct in not wishing to bear the brunt of direct Congressional responsibility for the entire range of economic and related military assistance programs which engender in many ways the most controversial issues in Congress. These controversies subject our foreign policy officials to the gantlet of the Appropriations Committee and of various other committees of the House and Senate. Ultimately, however, the Department has to bear the brunt of this legislative and budgetary scrutiny and the consequent policy decisions which must be made by Congress. If the Secretary of State does not himself carry this burden of persuasion and responsibility on the Hill, the issue often either goes by default or off on unpredictable tangents.

On this sort of reasoning, the Congress itself has insisted in putting more and more responsibility on the State Department itself for policies; for example, counterpart funds abroad are spent, if this law is followed, according to priorities in theory determined by the Secretary of State. Equally, the Secretary is now held responsible for integrating the policy aspects of mutual security programs. This has required somewhat drastic new assessments of the relations between the Department and the agencies which are by statute, as well as Executive Order, under its policy control, such as ICA and USIA. *It is obviously difficult to control effectively an agency when one cannot either hire or fire its head, or call the turn on its funding.*

This manifest difficulty has led to suggestions for creating a Secretary of State who is, in effect, Assistant President for Foreign Affairs (or, by extension, all National Security Affairs). Such a solution would divorce him more and more from the operating mechanism of the Department itself. There are many variations in degree on this scheme. But all of them would still leave the new official's relations with Congress to be faced, with many of the same difficulties. Stubborn agencies cannot be coordinated merely by repeating the word "coordination" in statutes or Executive Orders. The proposal to vest complete line-of-command responsibility in one single person for administering the foreign (or National Security) side of the government overlooks the basic fact that many of the problems are rooted in agencies whose primary functions are not even mainly "foreign," and whose political sensitivity is necessarily primarily domestic. Only the President can control his Cabinet members on such matters, unless he is to become a *roi faineant*.

Tactics in Dealing with Congress: Partisan or Bipartisan?

It is against this background—the nature of the Secretary's role and the difficulties of maintaining an integrated policy where so many of the roots of policy lie in domestic politics—that the Secretary must decide whether to adopt a partisan or bipartisan approach to Congress. At times it is inevitable that he has to deal with Congress as the representative and even the defender of the Administration in power. He cannot repudiate the farm program of an Administration (if it is an *Administration* policy) simply because its effects complicate his diplomacy and often do serious injury to his basic trade policies or to friendly nations on whose support a considerable part of our national security programs may rest. He has to make the best of the farm policy of the country, even in cases where the Congress may have rammed a considerable part of such a program down the throat of the Administration.

In this respect he also has to act as a defender of the nation, as does the President, even though both may be known to oppose a policy which has emerged out of the Congressional-Executive struggle as a compromise smacking of defeat. Any Secretary who fails to stand up for the national policies as against the "foreigners" tends to weaken his hold on Congress by seeming to appear, as he too often must, as the defender of foreign criticisms or foreign interests. This is one of the necessary hazards of the separation of powers; bipartisanship sometimes carries along a reluctant Administration in much the same way as it forces Congress to join, with at least budgetary support and some Legislative acquiescence, in policies which it may not approve in detail.

A crucial test of a Secretary's success with Congress comes when he asks for Congressional support on a bipartisan basis for such an issue as the defense of Quemoy and Matsu. Here he uses bipartisanship to bring Congress to the aid of a policy which may be subject to a considerable body of criticism and to some legislative opposition. Or he may have to rally Congress to the support of the United Nations as a vehicle for operating, as in the Korean hostilities, in ways that limit the effectiveness of United States forces and present the United States with a responsibility for which it does not have adequate freedom of action.

Secretaries of State start out with a large natural bank credit of Congressional support. No very clear-cut case of genuine hostility between the Congress and the Secretary of State can be shown, in my judgment, since the time of William Jennings Bryan; and even that one may be considered doubtful. But Secretaries of State do encounter periods of suspicion of motives: Whether Mr. Acheson, in the post-UNRRA and the Greek-Turkish aid programs, consciously employed the tactics of "dumping the baby in our laps," as many Congressmen felt, or whether the United States government was improvising to meet unforeseen contingencies which had to be suddenly presented without adequate warning, the temper of Congress was one of genuine suspicion of motives. A large part of Congress, both Democratic and Republican, thought that a more comprehensive and longer-range package of requirements, *in toto,* would afford the only sound way to maintain Congressional control of our national expenditures. The Herter Resolution (H.R. 296), in April of 1947, was the first Congressional demand for a study of the *total* aid needs and their effects on our economy and our ability to meet them for several years. The House Foreign Affairs Committee acted similarly by preparing a report of the Vorys economic subcommittee in June, 1947, before Secretary Marshall's proposals at Harvard in that month.

The debates on the floor of either house of Congress, especially of the House, do not reveal the full degree of Congressional suspicion produced by Mr. Acheson's very effective methods of getting programs approved by Congress when he was Assistant and Under Secretary of State. Many members who are really critical of a Secretary of State, and yet are members of his party, avoid voicing their opinion publicly. A feeling of the necessity of "keeping up appearances before the neighbors" governs the public behavior of many Congressmen of the opposite party, also, who feel the decent compulsion to retain a bipartisan unity of front.

The net effect of this critical attitude was to gain support for the inclusion of Title 4 (aid to China) in the ECA Act, in spite of the originally opposed judgment of the Administration, which had, for a time, the support of Senator Vandenberg. No doubt this attitude contributed to the ultimate effect of forcing the consolidation of all aid programs, except those of surplus property disposal, in the Mutual Security Assistance Act. *But what counted was that the Secretary's careful work in preparing the ECA Act, and seeing it through, won over a Congress, originally very critical, to the basic objectives.*

The reputation for sincerity and frankness in the Secretary's approach to the Congress, and his national reputation, combine to facilitate his dealing with the legislators, or to create liabilities. One Secretary of State may be successful by cultivating a wide range of personal relations and in some measure by trying to take Congressmen into his confidence about his policy, before finally formulating it. Another may succeed in presenting Congressmen with a strong line of policy, for which the ground has been carefully laid in public opinion support, so that they run no great political risks. Still another type of Secretary may appeal with confidence to the patriotism of Congress and to its good judgment in backing a strong national security policy, providing he shows that he respects their opinion and that he has given, with the aid of the President, a strong lead on which its members can rely in winning and keeping public support. A judicious combination is possible and useful. But a Secretary who courts favor with Congress at the expense of firmness in the defense of his policies suffers the usual fate of appeasers.

Three general observations can be made in reviewing the behavior of Secretaries of State from, say, Stimson's time on, as it was affected by the nature and habits of Congress:

1. Congress does not like to have to take the lead in defending a policy on which it has not been consulted and for which adequate preparation of opinion in the country has not been made. It does not wish to have to substitute its own advocacy for strong leadership. It is easier to defend a well-conceived policy than to substitute one worked out by legislative debate and compromise. Secretaries, almost without exception during

this period, acted on their insight, both in consulting and in giving good public support.

2. The fact that foreign policy issues are usually not *crucial* in the elections of about two-thirds of the House, and are rarely a determining factor in the elections of at least as large a proportion of Senators, allows for a freedom of action in supporting bipartisan foreign policies. Unless the policy of the Administration has antagonized very large and vocal and well-organized sections of the electorate that throw their weight in thin primaries, most Congressmen in both houses can vote their own consciences and estimates of national advantage.

But the mid-term elections, which affect the entire membership of the House and, over the course of time, the membership of half the Senate, are particularly dangerous to foreign policy issues. These normally thin primaries are deadly threats to the lives of politicians wherever strong racial, religious, or other minorities can be mobilized, or where the organized weight of great pressure groups like labor or farmers or the segments of taxpayers who oppose foreign spending can be brought into play.

This is an additional argument for getting rid of the mid-term elections for the House, by Constitutional amendment. This recommendation, which has been made not only by the present author since the early Thirties, but by many other political scientists, including the Committee on Political Parties of the American Political Science Association (1950), has also been recently endorsed by President Eisenhower. It is surely one of the basic points on Constitutional reform that now commands quite general agreement among students and should be pressed by anyone who wishes to strengthen public and Congressional support for a genuinely national foreign policy.

3. Finally, the more the Secretary can come before Congress and the nation as the defender of the national interest, even when he has to make defenses of policies that seem to benefit foreigners, the easier the work of rallying Congressional support becomes. Every British Foreign Secretary can pose in this light in dealing with Parliament; he draws on this mantle in defending his most conciliatory policies toward foreign nations.

That this is generally understood shows in the sometimes intentional exaggeration of the degree to which foreign aid programs directly contribute to the military defense of the United States. The very name of the Mutual Security Assistance Programs shows that blanketing in economic aid under this Act, in order to "make effective" military aid, is understood in this light. Indeed it is almost insisted upon as the shield for Congressional action. There is no real hypocrisy in this stance. It is just explaining the facts of life, as the Draper Committee Report emphasized, to a country which has had a long past of isolation and a natural suspicion of the machinations of foreigners in playing on "gullible Uncle Sam."

Neither is there any general rule for saying when the Secretary can best deal with Congress on his own responsibility, or when he can more effectively rely on having the President carry the ball or at least on getting a large degree of White House support. This choice of tactics must be rooted in his relations with the President and be subject to the President's own judgment as to the importance of the issue and the best way of developing it tactically with Congress. Mr. Truman, for instance, gave the widest possible latitude to each Secretary of State until he began to withdraw his confidence from Secretary Byrnes and so visibly showed it as to force Byrnes' resignation. He used Secretary Marshall to strengthen himself with the country, but did not hesitate to spring the Point Four program on the State Department without much, if any, clearance. Mr. Acheson not only enjoyed his full confidence, but was skillful to a degree in using it and keeping it.

Mr. Dulles apparently enjoyed the same sort of prestige and support with Eisenhower that Mr. Acheson had had with Truman; and perhaps to an even greater degree, where Mr. Dulles felt the need of exercising it. As he did not conceive the range of the Department's policies to require as wide a concern with military and economic programs as had Mr. Acheson, he seemed to think he was saving his strength for more dramatic and crucial matters. On these matters the President appeared normally to use the Secretary to deal with Congress instead of trying to carry the ball himself, and by preference. His respect for Mr. Dulles' experience and "professional" wisdom was unbounded—sometimes disconcerting.

To date, it appears that Mr. Herter, as Secretary, has attempted to get the President to "carry the ball" more, as a matter of policy. After a rather shaky start, due to President Eisenhower's state of shock at the loss of Dulles, Mr. Herter has apparently succeeded in winning both the confidence and support of Mr. Eisenhower as well as of the Congress and the country. He has accomplished this through a less dramatic but perhaps at least equally effective use of the Department and of his own negotiating and conciliatory powers. His long acquaintance as a colleague with the principal figures in the Congress (especially in the House) on both sides of the Floor, and the respect to which his record there entitled him, have been large assets in his dealings with Congress, by common agreement.

Nevertheless, on critical matters like the support of the State Department's own budget, it may be doubted whether either the President or the Secretary of State today is in a position to force what are perhaps

necessary increases to deal with the new programming control responsibilities of the Department, without raising issues that the Executive
Department is unwilling to test out with Mr. Rooney and the other
important figures like Mr. Passman on the Appropriations Committee in
the House. In some measure this is the natural byproduct of the budgetary policy of the Administration in forcing the maximum economies for
every Department.

How Can Congress Best Participate in the Formulation of Foreign Policy?

Bipartisanship, as Senator Vandenberg established quite early, does not
and cannot mean the slavish conformity of the opposition party to every
item of Administration policy, even in foreign affairs or national security.
Bipartisan support is justified only for those policies on which there
must be genuine continuity in order to establish confidence in the responsibility of the United States, and in its power to fulfill its international
commitments and its joint obligations under the United Nations or its
alliances.

If Congressmen are to give such support, they insist upon being consulted through some members, at least, before the event, before strikingly
new policies are announced in the newspapers or commitments are made
on international agreements of which even the Congressional leaders have
had little, if any, forewarning. It is not enough to work with the chairmen and the minority leaders of the Committee on Foreign Relations
and Foreign Affairs of the two houses, though this is the indispensable
minimum for clearing matters on which bipartisan support is expected.
Unless those two chairmen and two minority leaders are very strong in
their political position—a situation which occurs rarely enough even in
one house—it is even more imperative to have the support of the Speaker
of the House, the Majority Leader of the Senate, and their opposite
numbers in the other party. This is true whether the Administration's
party is nominally in control of one or both houses, or must depend, as
it generally does of late, upon a combination of support in both houses
from the opposition as well as at least a majority of its own party. This
situation has in effect existed for Democratic as well as Republican Presidents since 1946. Unless there is some strong figure to center consultation
on (Connelly, Vandenberg, or George) there is an almost impossible
range of consultation.

Sometimes one wonders how foreign policy can be as effectively formulated and sustained as it is in the United States, in view of the hurdles

which it must necessarily run. In the old days, one could complain merely of the Senate's extraordinary control over treaties and the chance that an unrepresentative minority of the nation (one-third of the Senate plus one) could refuse ratification and block foreign policy. Those were halcyon days, indeed, compared to the problems today of keeping the numerous committees of both houses "on the reservation," and preventing either resolutions like the Bricker Amendment, or the O'Konski resolution in 1948 (about the inclusion of Spain in the ECA), from jeopardizing basic national policy.

The Secretary of State, therefore, like the Secretary of Defense, has to call on the President to carry the big load. It has now become an established practice for every President to have fairly regular meetings, in times of crisis often on a weekly basis, with the party leaders of both Houses. These generally include the party in opposition, when that party controls one or both Houses, as well as the leaders of the President's own party. Generally, in addition to the Speaker and the Majority Leader of the Senate and their opposite numbers, it has been found useful to bring in the strong men of the party who can assure support for a bipartisan approach, to the degree that this is possible. A wise President would do well to include his Secretary of State and often of Defense, too, in these meetings.

Occasionally White House briefings are held for these members, giving them something like the information that the National Security Council gets in estimates of net capabilities, though discretion has to be used in view of the extremely sensitive character of some of this information. The kind of information which Congress must have in the Armed Services and in the Foreign Affairs and Relations Committee has, in general, to be made available to the key members of some of the other committees such as the Appropriations Committee, and Banking and Currency, and, at need, to some of the key figures in Congress outside these groups. But no standard criteria for choosing among members is possible.

There is no general rule that can be laid down for what kinds of matters can be discussed safely with committees in Executive sessions.

What should be the Secretary's attitude toward Congress on "full information" on issues of national security of high classification? The presumption is in favor of pretty complete disclosure, where it is technical information or general intelligence. But he cannot risk disclosing U-2 flights to several people or even their results beyond a general assessment of reassuring character or vice-versa. The Secretary must remember that allies can be stirred up or lost by some conversational slip, capable of being misunderstood. He cannot reveal plans for emergency action.

There have been only a handful of really serious leaks that meant harm done to the national security, partly because of this careful distinction. And it is very doubtful that these leaks added much to the fund of Soviet intelligence. What is really dangerous is to tip our hand in ways that prejudice our success.

From time to time it has been found useful, particularly in the House (in view of its unwieldy party control system and the weak position of the Foreign Affairs Committee), to establish select or special committees like the Colmer and the Herter Committees (the Post-War Economic Policy and Planning Committee, and the Committee on Foreign Aid, respectively). Such committees do have the great virtue of acquainting a considerable number of key Congressmen with the broad framework of the economic and, in some measure, of the military and diplomatic problems of foreign policy on which legislative support is going to be needed, often from several committees and certainly from the whole body of the House. The Senators, through their multiple memberships in several committees, are quite likely to get background repercussions of various foreign and national security policies without the benefit of special and select committees. Indeed, there is a certain jealousy among the Senate committees of any such committees. In any case, the individual Senators attach great importance to being consulted individually.

Congressional Organization, Elections, and Behavior

Every wise Secretary of State tries to learn to live with Congress, even if he can't reform it. What are the main facts about Congressional behavior that a Secretary must face? What can he reasonably hope to do about them, in dealing with Congress as it is? Is there any real hope of useful change?

There is a real difficulty involved in the organization of Congressional responsibility for the Department, in that the Departmental budget has to go through a subcommittee of the Appropriations Committee headed by Congressman Rooney, and in that all the approaches by the Department to the appropriations committees in both houses go through the administrative area of the Department. The Assistant Secretary for Congressional Relations is not really in control of this area. In other important budgetary areas, for example requests for appropriations for the mutual security programs (not the authorization), this Assistant Secretary has Executive Branch responsibility, but the Appropriations Committee, from preference and habit, looks to the controller of the Mutual Security Program as the official directly responsible and the primary spokesman on this matter. Yet the decisions made in this way can undermine the most valiant and wise efforts of the liaison officials of the Department who work with the other committees of Congress, and in particular with the Committees on Foreign Affairs and Foreign Relations.

And the administrative judgments of Congress are influenced by the visits of the somewhat miscellaneous groups which are sent overseas by so many committees of Congress—on the average about one hundred a year, from both houses together—with no control by the State Department. It is remarkable that as little friction is generated as appears now to be the case. There is a resulting tremendous burden on the time of our diplomatic overseas missions, already extended to their fullest, in times of almost continuous crisis, by the arrival of important Congressional groups. These visitors, who are known to have the powers of law and organization as well as the purse strings, have interests as diverse as the Mutual Security Assistance Programs (weapons, economic aid, and technical assistance), the operation of trade promotion for American exports abroad, protection of American markets against "dumping" and other trade practices of a like nature, the USIA and the rest of our information services, and agricultural services not only for marketing in the normal method, but also for use in technical assistance and for disposal of surplus agricultural products under P.L. 480. This is a very small part of the list. The appropriations committees are interested in the cost of American installations abroad, and both the appropriations committees and the committees of jurisdiction are painstaking in their inquiries into the competence, the staffing, and the usefulness of American instruments of diplomacy of every character.

When one remembers that any American mission in a major capital will have people who are concerned with the export of American movies (and a very important part of our impact this is), with the promotion of trade fairs, with the jobs of political reporting, with consular services of every sort, including getting and giving visas and the screening of prospective immigrants into the United States, one has just touched the surface of the complex job of modern diplomacy. The mission services and attempts to align with foreign policy all attachés or agents of most of the great departments: Defense; Treasury; Commerce; Agriculture; Health, Education and Welfare; and agencies like USIA, ICA, and CIA.

Naturally, when Congressmen go abroad they act as the most important corps of inspectors in the nation. What they do at home is partly conditioned by these tours. Their impressions of the way missions are staffed and run color their whole attitude toward the Department and many aspects of its foreign policy. They see great numbers of Americans, particularly in the underdeveloped countries, living in roomy houses, very comfortably—often complacently. They do not see the less pleasant side of family life away from home. They get too often the impression of American heads of missions living in a style to which the Congressmen themselves are not accustomed, and in many countries with servants and the ability to entertain Congressional visitors—which the Congressmen themselves relate to the entertainment allowances they suppose are used for the same sort of elaborate parties for others. This produces an ascendancy for Congressman Rooney in his strict views on cutting down "waste" in the conduct of missions abroad, and it often leads to an underwriting of the *Ugly American* stereotype which pictures overstaffed and not very usefully occupied missions, supported at taxpayers' expense which colors the views of the chairman of another sub-committee of the House Appropriations Committee—Congressman Passman—who deals with ICA.

Fortunately, the more serious committees of Congress which are on tour for genuine study missions have seen quite different sides of the missions' life. They have seen in many places, particularly in the capitals behind the Iron Curtain, an American mission, with much smaller numbers than their Soviet counterparts, kept under grave disadvantages in every aspect of their functioning and comfort by Soviet open antagonism and harassment.

Fortunately, too, Congressmen—when they are not on the political rostrum and making political noises for special consumption in segments of their constituencies—are quite reasonable and humane people. If they have a thorough exposure to our programs in the underdeveloped countries, they generally emerge with a sound conclusion, namely, that, for a variety of reasons, among them the insecurity of work abroad and lack of career opportunities equivalent to those available at home, it tends to be the exception rather than the rule to get in our officials the high level of diplomatic and managing skills, coupled with an ability to push through and safeguard programs involving vast sums of money, that they expect in business procedures. On the other hand, many of them recognize that we are not actually in a position to "run" these countries, and that our aid is in some measure conditioned by the ability of the countries to receive it and to use it wisely, most of all by the political stability and intelligence of the new governing groups, which in many countries have had little or no previous preparation. Congressional willingness to see funds spent to get better governments and more trained manpower is most encouraging.

But Congressmen learn many other things through what are miscalled "junkets." These trips, which I can testify are generally hurried, and with exhausting travel, long and intensive briefings, and much study, as well as the official rounds, are rarely very pleasant. There is no more important way to remove the misimpressions that individual Congressmen so often carry with them than these on-the-spot exposures to the problems of a mission and of its host country. At the same time, they are quick to sense any toadying or a "public-relations" approach that covers up real difficulties and inadequacies. One of the best ways for diplomats to get their sympathetic backing is to hail them for what they are—as in the best sense ambassadors of the American people—expecting and generally getting their sympathetic understanding of the problems concerned without inviting either their pity or their patronage.

One of the best and most frequently used devices for education of Congress on the realities of foreign policy is the association of both Senators and Members of the House in delegations to international conferences such as that at Bretton Woods (which drew up the proposals for the Bank and Fund) and the annual assemblies of the UN and related agencies. Congressmen and Senators earn prestige by their knowledge as shown in the debates. They have been "on the team," and generally back the results. Rarely do they present such a problem in negotiating sessions as to be counterproductive. Care in working out these selections with the House and Senate leadership *of both parties* is repaid manifold.

With all the organizational and management problems of the Department, as with many substantive problems, the Assistant Secretary for Congressional Relations, no matter how able he may be or how adequate his staff for contacts on the Hill, cannot succeed in covering up root problems of the Department or changing Congressional attitudes that are based upon an unerring instinct for finding political sore spots. The role of the Assistant Secretary, therefore, must be to accomplish some four main objectives. He must do so even with the minimal assistance available to him, and with all the turn-over of his own personnel as a result of the general "change posts" practice of the Department or the dissatisfaction with jobs that lead to no particularly brilliant future.

1. The principal job of any Assistant Secretary for Congressional Relations is to see to it that the Secretary, the two Under Secretaries, the Deputy Under Secretary for Administration, and the Assistant Secretaries all understand fully, and are willing to grapple directly and adequately, with Congressional relations in their own provinces. No Assistant Secretary can *make* a Secretary of State perform at this Congressional liaison job. He has to vie with the visits of foreign potentates and ambassadors, the meetings of the NATO Ministers, the perpetual crises of summit conferences and the like, to get the top policy officials of the Department to devote an adequate amount of time to meet the increasing demands for direct Congressional relations, including appearances before a large number of different committees and subcommittees of both houses.

A calendar of the meetings of Secretary Dulles (who was not supposed to be particularly active in direct conferences with individual Senators and Congressmen) shows that he averaged, from 1955 through 1958, six to eight conferences with important Senators a month, and two or three with Representatives from the foreign affairs committees, the appropriations committees, and others. In addition, his bipartisan Congressional appearances and meetings with the House and the Senate committees deeply concerned with foreign policy (including occasional meetings with the Congressional leadership group that also met with the President) averaged around six a month, while Congress was in session. Sometimes these ran to as many as twelve a month.

All these meetings required elaborate preparation not only by the Secretary, but by considerable segments of the Department. They spanned the main committees of Congress, including not only those of Foreign Affairs and Armed Services and their subcommittees, but the appropriations committees, the banking and currency committees, particularly of the Senate, the judiciary committees, the House Ways and Means Committee, the House and Senate Agricultural Committees, the Senate Minerals Subcommittee, Joint Committee on Atomic Energy, Senate Finance Committee, and meetings with many individual Senators and Congressmen. The Secretary also had a number of informal dinners and social occasions with important figures and made it a point to welcome newly elected Senators and Congressmen for briefing sessions and general discussions, aided by former members of Congress like Senator George, Congressman Dick Richards, and Senator Smith.

Other Secretaries and Under Secretaries have reckoned the time spent in this necessary "consultation" to run to one-sixth of all working days; of course at times the load is heavier. Phone calls are often not entered into the account; but they, too, eat time and require the utmost care. The complaint that a Secretary who becomes "peripatetic" is bound to sacrifice his Congressional relations probably meant, with Secretary Dulles, that he sacrificed his health and perhaps some measure of use or control of the Department instead.

2. This proper use of the Secretary himself and his principal policy officials is the first duty of the Assistant Secretary for Congressional Relations. He himself, however, must also maintain a broad intelligence service through staff contacts and friendly relations with Congressmen and Senators on what is happening in every part of the complex legislative mechanism that is of interest to the Department. He and his staff shoulder personal persuasion all over the entire Congress.

3. While keeping up his intelligence network in Congress and following the legislative programs as well as the committees of inquiry and the hearings, the Assistant Secretary for Congressional Relations has to arrange for both protective and positive action. He must supply Congress, through its committees, with the materials for reports and hearings, correct the records, and, in general, service this enormous apparatus that eats up time and manpower in almost the way that television programming does.

4. Small wonder, then, that he often has too little time left for the fourth function, which is to see that the feelings of Congressmen are not ruffled, that they are supplied materials that they can put to good use on broadcasts to their constituencies (now almost a normal practice through radio and television platters—often on a weekly basis). He must see to it that their constituents get a hearing in the State Department when they go abroad, and the appropriate elevated treatment by embassies already driven to distraction by the claims on their time. In other words, he must be in some measure a fixer and a go-between. But he cannot let this aspect of his duties substitute for more substantive achievement in seeing that the Department is never caught napping, and in promoting the legislation, including the Departmental budgets, for which he himself, oddly, has no direct presentation responsibility.

The main function of the office itself, as opposed to the personal responsibility of the Assistant Secretary, is to organize the Department so as to get immediate replies to 5,000 or 6,000 letters a year from Congress. Some range from post cards to searching and often hostile questions from committee chairmen which may require high-level consideration.

Channels of Review and Accountability

A highly responsible permanent official in the Department of State, who shall remain nameless, has permitted me to use a paragraph from a comment which he made on some parts of this study:

> A casual review of selected Appropriations Committee reports might startle the constitutionalist. The extent to which Executive operations can be, and are, influenced, curtailed or controlled through a one-sentence "directive" in such Reports prematurely ages the administrator who is trying to support his Secretary's policies with human and material resources. Ambitious and politically adept subcommittee Chairmen, frequently neglected in the larger power politics of winning authorizing legislation, make their influence felt through reductions in the amount of funds requested and the Committees' "views" as to how the program should operate. Seldom is the Secretary's personal prestige or political support brought to bear in the executive sessions of appropriations hearings. The glare of publicity is absent. The Chairman rules supreme. If damage is done it is almost too late to rectify it. Appeals in the Senate, even if successful, are mitigated by "trading" in the Conference.

A barrier has always existed, beyond the ordinary reach of treaties and Executive agreements, where foreign policy is made by legislation itself, as it was, for example, in the Lend-Lease authority granted by Congress and indeed, prior to that time, by the neutrality legislation and by various immigration statutes. The prime examples, already cited, were the Economic Cooperation Administration Act of 1948 and its successors.

Much of this legislation requires annual appropriations and some of it, as a matter of deliberate Congressional policy, expires after a short term and has to be either renewed or discontinued. In this process, limitations can be written in and the program so circumscribed that it emerges quite different from its intention as originally authorized. This is true of loan policies as they are worked out through the Export-Import Bank and through the Development Loan Fund. Indeed this grilling has a considerable bearing, through the tone of hearings and the reports of committees like the Senate Finance Committee and that on Money and Banking in the House, on the uses to which the (American) lion's share of both funds and policy can be used in international programs like that of the World Bank and even the Fund.

Congress has not been slow to learn, either, how to use, in addition to legislative initiatives and vetoes in legislation, or by appropriations, the "resolution of inquiry" which forces the Administration to produce papers if it wishes Congressional action of a favorable character. Even more sweeping have been the "committees of inquiry," or legislative investigations, which have often degenerated into a sort of man-hunt. When, by abuse, they become expeditions in headline hunting, they so increase the burdens of office that they have had a profoundly discouraging effect on the willingness of many otherwise patriotic Americans to assume the duties of Washington offices.

Still another device that Congress has increasingly used, and one which raises serious questions of constitutionality, is a statutory requirement for clearance of administrative action with and by individual committees, either of authorization or appropriations. If the Government Operations Committees continue this practice they can make the administrative process subject to a sort of perpetual suspensory veto by a single committee of Congress, or even by a subcommittee, and sometimes by an individual, occasionally even by a committee staff member who is given wide latitude. It would be invidious (perhaps dangerous!) to point out specific instances; but they exist. Sometimes they are tacit and implicit rather than matters of record. But they tend to control administrative behavior.

Since foreign policy often depends on instruments as much as on the formulation of attitudes or policy directives, the ability of Congress to force the expenditures of defense funds for particular types of weapons systems or particular amounts often has a very basic effect on foreign policy. It may be an unconstitutional usurpation, but Congress usually gets its way because of the danger to other programs from a stalemate.

Enough has been said to indicate how very numerous and varied are the normal forums for the review of foreign policy that are exercised by Congress. In addition to the committees already mentioned, the policy committees set up along party lines by the Congressional Reorganization Act of 1947 are now beginning to inject themselves into foreign policy and to try to work out coherent party attitudes on the entire area of national security policies. The House has adopted them only very lately. But there the Republican policy committee has already become more active on national policies and less on patronage and domestic partisan issues than that of the Senate, that goes back to 1948.

The two main "foreign" committees of jurisdiction have very unequal weights in their respective houses. The Senate Committee on Foreign Relations is regarded as a high prize in the Senate because of its long tradition. It acts generally with a greater sense of responsibility. Its Chairman very rarely fails to try to produce bipartisan backing, no matter what the party complexion of the Senate, for the Secretary of State in his main policies. In this respect the Senate is more used to the theory of shared responsibility and the implications of withholding the legislative hand, though it well may itch, like the peers in *Iolanthe*,

> To interfere with matters which
> They do not understand.

The House Committee, since it has set up a staff, shows some degree, at least, of policy continuity to parallel that of the Senate. Nevertheless, over a period of years, it has not been as highly prized for political importance and preferment in the public eye, perhaps because of the nature and interests of the domestic constituencies of the Congressmen concerned, as have other House committees like Appropriations, Rules, Ways and Means, and Money and Banking.

So much has already been said about the Appropriations Committee that only a few comments of a rather basic character need be added. The House Committee on Appropriations acts almost as a law to itself, and its staff relations with the Foreign Affairs Committee, as with most other committees of the House, are like those of a feudal sovereign to his unimportant lieges—frequently nonexistent. Nor do the Appropriations Committees of the House show much more regard for the Committee on Foreign Affairs' views on the needs of the Department in a budgetary way. The State Department's budget often fares very badly because it does not have spokesmen on the Appropriations Committee who are sympathetic with its functions or who know enough to stand up against the Chairmen of the principal subcommittees concerned.

One egregious instance may be cited. Senator Karl E. Mundt (R-S. Dak.) revealed to his constituents his negotiations with the Director of the Budget Bureau, by which he succeeded in restoring the sum of $8,250,000 to provide a budget for the Oahe Dam in South Dakota that had been stricken out of the annual budget by the Bureau. In return, as he put it, "last week I fulfilled my part of the promise. On motions made by me in the Senate Appropriations Committee, $8,000,000 was cut off from the funds approved for State Department personnel." [1] The Department is not often victimized to this degree, and Senator Mundt had been a true friend in the matter of the establishment of the information and exchange agencies through the legislation that bore his name (Smith-Mundt Act) when the Senator was still in the House. A Secretary of State may find himself whipsawed by a Budget Bureau deal where a Rivers and Harbors item seriously hurts the Foreign Service and the Department's programs.

General Conclusions

The questions that naturally arise out of this bare recital, even with the limited illustrations possible, raise fundamental issues about the whole nature of our separation of powers and its bearing on foreign policy. This is not the place for repeating the kind of proposals about constitutional reform which were raised in *U.S. Foreign Policy: Its Organization and Control*. Two of these reforms would obviously do much to relieve the Congress of some of the special political pressures that distort its approach to foreign affairs: first, to lengthen the terms of members of the House to correspond to those of the President; and second, to strengthen the President's protection of his own position with an item veto.

Short of such sweeping (and therefore difficult) reforms by amendment to the Constitution, how can Congress hold its own committees accountable, or even enforce some reasonable degree of policy harmony on them? Several proposals may be advanced, none of them involving sharp breaks with past practices, and all of them dependent on a realization of the essential unity of legislative and executive action, especially in the field of foreign affairs.

1. More could perhaps be done to give Congressional leaders a picture of Executive Branch insights and intentions. Conceivably some real progress could be made in working out, either through a combination

---

[1] This was quoted by Marquis Childs, "Washington Calling," *Pittsburgh Post Gazette*, June 4, 1953.

of the policy committees of both houses and representatives from such committees as Foreign Affairs, Foreign Relations, Appropriations, and the Joint Committee on Atomic Energy, briefing sessions, like those given the National Security Council, in which the Secretary of State might present issues of foreign policy and the Secretary of Defense some estimates of "net capabilities"; or the ICA an account of its operations, as well as the CIA of its basic intelligence findings. This does not involve bringing Congress into the President's decision-making and policy-forming structure (the NSC), but it should provide the kind of information to which Congress more and more feels it is legitimately entitled.

Unfortunately, there is no way to get a guarantee by such a selection that Congress will be bound by any views of these selected members. About all that can be hoped is that it will help to educate the Congressmen better as to the real nature of the problems with which the Secretary of State must grapple. It has been sporadically tried, with good results.

2. This process of education of Congressional leaders will be most effective, of course, if it helps to force the resolution of issues within the government and within the State Department. It should be used to force the setting up of some kind of Departmental and national program review and control, which, in my opinion, has been the weakest aspect of our national security policy, on a comparative basis.

The presentations of the Department and of its allied agencies like ICA and USIA and probably the whole MSA[1] program, including Defense, could be greatly improved if they were the responsibility of such a program review group of policy officials, advising the Secretary, or Under Secretary, rather than the joint responsibility of the Budget Bureau, the Department budget and administrative officials, and the various Assistant Secretaries of regional and functional areas. We do not have a systematic method for the allocation of resources according to policy priorities, even within the area covered by the Secretary of State. There is the usual tendency to repeat the same old formulae and to depend upon a certain flexibility in the reallocation of any funds that have been over-calculated to make up for the severity with which the Budget axe is used on quite essential new areas. The Secretary would make a better case, and could stand firm on it—as he can't if he is caught off base by bad staff work, or by staff administration unfamiliar with policy issues.

The Secretary of State can on his own initiative take the greatest load off the President by insisting in his own organization on a better packaging of the programs to carry out the policies of the United States abroad, as he now is attempting to do, with Congressional support and authorization, through a program review operation centered in his own Under

---

[1] Mutual Security Administration—successor to ECA, predecessor of ICA.

Secretary that applies and follows up the relation of policy priorities to the operation of all foreign programs, MSA, etc. His role in the National Security machinery and Council can be strengthened to the degree that the State Department is equipped to take this responsibility and to push the policy initiative in such security program reviews, as well as policy formulation, as the Council itself performs. The OCB could work more along the lines originally intended.

3. If such an increase in the intimacy of Legislative-Executive relations is to be useful, we must solve a general problem of the greatest importance: How can we protect the reports and opinions of subordinates from being produced through Congressional inquiries in ways that would compromise their frankness in advising or informing the Secretary of State? He tends to lose control of his own people if they have to write everything that they produce for him with an eye to having it put in the public prints by Congress. This is an area of privileged information, and it is one which the Executive Department must tenaciously protect if it intends to remain master in its own house and to have the nation well served by its civil servants and its subordinate officials of any kind.

That is not to say that the production of facts about the nature of expenditures and the confession of occasional mistakes, if they are truly our own, is not good policy. It is simply to say that the Congress has not the right to force into public view confidential reports which are intended to correct a situation within the Executive Branch, either for the edification of the general public (including Moscow and Peiping) or for partisan advantage in the legislative halls.

In the see-saw struggle between Congress and the Executive over the protection of their respective prerogatives, it is hard to drew a final constitutional or even discretionary political line. The general rule, however, must be to resist the intrusions of Congress where it tries to substitute its own judgment for that of the Executive in management and personnel problems as much as in the formation of policy. If Congress is to hold the Chief Executive responsible for the faithful execution of the laws, he must at least have the power to execute them. And the Secretary of State, who must be the chief agent of the President in all these matters, has to learn these lessons, and to keep them in the minds of his executive coadjutors, and to educate the Congress, as painlessly and skillfully as possible, to the sympathetic respect and understanding that preserve and develop a national unity of front to the rest of the world.

4. On the side of Congress itself, there is an equally difficult problem of organization, procedure, and discipline: How can Congress make better use of the information it gets? How can it keep its committees

more effectively working in concert? How may it restrict the number of appearances that high State Department officials are required to make before separate committees of the Congress? How can it curb Congressional abuse that deserves public contempt? At least some possibility of improvement may be found in the better use of the policy committees which Congress has established. These policy committees might be able to do on a continuing basis what the House has often done through special committees like the Colmer Committee and the Herter Committee, both of which succeeded in gaining support for radical reorientations of our foreign policy, through the serious work of leading members from all the principal House committees concerned.

5. More important, perhaps, than any suggestion of mechanics or procedure is the realization that the Secretary of State, or any other Presidential subordinate in the field of international affairs, can deal with Congress and with the wide range of government policy only as an agent of the President of the United States. The Secretary, in his personal relations with the President, has the delicate problem not only of dealing with a personality and a temperament, but an office. Indeed he has to build up the strength of the foreign policy of the United States through an appropriate use of the President's prestige and powers, while avoiding downgrading the role of the Secretary himself. If the thesis of this essay is correct, it is impossible to interpose by statute either a "Premier" or a "First Secretary" for national security affairs as a directing agent, in the President's stead, over either foreign policy or defense policy. The Secretary of State appropriately is already a First Secretary in the outward face that the nation turns to the world. He cannot treat for the President and carry the enormous diplomatic burden of this divided but still multilateral world without being himself a commanding figure and carrying the evident and consistent support of the President of the United States in all his actions and policies.

In this way he can be of the greatest assistance to the President. Without his knowledge, wisdom, and continuing energy, these ingredients cannot be supplied by finding someone to act as a super-Secretary of State in the White House staff. To downgrade the Secretary to a manager or a diplomatic agent is to cripple the President himself and to deprive Congress of that guidance and education under a firm hand which is the best contribution any Secretary of State can make to Congressional relations and, through them, to foreign policy.

6. The attitude of Congress itself, on the evidence of the past crucial thirty years, firmly supports a final conclusion: Nothing so strengthens the ability of Congress to support a foreign policy as to find, in the Secretary of State, not only a conciliatory and persuasive educator of

the nation, but one whose vision and courage raise the moral stature of Congress and the nation behind it to the necessary sacrifices which determine our ability to confront the alternating campaigns of nuclear terror, propaganda and blackmail, and massive political economic warfare for the control of this globe and its human inhabitants—to say nothing, for the moment, of projecting the struggle into the regions of outer space.

6.

The Secretary and the American public

The Nature of the Relationship

♦ JOHN S. DICKEY

The Department of State and the American public are neither old nor intimate friends. Fifty years ago, indeed only twenty-five years ago, a study of the Secretary of State would have taken little, if any notice of the public relationships of the office. Traditionally, diplomacy has been a relationship between rulers and, more recently, between nation-states. The agents who served and ministered to this relationship have generally, until relatively recent times, regarded themselves as answerable only to the highest executive authority. This circumscribed answerability of diplomatists has been fostered and the work of negotiation safeguarded by a tradition of

139

♦ JOHN S. DICKEY, President of Dartmouth College, held various positions in the Department of State and the Office of the Coordinator of Inter-American Affairs from 1934 to 1936 and 1940 to 1945. During the last two years of that period, he was Director of the Office of Public Affairs, and served with the U.S. Delegation to the United Nations Conference on International Organization at San Francisco.

secrecy in foreign affairs and of circumspection in the utterances of those privileged to deal with these affairs.

FACTORS FASHIONING THE RELATIONSHIP

This situation has changed drastically during the twentieth century; today the public's relation to our foreign affairs is a major, perhaps the major factor, in our diplomacy. In my view this revolutionary change is attributable to four broad factors that individually and in their interaction on one another have created within the past fifty years a well-nigh new dimension in the conduct of our foreign affairs, namely, the public dimension.

1. *An Enlightened and Extended Democratic Process*—The democratic idea, especially within the past fifty years, has gone very far toward drawing the American public as a whole, and its constituent interest-group elements, into a direct and rapidly mounting concern with foreign affairs. As it grows, this factor will itself be almost an irresistible force tending to reduce the "arm's length" relationship between the public and "its" foreign office.

A multitude of things have extended the democratic idea into foreign affairs. For example, the sixteenth (income tax) and seventeenth (direct election of senators) amendments to the Constitution, both effective in 1913, have played important roles. They have brought all voters and almost all citizens into a more direct relationship to foreign affairs. Moreover, such changes have put a political premium on the development nationally of strong, private-interest groups, and these in turn have promoted and exploited, in both good and bad ways, the influence of focused public interest on public policy.

2. *Modern Communications*—Inherently, mass media make public

140

affairs and public figures ever more public. This fact may or may not advance the democratic processes of our society, but there can be no question that it is a formidable new influence on the conduct of public business, particularly on that sector which traditionally has tended to avoid the limelight as well as the searchlight of probing questions.

Paradoxically, these technological advances seem to have stimulated both the rapacious and the professional tendencies of contemporary journalism. On the one hand, the mass appetite seems to demand more over-simplified, more highly personalized news than before. Circumstances such as a "cold war" are readily exploited for feeding this appetite, with the possibility of ultimately disastrous consequences in public misunderstanding of foreign affairs.

On the other hand, these same technological developments have brought so much more information to bear on public questions, particularly in foreign affairs, that the competition for professional penetration is also sharper. The journalists specializing on foreign affairs today as correspondents, editors, commentators, or writers are often so widely and expertly informed that they will not tolerate a governmental information policy that insults their competence and their sophistication in the field.

These pressures for more information and toward an ever larger public participation in foreign affairs are built into the circumstances of twentieth century life. Working with them, rather than trying to circumvent them, is the only realistic course for professional diplomacy in the future.

3. *The Changing Character of All International Relations*—The spread of the democratic idea and the modern mobility of persons and information are in fact changing the character of international relations throughout the world.

In all national societies, even within the communist countries, governmental policies and actions are being drawn or pushed more and more into the public domain. On the international scene the increased resort to summit meetings and similar highly publicized governmental exchanges creates public appetites throughout the world that all governments in their own self-interest dare not leave unsatisfied. Once called into being, public opinion throughout the modern world must be wooed by every nation and every statesman with an aspiration to power and leadership. From here on, any nation that permits a vacuum of information and understanding to exist anywhere (including at home) about itself can be sure that someone else will quickly fill that vacuum. Likewise, it must now be understood that anything of significance that is said anywhere is said everywhere. In the domain of public policy the free world can have no big secrets and there is truly no place for official actions to hide. As Lyman Bryson well put it in his last book, "In free countries problems of politics are problems of public opinion." From now on this is an underlying truth in the relationship of nations.

The international relations of our day seem destined to be paradoxically both more pervasively private and more prominently public.

4. *The Character of Contemporary United States Policies*—If this paper were to espouse any single theme it would be that the relationship of the Secretary of State to the American public is governed most immediately and directly by the content and the form of our contemporary foreign policies.

The Department of State's dependence upon public understanding and support was minimal when our policies were mainly negative or hortatory in content and declaratory or unilateral in form. Conversely, when our policies involve the positive commitment of national resources and manpower or changing the rules governing our domestic life (e.g., tariff rates), and when these policies must be carried out through international negotiation and agreement—at such times the dependence of a Secretary of State upon the public approaches the absolute.

The historical perspective of the past fifty years reveals a striking parallel in the development of positive, cooperative foreign policies and the realistic acceptance by the Department of State of the public as a rightful and necessary participant in the foreign affairs of the nation.

The Rise of the Relationship

It was President Taft's prematurely optimistic view that until 1909 "the State Department . . . has never been properly organized." The "properly organized" Department of 1909 was provided with a new "Division of Information," but the responsibilities of the division were confined to the internal distribution of information received from the field and to keeping our overseas missions better informed. The new division undertook a limited internal distribution of foreign and domestic press comment, but apparently no organized effort was made to service the public with information. The fact is that fifty years ago the State Department thought of "information" much the same way as "intelligence" is regarded today: as something for the use of officials in their daily work.

Although the organization of the Department did not reflect it, the public addresses of Secretary Knox and Assistant Secretary Huntington Wilson during the years 1910-1912 do reveal an awareness that the interest and understanding of the public and certain groups mattered in the conduct of American foreign relations. Major addresses were made to such citizen organizations as The Chamber of Commerce of the United States, The Third National Peace Congress, and The National Civic Federation.

1917—THE IMPACT OF WORLD WAR I

The circumstances and the imperatives of World War I, which moved America irrevocably out into the mainstream of international affairs, were mirrored in the information program of the government. Within a month after America's entry into the war, the Department of State, in May 1917, drastically reorganized the Division of Information that had been created in the for-the-first-time "properly organized" Department of 1909.

Among the unprecedented new duties assigned to the reorganized division were "the preparation of news items for the press," "the censorship and control of departmental publicity under the direction of the Secretary," and the "communication to members of Congress, governors of States, universities, magazines, chambers of commerce, and other organizations of bulletins and texts of official documents which will be helpful in understanding the foreign policy of the United States." An experienced newspaperman headed the division, assisted by a top Foreign Service Officer.

1920—THE NEW PRIVATE LEADERSHIP GROUPS

Organized public interest in American foreign affairs grew despite the isolationism of the postwar aftermath. Leadership elements in our society responded to Assistant Secretary of State Wilson's urging in 1911 that the way forward in foreign affairs depended upon a deeper "interest in and intelligent support of the everyday practical policies of government." Many of these leaders of the private sector of public opinion had made common cause during the Versailles Treaty fight through "The League to Enforce Peace." In the early postwar period this private concern was promoted on a national scope and a new level of maturity through the creation of new public-interest organizations such as the Foreign Policy Association (1918), the League of Nations Association (1920), the National League of Women Voters (1920), and the Council on Foreign Relations (1921).

1934—A TURNING POINT: RECIPROCAL TRADE

If there is any single point dividing the old from the new in the evolution of the Department of State's relationship to the American public it is the Trade Agreements Act of 1934. New foreign policies involving established domestic interests brought new information practices. Prior to the reciprocal trade program, the Secretary of State never bore the primary responsibility over an indefinite period of years for securing and sustaining public support for a foreign policy that had a widespread, continuing impact on domestic interests. The trade agreements program influenced the character of American foreign policy significantly; it also introduced the Department as a working partner to other departments of the government, and it introduced the Department to its own need for a strong functional staff to complement the traditional dominance of a corps of career Foreign Service Officers that was politically oriented (in the international sense) and geographically organized. But perhaps even more fundamentally, the trade agreements program introduced the Department of State and the public to each other.

Prior to 1934, and in most areas for another decade thereafter, the Department relied almost exclusively upon its press relations for its public relations. The top officers made the customary public addresses and they appeared as required before Congressional committees, but in an affirmative sense there was no comprehensive public information program except in the trade agreements field.

In addition to being comprehensive and sustained, the trade agreements information program was a two-way operation. The Department of State not only learned more about keeping the public informed; it also began to learn about keeping itself informed about the public.

Above all, perhaps, the trade agreements program forced the Department of State into sustained cooperation with the Congress as incomparably the best single two-way liaison with the American public on foreign policy.

In short, the trade agreements program began the monumental task of self-education about itself that the Department of State then faced.

Even so, the observable influence of the new outlook toward the public prior to 1943-1944 was largely confined to trade policy matters. Traditional foreign office ways continued to dominate the handling of our international political affairs. And in this area very little interloping from either the outside public (or, on the inside, from anyone not in the Foreign Service) was tolerated by the career diplomats until the pressures of public concern generated by war and the need for public support of the new postwar planning programs broke through the barriers of tradition and vested bureaucratic interests.

The Modern Period: Positive Policies

On June 29, 1943, with the last of his four successful fights for the Trade Agreements Act behind him, and with postwar plans for a United Nations organization shaping up into a major undertaking, Secretary Hull authorized the establishment of an office for the purpose of developing an organized, sustained liaison between the Department and the public. The aim of the new Special Consultant's office was "to be one of establishing a centralized two-way liaison with private and public-interest groups to service and to encourage their contribution in the formulation of foreign policy both within the Department and throughout the country."[1]

The genesis of the Special Consultant's office was the need to bring to the aid of our postwar policies the type of public liaison activity that had proved itself in the trade agreements program. For the next two years this effort focused mainly on postwar projects. However, it quickly became apparent that an affirmative information program, if it was to have integrity and sustained effectiveness, had to concern itself with more than the "sale" of specific projects.

1944—ORGANIZATION PARITY: AN ASSISTANT SECRETARY

The general reorganization of the Department of State of January 15, 1944, grouped all divisions under twelve newly created main-line offices, each responsible for the supervision of a group of operating divisions. One of the newly created offices was "The Office of Public Information" (shortly renamed "Office of Public Affairs"), which for the first time sought to bring together under one operating head all domestic and overseas information and cultural affairs work of the Department. The director of the new office was made a member of the two principal committees of the reorganized Department: Policy, and Post-War Planning. The office of the Special Consultant, with its pioneering activities of "public liaison" and "public studies," was incorporated into the new office and these two fundamental functions have since remained a basic part of the public affairs work of the Department through ensuing reorganizations and many changes of name.

In December 1944, with the advent of Edward Stettinius as Secretary of State and another round of reorganization, this side of the Department's work was brought to "organizational parity" by the creation of

---

[1] Departmental memorandum by the Special Consultant, July 10, 1943.

the first assistant secretaryship for information and cultural relations (subsequently and currently designated "public affairs").

1945—THE UNITED NATIONS CHARTER AND BIPARTISANSHIP

If the new assistant secretaryship meant "organizational parity" within the Department, it was the UN project that brought the public affairs function to full flower in American foreign relations.

The UN Charter project represented the culmination of expert studies, political consultations and international negotiations that reached back over five years of war. For Roosevelt and Hull it represented the resurrection of a prospect of peace they had seen fall with Wilson in the Versailles Treaty fight. For everyone it represented the most momentous foreign policy commitment the nation had ever contemplated. It clearly would require approval as a treaty by a two-thirds vote in the Senate and this, in view of the League's rejection twenty-five years before, presented what seemed to be a challenge of unprecedented magnitude. A broad base of public understanding and support was imperative.

Throughout the UN effort, from the early explorations to the final action in the Senate by an almost unanimous vote, Secretary Hull insisted upon a nonpartisan approach. Whenever possible he drew the Congressional leaders from both parties into active participation, including ultimately service on the United States delegation to the San Francisco Conference.

Secretary Hull's efforts to keep foreign policy out of partisan politics and especially to enlist strong bipartisan support for the UN project had a powerful bearing on the character of the information activity the Department could carry on behind this project. The Congressional leaders and many others on both sides were so strongly committed personally that in their political self-interest they welcomed all reasonable efforts to assure broad public understanding and support for the project (and perforce for their personal positions). Few instances illustrate more vividly than the UN Charter the interlocking relationship between bipartisan policy and a strong public information initiative by the Department of State. Bipartisan policy not merely permits, in fact it engenders affirmative information activity on the part of the Department. Perhaps to a fault.

Following the formulation of the UN proposals at the Dumbarton Oaks conference in the fall of 1944, the Department organized a comprehensive program to bring the proposals before the American public. For example, arrangements were made to enlist the cooperation of the motion picture industry in an effort to bring the essence of the UN idea as a peace enforcement agency before the movie-going audiences of America. The result of this unnatural union of Hollywood and the Department of State was a film entitled "Watch Tower Over Tomorrow." As the apogee of the Department's effort to take this foreign policy to the "people," it is an historical exhibit meriting study more than emulation.

On a more critical level the Department's liaison activity with citizen groups reached an all-time high in intensity and coverage in such fields as adult education, business, agriculture, labor, race, religion, veterans, women's organizations, service clubs and, of course, the specialized foreign affairs groups. Explanatory literature at all levels was prepared; briefing conferences were held for representatives of citizen organizations, and speakers were sent out to address their memberships. In turn, the secondary impact of these organizations on the general public was far greater than anything the Department of State could have achieved alone through any direct approach.

At the same time, the representatives of these varied interests brought back to the Department realistic interpretations of the state of public opinion. This liaison with leadership elements was an invaluable supplement to the Department's analysis of Congressional sentiment, press comment, and the public-opinion polls as indicators of public support or criticism.

The liaison work with private groups culminated in a decision by President Roosevelt and Secretary Stettinius to invite citizen organizations to be represented at the San Francisco United Nations Conference with officially accredited "consultants" to the United States delegation. Forty-two organizations representing a cross-section of citizen groups from all major fields were invited by the Department of State to send such "consultants"; and throughout the Conference, from April through June, most of these organizations were constantly and conscientiously represented. The "consultants" directly influenced the terms of only one section of the Charter, i.e., the elevation of the concept of "human rights" to a position of central concern in the United Nations. This group liaison activity, however, played a major part in creating our overwhelmingly favorable public climate for the UN. Mr. James B. Reston has said of the San Francisco "consultants": "Their presence at San Francisco induced conviction, and their conviction produced support throughout the country which was reflected in the overwhelming ratification of the Charter in the Senate." [1] This was the major aim of the undertaking. Incidentally, it also paved the way for the concept of nongovernmental observers at the UN and for the later development of the group liaison work in the Department of State.

---

[1] *Foreign Affairs*, October, 1945, p. 52.

Ever since the establishment, early in World War II, of the Office of War Information and the Office of Inter-American Affairs, this government has been committed to a world-wide information activity. This commitment has done more than any other single factor in recent years to enlarge the public dimension in American foreign affairs and to "set" the problem.

No Secretary of State can ever again risk leaving any major policy of the nation publicly unexplained to either our friends or our foes; nor can he risk having the American people and their Congress get their first and fullest information about American policies from abroad. From here on, silence is rarely a realistic alternative for a Secretary of State. The point requires no laboring, but it is one of the relatively new and fixed "givens" in any contemporary study of the public relationships of an American Secretary of State. It is the ever-present reminder to every Secretary of State that the world is always his audience, and in this sense he is a party to all the political processes of the world, whether of a democratic or dictatorial character.

The Bureau of Public Affairs

The public affairs program of the Department today is the product of the foregoing evolution, of perennial reorganization, and of the retrenchment effort of 1953, when a Republican administration took over responsibility for something that had perforce been the creation of Democratic administrations. Despite a cutback in personnel of over 30 percent, the public affairs concept survived what must be assumed to have been a critical, even suspicious, appraisal. It thereby achieved bipartisan acceptance as an integral part of our foreign affairs work.

The domestic public affairs work of the Department is presently consolidated in the Bureau of Public Affairs, under the direction of an Assistant Secretary of State.[1]

The operations of the Bureau are organized into the Office of News, the Office of Public Services and the Historical Office. In addition to these operational offices, the Bureau includes the Public Opinion Studies Staff; the Mutual Security Information Staff (a specialized, semi-detached group); the Policy Plans and Guidance Staff (mainly concerned with

---

[1] I am indebted to Mr. Harrison C. Dunning, of the Class of 1960 at Dartmouth College, for general assistance on this project and specifically for much of the data in this section, which he gathered for a senior thesis on this Bureau.

policy guidance for United States overseas information and cultural affairs); and an executive staff handling the over-all coordination of the Bureau's fiscal and personnel affairs.

The current Assistant Secretary was trained as a journalist and has had considerable experience on the press side of foreign affairs. He is assisted by a Deputy Assistant Secretary, an experienced Foreign Service Officer on assignment to the Bureau. The Bureau's domestic work employs about 140 people with an annual salary budget in excess of $1,000,000. Twenty years earlier the salary budget for the news and publications work totaled about $200,000 for some 70 people.

OFFICE OF NEWS

This office services all the "fast news" media, newspapers, radio, television and motion pictures. It manages the Secretary's press conferences; and the head of the office, a man who has made it his career, holds daily briefings for about forty reporters covering the Department on a regular basis.

The questions in this area that need asking go mainly to policy and personnel issues above and beyond the efficiently performed operating responsibilities of the news office.

THE PRESS

Is the catch-as-catch-can press conference a satisfactory forum for responsible utterances on foreign affairs? Almost certainly the answer is "no." But the answer is also "no" to the next question: is a better and generally acceptable alternative available?

Secretary Hay began the press conference practice at the turn of the century by occasionally seeing four or five trusted correspondents for informal, private chats on his policies and problems. Today the Secretary's press conference is attended by 150 or more reporters; although theoretically the conference is a weekly affair, in recent years the schedule has become increasingly irregular and infrequent. The range and penetration of the questioning has certainly not diminished. To the contrary. The protocol remains basically respectful of the Secretary's position; but today there is little or nothing else, except his judgment and wit, that stands between him and the embarrassment of the "unanswerable" question or the misfortunes of a "do-it-yourself" foreign policy that can come with the too-ready response.

Moreover, the dangers and difficulties facing a Secretary at these conferences are neither wholly of his making nor wholly his to risk. He must align his utterances with the practice and policy of the President.

If the President tends to be "free-wheeling" in his press conferences, a Secretary of State finds it difficult, if not impossible, to be less open. The fact that the President has spoken on a matter rarely saves the Secretary from having to deal with the same subject in his press conference. On the contrary, comment by the President usually simply assures that the Secretary will later find himself pushed further by his questioners toward the dangerous edge of the subject.

COORDINATION

Coordination of the public utterances of the President and the Secretary of State is a central, continuing problem.

Louis Brownlow, in his *A Passion for Anonymity,* tells how, early in World War II, President Roosevelt explored the idea of bringing Harry Stimson into his administration to be the public spokesman on all foreign policy questions. The idea was generally rejected as impractical by press and officials alike. Later an experienced, senior Foreign Service Officer was assigned to serve as a top-level liaison between President Roosevelt and the Department. This officer, in addition to other duties, assisted with the coordination of press conference statements and also did considerable background briefing of the press and others on major matters. This practice has not been followed in recent years.

THE AVAILABILITY ISSUE

The problem is not wholly one of coordination. It is also one of availability. There is a strong opinion among some of the most experienced Washington correspondents that an acute need exists today for greater regular access to the knowledgeable sources of information on foreign policy. These men are unable to regard a weekly, or less frequent, general press conference as an adequate diet of information to sustain the kind of journalism to which they are personally and professionally committed. Neither do they believe that such limited-access news is adequate to sustain a healthy public understanding and opinion on foreign policy.

There is relatively little disagreement that neither the President nor the Secretary of State can be expected to be more available personally to reporters. But neither do these correspondents believe that what they want can be provided through the conduit of a news office, however skillfully run and however sympathetic it may be with their desire for more. These men insist on direct discussions in some depth with people possessing professional knowledge and the discretion to use that knowledge. This, these press critics insist, is largely lacking today in both the White House and the State Department.

Others are less critical. They say the situation never has been very different from what it is, and they incline to a philosophical view that nothing very much can be done to alter what is essentially a continuing "trial by battle"—he is right who prevails. This opinion recognizes that to a degree (the extent is always at issue) there is a real conflict of interest between any negotiator who wants a calm sea to sail and an aggressive press in search of a storm that will catch reader interest.

"STYLE" AND CIRCUMSTANCE

Considerations of person and circumstance also enter into the problem. For example, there is a widespread view among correspondents that since the death of Secretary Dulles the focus of significant foreign policy news has shifted from State to the White House, that this has tended to "dry-up" down-the-line sources in State who are reluctant to outguess the President and that the over-all press treatment of foreign affairs suffers because there is no one in the White House available and sufficiently knowledgeable about foreign policy to do the daily, systematic "backgrounding" demanded by modern journalism.

The practice of Presidents and Secretaries will vary with persons and circumstance. One need, therefore, is to recognize this fact and to see that the situation is adjusted organizationally to take full account of the "style" of the men involved and the circumstances governing at the time.

Secretary Dulles' news conferences were frequently "free-wheeling" to the point where his colleagues in the Department are said to have often found fully as much news in one of these press conferences as did the reporters. Secretary Dulles probably used the press to make policy more than most Secretaries would care or dare to do, but it would be highly unrealistic to imagine that the wide-open type of press conference is ever merely a news mechanism and not also an immensely important policy-forming catalyst. It is in the press conference that even the most professionally disciplined Secretary learns how often it is true that he really knows what he thinks only when he hears what he says. Both for better and for worse this generative quality is inherent in the open press conference. It is a wise Secretary who recognizes this fact, and a fortunate Secretary whose colleagues are able, through shrewd, disciplined preparation, to protect him from the worst and, through a resourceful follow-through, to exploit his unexpected best as revealed by a reporter either too smart or too ignorant not to ask the right question.

Secretary Dulles was also to a degree atypical in his insistence on doing a great deal of background briefing of the press himself. He was highly skilled at exposition and he enjoyed expounding his problems and policies to small, invited groups of correspondents, either at an informal dinner meeting or elsewhere. The press people who were favored with these invitations generally valued the opportunity because, as one such participant put it, "Although we knew we were there to get his story, we were also able to get ours." These invitational briefings undoubtedly displeased some who felt left out, but on balance they seem to have been on the plus side for both the Secretary and the press.

Effectively done, such briefings take some pressure off the Secretary for exclusive interviews and reduce the incentive to "leaking" down the line that builds up in the Department when the top lid is too tightly fitted. The line between such briefings and the familiar Washington phenomenon of a vessel leaking only at the top is mainly one of judgment in fairly selecting those to be invited and in confining the information being discussed to genuine background, rather than using the occasion to release a news story surreptitiously. These things are difficult and occasionally they will fall short, but this is the lot of judgment in all affairs. Certainly there is a place for this type of briefing in the information strategy of the Department.

TO LEAK OR NOT TO LEAK THE NEWS

Seasoned practitioners in both the government and the press feel that a practice of leaking out official news to favored reporters or papers is dangerous and self-defeating.

This judgment holds generally for international conferences as well as for the operations of the Department in Washington. There is more likelihood, however, of departures from this policy at international conferences where the circumstances and the personnel of both the press and the government are largely *ad hoc* in character. Likewise, the competitive atmosphere of conferences involving negotiations between a number of national delegations is itself conducive to leaking stories to friendly correspondents. If one delegation does it, the pressure on the others to do it may be irresistible. The temptation is especially great in the cold war where our opposition regards "news" as a weapon.

Recognizing the realities that may influence *ad hoc* practices at international conferences in ways that conflict with sound information policy, it is in order to caution against permitting such practices to become the presumed good or even the presumed necessity. This is especially true as we enter a period in which international conferences are becoming continuous forums rather than special occasions for the transaction of international business. The permanent international organization is even a sharper case in point where widespread policies of putting out significant information mainly through leaks to a partisan home press could seriously poison the climate of daily work. The United

States mission at the United Nations, for example, could not for long follow principles and practices in these matters that differed fundamentally from those of the Department of State.

HIGH-LEVEL BRIEFINGS AND LIAISON

One of the basic objections to a policy of leaking news is that it tends to exaggerate tactics at the expense of policy. A preoccupation with beating the other fellow in the press tends to distract the Department or a conference delegation from the main business, namely, working out the best policy possible. Perhaps most fundamental of all for us is the objection that the practice of leaking news is rooted in an information philosophy of secrecy. Leaks are effective only under conditions of secrecy, and the essential story told in this paper is that a climate of secrecy is no longer compatible with the conduct of the office of the Secretary of State.

One antidote to pernicious leaks is an enlightened program for providing background information in depth. As indicated above, providing this type of interpretive news at top levels is closely related to the problem on maintaining an optimum liaison between the White House and the State Department on the issuance of public information.

The answer to these two needs can probably not be institutionalized as yet. It will vary from administration to administration, at least for a while. Occasionally adjustments will be necessary to meet changes of personnel and circumstances within the same administration.

The following is a possible approach to the problem:

(a) One individual based either on the White House staff or in the office of the Secretary of State, preferably the latter, might have responsibility for this liaison and for top-level background briefings, whether given by him or by others.

(b) The person performing this function should be one seasoned in public affairs, with broad knowledge of American foreign policies, who holds the personal confidence of the Secretary and the President for his judgment, integrity and wisdom. The position would be comparable to a first-rate ambassadorship and within the Department would carry the rank, if not the title, of an undersecretaryship.

(c) This official should be politically loyal to the administration and normally, therefore, not a career FSO. He should, however, have the professional background that would command the respect and close cooperation of the top career personnel. It is likely that this official would also be drawn into policy liaison work with key Congressmen who want and need the same type of high-level briefings. Here is one of the most delicate situations in the entire public information complex, since there is a fast, continuing give-and-take between the press and "the Hill." When either "the Hill" or the press learns from the other about the Executive's business, it tends to taint both the information and the relationship of the Executive with "the Hill" and the press.

The problem of bringing authority and availability together is by definition one of squaring the circle; all that can be hoped for is an intelligent effort with a willingness to learn from the effort itself. The success of any such effort will depend mainly on the man, plus an information policy on the part of the President and Secretary of State that is prepared to take its chances on the side of openness.

The Bureau of Public Affairs: Office of Public Services

This Office, historically and functionally, exemplifies the growing public dimension in the conduct of American foreign affairs. A lineal descendant of the Office of the Special Consultant established in 1943, the Office of Public Services today employs roughly one-third of the Bureau of Public Affairs. The work of the Office is to service the public through four principal channels: pamphlets and other publications for general distribution, speakers, public correspondence, and liaison with private organizations.

THE CLEARANCE PROBLEM

The writers and the editorial workers in any governmental publications program live and work under the omnipresent cloud of getting "clearance" for what they would like to write and publish. It is well for all concerned to realize that it never has been and never can be otherwise.

The official in charge of a publication project may have trouble clearing everything he wishes with the policy people, but he in turn must remember that clearance by a policy officer is not of itself proof that something is fit to print. Clearance is a negative not a positive certification. It is bought at too high a price if it results in sterilizing either the life or the truth out of a piece to be issued by the government as a service to the public. The Secretary of State has fully as high a stage in having this side of his business well performed as he has in the clearance of information by the policy officials. Here again, the basic point is that the earlier alternative of publishing nothing is increasingly no alternative.

The Secretary must use publications more and more to expound our problems and his policies, and these explanations, at whatever level they are aimed, must possess both integrity and substance.

One procedural principle is relevant to both the negative and positive aspects of the clearance process and that is to require that disputes between publication and policy officials be referred to the next highest authority on both sides. These are ultimately problems of judgment, and the Secretary should be protected so far as possible from having to stand before the world in print on the judgment of *either* a too-fearless penman or a too-frightened junior country-desk FSO.

HISTORICAL PUBLICATIONS

Parenthetically, since it will not be possible here to discuss the Historical Office separately, it should be said that the clearance problem is also of central concern to the scholarly integrity underlying the long-range publications work of that Office. Here the principle should be followed of having the publications work constantly advised and audited by a semi-independent board of outside scholars. The temptation to use or to suppress historical material for policy or political purposes is always great, and the safeguards against such misuses should be made correspondingly strong. The kind of political debate and innuendo that surrounded the leaked publication of the Yalta papers shakes public confidence in the integrity of the entire information operation of the Department as well as its sense of responsibility to the nation's history.

THE DISTRIBUTION PROBLEM

As every publisher knows, even the best book needs marketing if it is to reach a large public. The Department of State operates its publication program under the watchful supervision of the Congressional Joint Committee on Printing. The policies and prohibitions set by this Committee put effective limits on the promotion of governmental publications, especially on their free distribution. These very understandable Congressional policies are rooted in both the fear of unrestricted propaganda by an Executive agency and in the budget. These restrictive policies and related legislative prohibitions against the expenditure of funds to influence legislation might well be made the subject of a broad, dispassionate study under nongovernmental auspices. The effectiveness as well as the integrity of our democratic process is at issue in this critical area of public policy. As of today the distribution problem must be left to the good sense of the Congressional Committee and its staff, the ingenuity of the producers, the tenacity of the consuming public, and the vagaries of trial by Congressional wrath.

LIAISON WITH PRIVATE GROUPS

The private association has long been a familiar participant in the American democratic process. Every private interest and every public cause at some point, in some form, is personified and served by an organized group. The dual public-private character of foreign affairs attracts the attention of every type of organized interest.

Fifty years ago the range of this interest was witnessed by the personal attention given by high officers of the Department to both the Chamber of Commerce's hard-headed concern with trade promotion and the idealistic devotion of the peace societies to the cause of Peace—with a capital P. Today the outer edges of organized self-interest and idealism have been extended into outer space, and the spectrum of organized private interest in foreign affairs is now filled with groups defined by sex, religion, race, calling, geography, education, military service, community service, and every form of previous or present condition of political servitude and national affiliation.

Manifestly, the relationship of the Department of State to this complex of organized interests is an immense reality in the conduct of American foreign affairs. It is a reality that cannot be ignored since most of the American people seriously concerned with foreign affairs are identified with these groups.

Since 1943, liaison with private groups, particularly the public-interest organizations, has become a permanent, major aspect of the public affairs operations of the Department. About 3,000 organizations are represented in the files of the Organization Liaison Branch of the Office of Public Services. Active contact is maintained with about 300 of this list and upwards of 100 of these receive the attention accorded "important customers."

Few students or practitioners in this field have any doubt about the value of the relationship between the Department and these groups for the purpose of promoting public understanding and support for our foreign policies. Since many groups exist primarily for this educational purpose and since the President and the Secretary of State are constantly in need of understanding and support for their aims and policies, this function of the relationship is itself an imperative in the policy process rather than "one of those nice things to do if you have the time." Even so, the question remains whether such an essentially one-way relationship is enough; indeed, more basically the issue is whether the imperative need to "export" information and create understanding can be sustained at adequate levels unless there is also an import from the public into the Department and thereby a genuine reciprocity in this relationship.

The traditional view assuredly focused almost exclusively on the "export" of understanding, and recent studies on the "import" side indicate, at least up to now, little evidence that nongovernmental groups have had an extensive, discernible impact on the formulation, as contrasted with the implementation, of American foreign policies. (See "Americans in World Affairs" surveys of the World Peace Foundation. Cf. Thomas Bailey's *The Man in the Street*.) However this may be, there are considerations that counsel against a hasty rejection of the idea that reciprocity in both form and intellectual substance is possible and may be essential to the future good health of this public relationship of the Department.

The dividing line in our democratic process between the formulation and the implementation of public policy is veritably "a seamless web." It is difficult for any of us to be sure how much of any idea or judgment is our own and how much we have picked up along the way, as it were, out of the atmosphere of the problem. Certainly the capacity of public officials at all levels to let their minds be bold is consciously and unconsciously affected by the climate of public opinion. And the climate of public opinion is always related to its constituent elements. In fine, public interest, understanding, and opinion, whatever may be their discernible contribution, do play a role in the formulation of foreign policies and, both directly and indirectly, the private groups are indispensable to this role.

Whatever may or may not be the impact on policy of any private group's ideas, it is certainly true that a willingness by the Department to listen to such ideas helps greatly when the Secretary of State in turn needs a listening public.

Finally, it must be emphasized that in large measure this issue turns on the selection of the private groups and persons to be consulted and the circumstances of the consultation. On the one hand, the Department discovered early in the past decade that it was distinctly dangerous to attempt genuine consultation on something as politically inflammable as the China problem with a large group of private persons and group representatives of varied background and responsibility. The abuse of the Department's confidence in this unhappy instance is credited by many with setting back for a decade or longer any serious effort to extend and deepen the consultative relationship between the Department of State and nongovernmental organizations.

National conferences for representatives of 200 or more organizations are still held by the Department, but since 1952 they have been fewer in number, the information imparted has been of a lower proof and the quality of candid give-and-take consultation has largely disappeared from these occasions. At the same time most observers share the Department's judgment that these efforts are still worth-while. The opportunity for the groups to be exposed to each other's views is itself regarded as a valuable by-product of these gatherings.

Aside from the dangers of abused confidence illustrated by the ill-fated conference on China, the Department faces the dilemma of being criticized either by the organizations for "not telling us as much as we get from *The New York Times*" or by Congress and the press for giving these "favored few" confidential information. Members of Congress not in sympathy with State's policies are also likely to complain that such conferences are mainly "sales meetings."

In particular, it seems clear that serious substantive consultation with outsiders (even with unclassified material) can only be carried out with relatively small, highly selected groups, gathered under circumstances that command a sense of responsibility from the participants. This was done in the postwar planning studies carried out during both World Wars I and II. More recently, the Senate Committee on Foreign Relations has tapped the resources of private thought in ways that could just as readily be used, perhaps with some modification, by the Department of State. There is some opinion in academic circles and the professional groups that State has not been nearly as resourceful or as much interested as some other agencies of the government in supplementing its expertness with outside help of this character. The problem of organizing and using outside "professional" advice on a continuing basis is probably more difficult in diplomacy than elsewhere, but, in the judgment of the writer, the potential advantages make the effort, the risks, and an inevitable measure of new trouble worth-while.

THE "HARD-SELL" GROUPS

The Department's ability to enlist the aid of private groups on behalf of its work is sharply restricted by the line the tax laws draw between educational enterprises and those trying to influence legislation. Established public-interest groups possessing tax-exempt status are naturally chary about pushing their educational activities to the point where they could be charged with propagandizing.

And yet a Secretary of State today quickly comes to realize that education and its ways are not alone enough or not fast enough to meet the imperatives of his public leadership. He frequently needs help from groups organized out of a commitment of conviction (even of self-interest) and free to pursue their aims of public policy without the inhibitions against salesmanship imposed by law on tax-exempt enterprises.

American society is the world's most fertile spawning bed for direct-action groups. In recent times many leading citizens have entered the lists of foreign policy under such vivid banners as: *The League To Enforce Peace, America First, Committee to Defend America by Aiding the Allies, Americans United for World Organization, Committee on the Present Danger,* etc. Similarly, foreign economic programs such as Reciprocal Trade Agreements, the Marshall Plan, and foreign aid have been supported and opposed by both established interest groups and a variety of *ad hoc* organizations created for the particular projects.

In the business vernacular, these are the organizations that can do the job of "hard-selling" or, perhaps, of "hard-opposing" when the democratic process approaches the point of decision on great issues of public policy. As agencies for influencing public opinion at their best these groups have many unique assets: the strength of purpose that flows from focused interest, conviction, and commitment; and the power that goes with prestige sponsorship by leading citizens, skilled direction by professional publicists, and any all-out action.

Such enterprises also render incalculable service to our democratic process by creating bridges of bipartisanship throughout the American public on the great overriding issues of public policy. Of itself, this characteristic makes such groups of especial importance to a Secretary of State. And they are of peculiar importance to him in another respect, namely, their purpose, their organization, their personnel and legal status are usually such that direct, "down-to-cases" cooperation with them is more manageable than with other types of groups. At the same time their demands of the Department are likely to be correspondingly greater and more insistent for information, prestige speakers, and the like. A wise Secretary will not ignore the returns that an investment of such assistance can bring to his program.

PUBLIC OPINION STUDIES IN STATE

Over the years, the Department of State has shown a more sustained, systematic interest in public opinion than it has in private ideas. For at least fifty years, excerpts from the daily press at home and abroad have been circulated to the policy offices. Since 1943, the study of American public opinion on foreign affairs has been carried on in the Department by a small staff of specialists.

The public studies staff is headed today by a political scientist with upwards of twenty years' experience in the field, and his predecessor was an established scholar in international affairs. The staff prepares analytical reports for distribution throughout the Department and to our overseas missions. These reports, which range from daily opinion summaries to a monthly survey, deal not only with the general climate of opinion on foreign affairs, but also with specific issues where the study must focus down onto a relatively narrow band of the opinion spectrum.

The writer and others differ with the present policy of the Department in its refusal to seek appropriations to permit the public studies operation to employ on a limited basis the services of outside polling surveys. Congressional unhappiness in 1957 over the alleged discrepancy between the critical opinion on foreign aid in the mail of Congressmen and the results shown by the polls led to discontinuance by State of the polling studies it had employed on a limited basis from 1944 on. It is difficult to believe that as this technique of the social sciences is perfected and becomes a generally accepted aid to public opinion study American diplomacy will not once again use it.

TV AND RADIO

It is believed that the location of the Department's television and radio personnel in the News Office is a mistake. The news operations of the Department are naturally dominated by their traditional function of servicing the press. In so far as TV and radio are conceived of as being simply news operations in another form, the present setup makes sense. But there is a large body of opinion that regards this as an unduly limited and outmoded view of the role these media can and should play in a comprehensive information program based on public service principles.

If the full potential of radio and TV for serious public education is to be realized by the Department, they should be more closely associated organizationally with the longer-range, educational information activities of a strong Office of Public Services. The news aspects of TV and radio might be retained as a function of the Office of News, but the evidence to date is very strong that this is not the organizational climate in which these immensely important facilities will flourish as aids to a public service program aimed at bringing a deeper understanding of foreign affairs to the American people.

Issues at Large

Two issues will always confront the Secretary of State in formulating news policies and in developing information programs to assure understanding and support of our foreign policies.

The first is rooted in the peculiar nature of the Secretary's responsibilities. The issue is—does the Department's news policy hinder or promote foreign policy? In over-simplified form it is the issue of diplomacy vs. news.

The second issue relates to the role of the Executive in the American government and the nature of our democratic process. It is—does the Department's over-all information program serve and not subvert the American democratic process? The over-simplified form of this issue is information vs. propaganda.

Manifestly, the answers given to such questions will involve both the boundaries of philosophic outlook and the context of circumstances within which a Secretary operates.

These issues can be decided only in the context of the specific foreign policy aims, the American political situation, and the world conditions faced by a particular President and his Secretary of State. What must be said is that any future Secretary of State who fails to grasp these issues will impair the conduct of his office. They are henceforth inextricably a part of every major foreign policy problem.

THE NEWS ISSUE

It is reasonably certain that the "news" policies of the Department will be increasingly complicated by the number of interests that must be dealt with in reaching a foreign policy decision and in clearing what is to be said about it to the public: the other governments and the international bodies involved, the other interested departments and agencies of our government, usually at least two Congressional committees—all of these probably must be in on any major-policy move before it is made public.

A foreign policy dependent upon multilateral negotiations, interdepartmentally cleared policies, and Congressional authorization or appropriations is highly vulnerable to news troubles, especially "leaks along the way." Prime Minister Macmillan recently advocated direct discussions among the leaders rather than elaborate diplomatic procedures involving an "opening" position, a "middle" position and a "fallback" position because, as he put it, "by the time the experts reached the 'fall-back' position to be held in reserve until the summit, some one inevitably leaked it to the reporters, and then the 'fall-back' position became the 'opening' position." [1]

The pressures toward more "open diplomacy" all along the way are built into both the political and technological structure of today's international community. There is little prospect that these pressures can be reduced. The hope of the neo-Wilsonians during the inter-war years that

---

[1] *N.Y. Times,* April 1, 1960.

"open diplomacy" could be restricted to the public ratification of privately negotiated foreign policies seems to be increasingly a lost cause. The *New York Herald Tribune* headline of June 18, 1960, was as authoritative as it was melancholy on this prospect: "Eisenhower on Summits: Here to Stay but Why? President Sees World Opinion Demanding Them; Doubts Value."

"Open negotiations," whether at the summit, on "the Hill" or in "Foggy Bottom," understandably are not regarded as progress by experienced diplomatists. This tendency will inevitably be met within a foreign office by more stringent secrecy, which in turn may isolate the policy makers even further from responsible private persons and groups. This downward spiral of trouble leads only to greater dissatisfaction of the public and the press.

These built-in dilemmas cannot be banished; the Secretary of State's best hope is to understand and manage them.

Another continuing influence on news policies will be the "cold war." Its impact is paradoxical in several ways. On the one hand, the level of candor in talking about the other side has risen (or fallen) to the point where there is little left to be said in this respect "off-the-record." Inevitably the influence of this kind of candor gradually seeps over into other areas of the Department's public behavior.

On the other hand, the influence of the cold war also cuts the other way. The "spy flight" affair is a prime illustration of two serious dangers. First, when the Department of State gets entangled in falsehoods, whether of its own contriving or not, the damage to our foreign policy is incalculable both at home and abroad. Second, in any explosive situation, the press, public opinion leaders, and the general public tend to patriotic restraint to the point where essential information and the issues at stake may not be laid bare for public deliberation. Such restraint is tolerable, even necessary, in war, but in the undefined and endless twilight of "cold war" too much of this could weaken our democratic process.

The "spy flight" and the ensuing abortive summit meeting are too close to this writing for definitive appraisal, but it is not too early to say that both we and the Soviet now have instructive case studies in what can happen when the public relationship is abused: by us in the use of deception and by our foe in the misuse of public diplomacy at the summit.

THE PROPAGANDA ISSUE

The issue between the desirable promotion of public understanding and the abuse of our democratic process through government propaganda is a more difficult problem than whether to tell the truth about the news, or how much to tell to whom and when. The judgments that must be made as between information and propaganda are more subjective and the consequences of mistakes in this area are less readily perceived and corrected than in the area of news policy.

The Secretary of State must sell as well as negotiate American foreign policies today. He is a contender in the publicity marts of the world for support. It would be naive in the extreme to imagine that the American public could be kept quarantined from and uncontaminated by such efforts even if that were desirable, and it is not.

If our national interest requires positive foreign policies involving men, money, and other forms of national commitment, then it is clear that the Secretary of State must assume a major responsibility for seeing to it that the American public is willing to assume such commitments. Understanding of these matters can be achieved only in relation to specific problems and concrete proposals for dealing with them. This in some measure means "selling" the public. The polite word for this type of information activity on the part of the Secretary of State is "leadership." The alternative is to forgo such policies and forfeit the national interest.

The immediate arbiter as to what is and what is not permissible in this area is the Congress. If existing statutory prohibitions were enforced literally, there would be an immediate outcry from all quarters, including "the Hill." As it is, all parties are generally content to leave the *status quo* undisturbed in theory while *de facto* practice responds to realities as they become imperatives. The gun of Congressional wrath is always behind the door to be used or threatened to curb propagandistic excesses that stray beyond the sanctuary of bipartisanship.

Issues of public information cannot be resolved by a constitution. Ultimately they are matters of self-confidence and self-discipline for the public to decide through its democratic processes.

Two generalizations are warranted about the public attitude in these matters. The first is that for some time now the public tolerance of governmental information activity has been increasing. The outlook is for more rather than less public tolerance of such activities.

Secondly, the public demand for greater leadership on the part of the United States in world affairs and on the part of the Executive within our democratic process will require more governmental information activity. It is no longer true that the Secretary of State is the only cabinet officer without a special interest constituency. The number of Americans with some personal knowledge and a sense of personal involvement in world affairs has grown greatly, will continue to grow, and this element will be constantly more insistent on strong leadership from the Secretary of State. Leadership means positive policies, positively presented, and this means being constantly at grips with the propaganda issue.

COUNTERVAILING SANCTIONS TO PROPAGANDA

There are countervailing safeguards within the foreign policy process itself. The most pervasive safeguard is the growing multilateral character of both our foreign policies and of the processes, at home and abroad, for the conduct of foreign relations.

Any foreign policy fashioned out of a painstakingly negotiated mutuality of interest usually has inherent safeguards against being distorted or falsified by over-zealous home salesmanship. These safeguards do not protect against the situation where all concerned—the other nations involved, the other departments and agencies of our government, and both parties in Congress—want the same thing. But short of such relatively rare instances of unanimity, we can rely importantly on this mixture of interests and the multilateral character of our international and domestic foreign policy processes to keep the Secretary of State's information efforts within tolerable bounds of truthfulness and restraint.

Leaving aside the aberration of the so-called spy-plane episode, (which, incidentally, was probably in no small part attributable to the secret, unilateral manner of its handling) it is still reasonable to expect that the Department of State will aim at telling "nothing but the truth." What is less likely is that any governmental information program can be expected to meet the other sworn obligation of a witness, namely, to tell "the whole truth." Government information activity will inevitably always be circumscribed by the purposes of government

It is at this point of "the whole truth" that the public, as well as the Secretary of State, might well be more concerned with the well-being of the private organizations that are so essential to the climate of American understanding and opinion on foreign affairs. The limitless variety of background and interest represented in these private cells of our body politic can itself be a powerful safeguard against having American opinion become dangerously rigid. These private agencies can reach out for the growing-point ideas and for the reconsideration of error, both of which are hard reaches for government. The health of these organizations cannot be taken for granted; they are not as alert and strong as they could be; and they will not be, without the positive interest and encouragement of both the Secretary of State and the full private leadership potential of the American public.

In pursuing an honest, continuing development of a "two-way" philosophy of both speaking and listening to the public, a Secretary of State may find encouragement in these wise words of the late Alan Gregg:[1]

---

[1] *For Future Doctors*, p. 55.

. . . speaking and listening have, like most opposites, a curiously close relationship . . . for it is by listening to the orienting echoes of their supersonic shrill cries that bats steer their flight in the dark. By a not dissimilar process, politicians often steer their zigzag courses by the popular responses to their speeches and editorials.

7.

The Secretary and our unwritten Constitution

♦ Don K. Price

It is comfortable to be able to think in simple, clearcut categories, and disturbing to have them upset by the ruthless course of events. In thinking about foreign affairs, Americans have been going through some such shake-up. As a nation, we used to make a neat distinction between domestic and foreign problems; the main interest we had in foreign countries outside of Western Europe was to send them missionaries, of either the religious or technical variety, while we went ahead with our business at home. We made a clear distinction between peace and war; force was immoral, except when the Marines had to be called out to preserve order abroad, or unless foreign aggression led to war, in which case there was no substitute for victory. Most important in practical issues, we made a distinction between public and private affairs; government and private business should not interfere with each other, and we could be almost upset by the notion that munitions makers were influencing international policy as by the possibility of governmental interference with international commerce.

Breakdown of Old Boundaries

We have been shaken out of this easy kind of thinking by the events of the past two decades. Among the scholars and the professional policymakers, the evidence is obvious: the new realism dominates the advanced thinking on foreign policy; it emphasizes the impossibility of reforming the world completely, the limitations on our ability to control our environment, and the necessity of facing up to the moral issues involved in the application of force to international issues. Among the politicians, the evidence is equally obvious: a willingness to support alliances and commitments abroad, and to tolerate a program ranging from technical assistance to avowed espionage, which any normal legislator would have thought it immoral to vote money for a short quarter-century ago. The all-out isolationists are as extinct as the one-worlders.

But if we have come to a more responsible (though less idealistic) way of thinking in our foreign policy, we have done nothing of the kind with respect to the measures that are necessary to carry it out. We do not still believe, as Mr. Wriston reminds us that the early Jeffersonians did, that the governmental machinery for the conduct of foreign affairs is going to become unnecessary and wither away in the new age. We do not propose to dismantle the Department of State or the Foreign Service. But we have been guilty of almost as unrealistic an approach—a tendency to substitute slogans for policy, and reorganization charts for the practical and expensive measures needed to improve the competence of our government officials and their administration.

The importance of the position of the Secretary of State, as the essays in this volume all suggest, is not that any single officer carries the main burdens of America in world affairs. Instead, it is that his position, by standing at the center of our system of constitutional and political and administrative responsibility, reflects so clearly the practical issues that we have to face but wish we could avoid. It is no longer possible for the Secretary to think only about the missionaries, and to leave the Marines and the munitions makers to someone else's conscience. But while he may reconcile all their roles in his own personal system of morals, it is harder

167

for him to get the government as a whole to think and act with unified responsibility. Institutionally, we have not quite caught on to the fact that the conventional categories have crumbled—it is hard now to recognize the old boundaries between domestic and foreign problems, between peace and war, or between public and private affairs.

It is much easier to realize this in theory, or even to appropriate money to pay for its consequences, than to change our thinking with respect to the way our government operates. But each of these three changes calls on the Secretary of State to make radical changes in the way he runs his job—and each of those changes involves readjustments of a fundamental nature in our administrative, political, and constitutional system (though not necessarily in our written Constitution).

Take, for example, the distinction between domestic and foreign affairs. It is significant that none of the essays in this volume paid much attention to treaties. The awkward arrangements in our Constitution with respect to the Senate's advice on treaties—which have never worked as originally intended since President Washington stamped out of the Senate in disgust and swore he would never go back again—are among the least of the worries of the Secretary of State; his main instruments of foreign policy are now indistinguishable from domestic policy. Mr. Dickey and Mr. Elliott independently noted that the Reciprocal Trade program was the decisive turning point in American attitudes toward foreign affairs; before it, the terms of our trade with the rest of the world were considered purely a domestic problem (and for that matter, a Congressional rather than an executive problem, and in practice within the Congress sometimes to be settled by laws drafted by representatives of private interests rather than of the government). After Reciprocal Trade, no one could ever suppose again that our domestic and foreign affairs were separable. But we are interested in what that did to the Secretary of State: from that time on, it was clear that commerce and industry and labor and agriculture and natural resources were not matters that he could ignore and leave to his Cabinet colleagues. And, in view of the way in which the Federal Communications Commission and the Civil Aeronautics Board were set up, neither was the system of independent or quasi-judicial commissions.

Next there is the distinction between peace and war. The Ludlow amendment, which as recently as the late 1930's proposed to require a popular referendum before a declaration of war, is a distant memory; we even look back a little ruefully at our innocence during the second World War in not being more alert, in the control of our strategy, to its implications for postwar power relationships. We may not, as a nation, have learned the theoretical lesson that power relationships in politics do not disappear in time of peace or even under the rule of law, but there are some practical things that we do understand—communist threats, and the technical feasibility of ICBM's and H-bombs—which lead us to the same end. Then consider the effect of the disappearance of this boundary on the Secretary of State: he can no longer, like Bryan and Wilson, assume that war plans are immoral, nor can he be set aside like Hull from strategy councils when the shooting starts. On the contrary, he is obliged to consider the nature of our military forces and our weapons systems as indispensable factors in the diplomatic equations that he tries to bring into balance; the machinery for the conduct of his relations with the military, and his Department's must work smoothly and responsively if he is to succeed in his job. As Mr. Acheson, Mr. Bowie, and Mr. Nitze have all suggested from different experiences, this takes some doing.

But much more far-reaching in its consequences is the breakdown of the old boundaries between public and private affairs. I do not mean to suggest that there is not going to be any difference between the two in the future, or that there ought not to be; indeed one of the great needs of civilized society is to protect each citizen in his essential privacy. But the old boundaries have collapsed, and this is a source of great embarrassment to those who have committed themselves too uncritically to an identification of democracy with unregulated corporate enterprise. The conservatives who did so, and who objected to the regulation of private corporations in the interests of foreign policy, had their counterparts on the liberal side in those who thought of the munitions makers as "merchants of death" and assumed that it was immoral for the government to be concerned with the fate of the international oil companies.

These issues still remain, but they are no longer issues in which the interests of government and those of private companies are thought of as antagonistic; our moral dilemmas are now part of a single system. If anyone doubts that the boundaries are different today, let him reflect on the facts that Mr. Francis Powers, who flew the ill-fated U-2 over Russia, did so (or so NASA announced) on the payroll of a private aircraft company; that technical assistance and international educational exchanges, which have become important arms of foreign policy, are largely conducted by universities and private institutions under contract for the government; and that some of the most important strategic studies are being made for the military not by staff officers in uniform but by a series of private institutions which began work under the somewhat narrower concept of operations research.

The Secretary, of course, has to worry about all this. He has to be concerned with the extent to which private institutions are supporting the international activities of the government, particularly of the Department's closely affiliated agencies like ICA and USIA. Moreover, he must be equally concerned with the way in which the breakdown of this boundary between private and public institutions is affecting the public agencies themselves. The basis of our old approach to government service was that it was a separate calling. Politicians were expected in theory (though not supposed in practice) to serve out of a sense of duty; members of the Foreign and military services were separate groups, dedicated by their *esprit de corps,* their special education, and their isolated assignments to a career of poverty, anonymity, and obedience; and the civil service was not very important and could be disregarded.

But what happens to all this when the pleasures of working on public affairs are extended to the employees of private institutions, who may be paid under government contracts far more generously than their government counterparts? If this process continues, why should a promising young man interested in international affairs work for the State Department or the Foreign Service when he can work on the same problems, and go to the same exotic places, on the more generous payroll of a research institution, a foundation, or a private corporation? And then what happens to ability of the Department of State, and its Secretary, to play a controlling and responsible role in the conduct of foreign affairs? Private institutions are doubtless being brought within the orbit of government policy, but their superior attractions as employers might unbalance the political system of gravity, and make the Department of State their satellite, rather than vice versa. General Gavin (in his *War and Peace in the Space Age*) has asked rather pointedly whether our strategy is being set by the military staffs or the manufacturers of missiles.

There is no such single lobby with which the Secretary of State must contend, but he may well worry whether, as so many private institutions have become involved in foreign affairs, he can continue to compete for the best talent and maintain as competent a Department as he needs to meet his responsibilities.

In our general approach to international affairs, we have changed from utopians to realists. Morally and politically, we are not so likely to think in watertight compartments about the use of force to safeguard our policy objectives, about the subordination of domestic habits in the interest of national security, or about private and corporate interests as things to be kept quite apart from governmental concern. But we have not yet taken the same step with respect to the ways by which our policies are to be made and the means by which they are to be carried out. Here is an equally difficult set of problems for the Secretary of State. To solve them, it may be necessary to think in the broadest possible terms about the way in which he fits into our governmental system as a whole.

The Constitutional Consequences

Just as it has become harder in recent years to draw the old sharp distinctions between domestic and foreign problems, between peace and war, or between public and private affairs, so it has become harder within our constitutional system to distinguish between the functions of the legislative and executive branches, or between questions of policy and those of administration. Indeed, it is because the former boundaries have broken down that the latter have become almost useless for defensive purposes.

This is not to say that the Constitution of the United States is being flouted or ignored. It is the basic instrument of our government, and controls the basic distribution of its powers and functions. But as a matter of practical politics, we have fortunately recognized that the basic framework can be preserved best if we do not worship all the incidental apparatus and procedures that the Founding Fathers had in mind. Back of our written Constitution we have developed an unwritten constitution that is much more complex than the unwritten British constitution, and equally responsive to adjustments in the balance of powers and prestige among its several branches.

This is the significance of the point that has already been noted: the most urgent problems of the Secretary of State are no longer connected with the ratification of treaties—a matter governed by rigid Constitutional formula—but are those connected with his relationships with the appropriations and legislative committees of the Congress and with his relationships with the President and his fellow Department heads—and on these matters the written Constitution has comparatively little immediate bearing. This development has not been brought about by sheer perversity or a desire of any branch of government to encroach on another. It rather came about because the Constitution had never foreseen what the new constitutional problems would be, and it has been quite necessary, in order to maintain the general spirit of the Constitution, to work out an unwritten Constitution on new lines.

Take, for example, an economic aid program in, say, Taiwan. If the Founding Fathers had been able to imagine such a thing, they might have thought of it first of all as a matter of foreign or military affairs; in such matters the early Federalists were willing to turn full authority over to the President, whose responsibility was spelled out in broad terms by the Constitution. On the contrary, they might have thought that the appropriation of funds for such matters made them the responsibility of Congress. If they had differed on the exact way in which such responsibility would be shared between the two branches, they would have been doing exactly what we are doing today. And the precise distribution of responsibility is adjusted from time to time by a process of bargaining in the light of the balance of various factors—the political leadership of the President, the weight of the expert advice from various parts of the Executive, the power of various parts of the Congress to influence the granting or withholding of money or authority, and many others. We are, at times, legalistic and doctrinaire enough, but on issues of major importance we have tended to work out our unwritten constitution pragmatically enough to please a Walpole, and with enough formal deference to tradition to satisfy a Burke.

In general, the balance between the respective influences of Congress and the Executive Branch with regard to international affairs has probably shifted somewhat in favor of the Congress since the second World War; at least, as Mr. Elliott has noted, the Congress has invented new techniques and procedures to give its members and committees a greater share of influence in the rapidly growing business of foreign affairs. But any attempt to assess such a balance in any precise way is rather meaningless, for several reasons.

First of all, neither the Legislative nor Executive Branch functions apart from the other. A public recommendation by the Executive may be supported by the Congress; the general public impression may then be one of harmony and teamwork, even though the executive in question may have been thoroughly browbeaten by a legislative opposition and scaled his recommendation down to what he thought the political traffic would bear. Alternatively, an executive may be forever in the headlines for quarrels with "the Congress," when actually he has the firm support of an overwhelming majority, but comes under the implacable enmity of a tiny minority.

The second point is related to the first: neither the Executive nor Congress is itself completely unified. The Foreign Service, or any of the military services, may act almost as independently in dealing with the Congress as any private interest, especially when its corporate interests are affected, and so may various departments and bureaus. This is partly because of their special professional or technical outlook, but partly too because of the pressures that support them and push them in particular directions. These pressures—whether they come from the farm bloc working on the Department of Agriculture and on the agriculture committees of the Congress or from similar interests in other fields—create extreme difficulties for the Secretary of State, whose responsibilities and political position force him to take the most general view in the government of our national interests, short of the President himself.

Third, the distinction between policy and administration is un-

government is not responsive merely to the executive directions of the President, or organized according to his wishes. It has political traditions and interests and policies of its own. Some of our greatest political errors have resulted from thinking that these elements of stubbornness were based only on partisan connections and motives. In this respect, a Presidential election settles comparatively few of the political issues that the government faces; only the most conspicuous (not necessarily the most significant) ones can come to public attention in a campaign; and in practice the new President and Secretary of State are then faced with much of the same recalcitrance from the Executive vested interests, and have the same difficulties in reconciling or adjusting or removing them as would have plagued their partisan competitors.

One thing is clear: the problem cannot be solved by transferring all the international activities of the government to the Secretary of State. That would be as difficult as transferring to the Department of Justice everyone concerned with the interpretation or execution of laws. The disposal of agricultural surpluses abroad is a domestic problem for the Department of Agriculture as well as an international problem for the Department of State. The same principle applies to the Atomic Energy Commission in connection with locating reactors abroad, or exchanging scientific data with foreign countries; or to the Department of Commerce in its administration of the Export Control Act; or the Civil Aeronautics Board with respect to the licensing of airline routes abroad. The problem is not one of organization in the sense of locating boxes on charts; it is one of organization in the sense of adjusting the various political pressures and bureaucratic interests to produce an integrated program.

In this process, the President and the Secretary of State have all the conventional problems of organization and administration—span of control, the grouping of related functions, communications, specialization, and so on. But they have in addition two broad types of problems that an industrial organization does not: one is the way in which, legally and politically, bureaus and agencies are linked to particular committees of the Congress and to particular interest groups within our economic and social system. The other is the special view of policy that is consequently characteristic of the responsible personnel of each bureau or agency. This is not a matter of "corrupt interests." Some of the most difficult problems come from strict professional and moral standards; Secretary Ickes, to take an example from ancient history, refused to take orders even from the President with regard to the sale of helium to Nazi Germany, since statutes had given the Secretary of the Interior full legal responsibility for that decision.

The most feasible way to help the Secretary of State solve this problem is not by reorganizing the government to put more functions under him.

or even to give him more formal authority. It is, I think, to try to deal with the two underlying causes of his problem noted above.

First, how can Congress, as it deals with a problem that is both foreign and domestic, be induced to give adequate attention to its foreign aspects —when jurisdiction over the controlling elements of that problem will probably be assumed (as Mr. Elliott's essay so clearly points out) either by a legislative committee other than Foreign Relations or Foreign Affairs, or by a subcommittee of an Appropriations Committee. The problem that is usually seen in terms of executive organization is thus, at its roots, often a problem of legislative organization.

Second, how can the top officials of the departments and agencies be induced to take a more comprehensive view of their policies, with due regard to international considerations and the policy of the President and Secretary of State? The primary answer to this question—especially with respect to the top layer of political officials—undoubtedly lies in political vision and political leadership. But an almost equally important part of the problem, and probably the only part that institutional planning can reach, has to do with the career or relatively nonpartisan officials. Reformers are quite properly beginning to worry not only how to protect the career officials from the politicians, but vice versa. And the main aspect of this problem is not the danger of partisan sabotage, but the narrowness of vision with respect to policy and national purpose that is necessarily characteristic of most officials of predominantly specialized education and background, whose career in government offers them no incentive to think of their problems from a broader point of view.

Within each military service, if not within the Defense Department as a whole, an effort is made to give a promising officer varied experience to keep his outlook broad, and to plan his career so as to hold out for him the opportunity for promotion to high command, and thus to give him an incentive to think in terms of the total mission of his service. The Army general officer may not be able to see things from the Navy or Air Force point of view, but he will at least have had some training and some job assignments deliberately designed to get him out of a specialized rut. The Foreign Service tries, of course, to do the same kind of thing. Amid the somewhat greater political uncertainties of the civil service, however, the civilian officer finds more career safety in distinguishing himself within as technical (and therefore nonpolitical) a specialty as possible. And this makes it extremely hard for him to adjust his thinking to the kind of policy considerations that ought to be responsive to politics. On the other side, the typical Foreign Service Officer of a decade ago was equally likely to think of problems mainly as diplomatic problems, with little awareness of their impact on domestic problems, and little interest in the ways in which new techniques of international action could be brought to bear on foreign problems.

Senator Mansfield, in his evaluation of the U-2 incident (Congressional Record, June 23, 1960), came out for giving the Secretary of State "centralized and firm control over the policies and activities of the various agencies with significant functions in the international field . . ."—and over their public speeches as well! There would be little disagreement, perhaps, over the desirability of giving the Secretary more effective influence in these respects. But what does "centralized and firm control" mean in practice? It is hard to see how the Secretary could be given such authority without the right to discipline those department heads who resisted his authority, and the right to control their relations with the Congress. Could those elements of power be given him without making him into a Prime Minister, and reducing the President to the role of a constitutional monarch?

A second problem is the relation of the Secretary to those federal agencies operating exclusively in the international field, especially the International Cooperation Administration and the United States Information Agency. The debate has raged for years whether they should be in or out of the Department of State. Each has tried it both ways; it is hard to say how much difference the position on the organization chart has made. One is now in, and one is now out of the Department, and the essential problems of organization of both remain the same: how can they be set up so as to be responsive to the guidance of the Secretary of State, while still relieving him of the operational burden of detailed management, or the political burden of accepting responsibility for them before the Congressional committees? This is a much more tractable problem than the relationship of the Secretary to the major Executive Departments, for neither in their political strength nor in the substance of their policies do these agencies have as much of a case as do the other Executive Departments for a right to compete with the Secretary of State in the shaping of national policy. It should not surpass our political ingenuity to put them firmly under his control with respect to issues that he considers important, while giving them the separate machinery for such matters as personnel and budgetary and financial management that are required if their executive directors are to be held responsible for their operation.

This problem is closely related to the third major problem of organization with which the Secretary deals: the organization of the Department of State itself, and of the Foreign Service. For the relationship of either ICA or USIA to the Department is much like the relationship of one of the functional subdivisions of the Department itself to the geographic

Branch. For the time being, the case is even stronger; in many fields, to ask the Secretary of State to rely on the other Departments' experts would be like asking a man with a lawsuit on his hands to take the advice of the other side's lawyers.

This is not to say, of course, that all the Secretary's problems of this kind have come from outside his Department. There have been in the past plenty of cases of lack of sympathy within the Departmental and Foreign Services for the policies of a Secretary. These, however, were subject to reform by the processes that Mr. Wriston has described, and in general were less likely to be beyond the power of a strong Secretary to control.

Along with the general distrust of committees has developed an awareness of a much more specific difficulty. This is a modern version of the old query, *Quis custodiet ipsos custodes?*, which, being freely translated, means "Who coordinates the coordinating committees?"

If I have complained about the insubordination of Executive Departments and the independence of Congressional committees, it was only to complain of an excess of a desirable quality. It is necessary to departmentalize a great operation, and impossible to do so without having great overlaps of interest. Hence it is necessary and desirable for strong and aggressive Department heads to state the case for their respective Departments, to see policy from their special points of view, and to be called to account by Congressional committees for their discharge of statutory responsibilities. The overlaps and inconsistencies in this process can be adjusted by political leadership, and tolerated in reasonable degree. If an interdepartmental committee is set up to help the President adjust those overlaps or inconsistencies, it can be quite useful. But if such a committee acquires legal status, *esprit de corps,* and jurisdictional interests of its own, and is looked to by the Congress and the public as the source of policy, the only outcome can be a muddle.

For a Department head assumes political responsibility to the President and the Congress not only for thinking great thoughts about policy, but for seeing that they are put into effect. That is a sobering discipline. But a committee that has a public and statutory status is another matter. It acquires an influence of its own even though it has no responsibility for getting things done, and its responsibility even for advice is diffused. Even if its statutory function is nominally advisory, it feels it has something of a right not to have its advice disregarded, and the executive to whom it reports is never able to decide against its advice without considering the political consequences. Moreover, the formality and slowness of committee procedures are enhanced by the political self-importance that goes with formal status. Most troublesome of all, it is even more difficult to distinguish between the terms of reference of committees than the functions of departments, for the policy questions that ought to be considered by any committee are so broad that they must overlap with the interests of other committees in related fields.

This overlap is only a minor technical problem to be taken care of by good staff work, if the committees in question are merely auxiliary to a responsible system of executive organization—that is to say, if a responsible executive sets them up without fanfare, and can change their assignments and membership and disregard their advice when it suits him to do so. But if they acquire a right in the eyes of the public and of the Congress to formulate policy in a given field—and statutory status can hardly mean anything else, no matter how carefully that status is limited to an advisory role—the channels of executive responsibility to the electorate and the Congress are inevitably confused.

The Secretary of State has been the chief loser from his tendency to set up highly formalized committees at the policy level. It may have been inevitable, since the Department of State at the end of the second World War was certainly not equipped by its experience and traditions to become, in effect, the President's chief coordinating agency for Executive Branch policy. Since something had to be done, in several important fields, the result was statutory committee machinery: the National Security Council in 1947, the National Advisory Council on International Monetary and Financial Problems (NAC) in 1945, and in 1958 the National Aeronautics and Space Council.

The NSC was originally set up as the key instrument in an effort to integrate national security policy while avoiding the complete unification of the armed services; the result was to put into a committee—and a committee in which the military departments were equipped by their massive staff facilities to play a disproportionately influential role—much of the responsibility for policy formulation that might have been assumed by the Secretary of State. Similarly, the NAC was set up by statute in 1945 to coordinate all departments' policies "in the making of foreign loans or . . . in foreign financial, exchange or monetary transactions." The statute was a victory for the Treasury over the State Department; the Secretary of the Treasury was made chairman of the NAC, and his staff became its secretariat.

The Hoover Commission in 1949 supported the traditional opposition of the Bureau of the Budget to the creation of other statutory committees with fixed membership and agenda, and raised the question how the President might bring the committee system under control. In the meantime, ways had been found to keep the worst of the potential difficulties of the statutory committees from developing. From the beginning of the NSC, the President and the NSC staff took pains to make it clear that the President could invite additional members to the NSC as he wished, and that its recommendations were purely advisory to him. The issue had become clear by 1958: when Congress forced the Space Council on the President, it soon became obvious that this was to be given little importance in the policy councils of the White House. On major issues, of course, the Secretary of State can always appeal personally to the President against any committee recommendation. But we are still far from managing our interdepartmental committees with the flexibility and coordination of the British model, which we tried to imitate rather uncritically at the end of the War.

THE PRESIDENT'S OFFICE

For the purpose of coordinating the international aspects of government policy, the obvious alternative to the creation of committees is the development of the President's staff. The Executive Office of the President was created in 1939, absorbing the Bureau of the Budget which had served as Presidential staff (although formally in the Treasury) since 1921. Its location in the Treasury had been a handicap, since other Executive Departments, who naturally disliked budget reviews anyhow, objected especially to being reviewed by a Department of equal status. It was much easier for the Bureau to help in the exercise of Presidential authority when it became formally attached to the Presidential Office.

The same argument has been used to justify machinery in the Executive Office for the coordination of international policy: the Department of State, being merely another Department, cannot be given the job of coordinating its sister Departments; that job has to be assigned to an agency in the Executive Office. It was partly on this logic that the Office of the Director for Mutual Security (the Harriman Office) was set up in the Executive Office in 1951; similar arguments have held that in interdepartmental committees (like the NSC, or the Operations Coordination Board which is now subordinate to it) the Department of State is merely another member.

The difficulty with this line of reasoning is that it would lead the President, for the control of international policy, to set up in the Executive Office a competing Department of State. Special Presidential assistants in the field of foreign affairs have, to put it mildly, found it somewhat difficult to work out their role without encroaching on the Secretary's jurisdiction.

But the problem remains: how can the President be given more effective assistance in the direction and coordination of the international aspects of national policy? Is this a job for the Secretary of State, or should some new office be created? Several proposals have recently been put forward. Generally they fall into four types:

1. Some recommend, as did former President Hoover in 1955, an appointed vice president for foreign affairs. This usually means the creation of a new position, and the granting of its basic powers, by statute.

2. Others (like Senator Mansfield in the speech already quoted) would give the Secretary of State definite authority over other Departments with respect to their international policies or decisions.

3. Governor Rockefeller, drawing on his former studies as Chairman of the President's Advisory Committee on Government Organization, has recommended the creation by statute of a new officer—the First Secretary of the Government—who would not have statutory power in his own right, but exercise authority only by delegation from the President. Statutory provision would be necessary, however, to let him be confirmed by the Senate, serve as Executive Chairman of the National Security Council, and have the power to reorganize and direct all of the inter-departmental planning machinery of the government relating to national security and foreign affairs. While he would not be directly in command, in his own right, over the Department heads, he would be superior to them in status, and would be expected to attend for the President international meetings of Prime Ministers.

4. The Brookings Institution, in a study for the Senate Foreign Relations Committee, rejected the idea of a super-Cabinet officer, and recommended instead (a) a somewhat stronger grouping of staff functions in the Executive Office, and (b) the creation of a Secretary of Foreign Affairs, to be Vice Chairman of NSC and to have actual power of direction over three Cabinet colleagues: the Secretary of State, in charge of the State Department, and a new Secretary (and a new name) each for the ICA and USIA.

The first two types of proposals run into the obvious difficulty of defining just what issues are international. An issue can be stated as purely international in abstract terms, but the actions to carry it out almost always involve domestic policy as well. How can a Presidential deputy be given real authority over international affairs, without almost unlimited authority over the Departments? But to give a single officer full authority over a major part of all government business might well leave the President wondering what he was elected to do. The power of appointment and removal, especially when complicated by Senate confirmation, is hardly enough to let the President feel comfortable in keeping on top of such an officer, when political factions might group around him to seek to exploit any shade of difference between his policy and the President's.

The third and fourth proposals are, of course, more sophisticated. Both seek to make it clear that it is not possible by statute to put another officer in the chain of command between the President and the Secretary of Agriculture, or the Secretary of Defense. Both would create a new office, of higher rank than the Secretary of State, in order to symbolize the supreme importance of international affairs in our national policies. They differ as follows. Governor Rockefeller's proposal would give a new First Secretary no direct command of any operating Department, and would justify his status only by making him the President's staff agent for all international interests, and by putting him in charge of all the committees and staff agencies that deal in that field. The Brookings proposal, on the other hand, would give a new Secretary of Foreign Affairs "general directive authority" over what are now State, ICA, and USIA: by making him Vice Chairman of NSC, it would try to enhance his ability to give leadership to other Departments, especially Defense; but it would create a separate officer to head the staff units for international affairs in the Executive Office.

One obvious difficulty with the "First Secretary" proposal is an ambiguity in the status of the office: To give an officer higher rank and pay by law than the Department heads, and to send him to meetings of Prime Ministers, suggests a role quite different from that of staff officers who operate only as a part of the Presidential Office—such as The Assistant to the President, or the Director of the Budget. If he cannot make decisions and give orders to the Defense Department, for example, could he qualify as a representative of the United States at a meeting of heads of governments? Or for the higher rank and pay that proposal implies? And if he does pretend to this degree of influence, can his role be acceptable either to the President or to the heads of the Executive Departments?

By avoiding this difficulty, the Brookings proposal runs into another one. The Secretary of Foreign Affairs would, like the present Secretary of State, be only first among equals among the Department heads, but he would have under him three operating departments also headed by Secretaries of Cabinet rank. The analogy of the National Military Establishment, before the creation of the Defense Department, suggests the obvious problems that he might encounter. Congressional committees are not always willing to listen to the head of a subordinate Department as long as they can summon the occupant of a higher office that has been made responsible by law, and hence publicly accountable, for the conduct of a program.

The source of this difficulty, therefore, is the same principle that complicates the "First Secretary" proposal: if Congress gives an officer definite functions and powers, it is natural to consider him publicly accountable for their exercise. It is likely to cause confusion, therefore, to give responsibility for a certain decision by statute to a Department head, and by statute to give another officer (or worse, a committee) the duty of determining the policy to guide that decision. That difficulty does not arise—or at least it arises in much less acute and more acceptable form—if a Department head is obliged to make his decision conform to an authority that derives unmistakably from the President's constitutional power. The Department head, as a politically responsible member of the President's Administration, cannot then refuse to accept responsibility for whatever he has done or failed to do.

The most important question, therefore, to ask about all these proposals is not whether the President's coordinating authority should be organized in one detailed fashion or another, but whether such matters should be governed by statute at all. What is being considered here is the inner working of the President's Constitutional authority to supervise and coordinate his subordinates, especially in a field in which the fullest executive discretion has always been considered proper. From the beginning, Congress has always considered the Cabinet, for example, as an institution which had no statutory existence, and could be managed secretly by the President as he saw fit, and it has never undertaken to define the functions of the Secretary of State except to say that he was the President's man, to do as the President pleased. All this was recognized from the beginning as essential to the unity and dispatch of executive business; moreover, it was a deliberate choice, in sharp contrast to the practice of several of the States which had formal executive councils to restrict the governors' discretion.

If this original principle is sound, and if it should be applied to the modern working of the President's inner councils, the only legislation that would be required would be to grant the President authority to organize his Executive Office, and assign duties within it, in any way that he sees fit; and to fix responsibility on the President, rather than on any subordinate, for any exercise of authority over the operating Departments. This is not particularly novel doctrine; it was recommended explicitly in 1949 by the first Hoover Commission. If it were put into effect today the President could work out the delicate balance between the use of his immediate staff, and the use of the Secretary of State (by whatever title the man in charge of our foreign affairs department might be known), to help guide the development and execution of policy. If this can be done, the practical requirements of the situation might show that the State Department is, by necessity, as much a staff agency to the President as any part of his Executive Office. The title of the Secretary of State, and his symbolic custody of the Great Seal and counter-signature of every Presidential appointment, show that he was originally thought of as the President's first minister and chief of his secretariat; the intricate interweaving of international affairs with domestic policies may require him to move back toward that combined position, or toward an agreement by which his influence is the most weighty—short of the President's—in guiding the policy judgments of those who manage staff work and committees for the Executive Office.

Personal and Political Responsibility

Such a development would add to the obligations of an official whose job is already too demanding. But the nature of his responsibilities are such that he cannot carry them unless his influence in the policy councils of the President is strengthened, and unless the policies which he helps make receive more systematic support in the Congress and the nation.

In one sense, any executive's job is "too big for one man"; that is why he organizes it, and delegates duties and functions. But the job of the Secretary of State has been too big in another sense: he has been expected to do what nobody could, for he lacked the command over the personnel and the resources to do his job. The reason was that the American people—and consequently, the Congress—did not realize that his job required the use of the best of our human and material resources, and major changes in the ways in which all parts of the government, and nearly all parts of society, were going about their affairs. The breakdown of the old boundaries between foreign and domestic affairs, between peace and war, and between public and private concerns changed the Secretary's job in a fundamental way, and only some considerable changes in our unwritten constitution could make it tolerable.

It is important to make it tolerable, of course, not in order to spare the Secretary as a human being, but because his job is a barometer of how well our constitution is meeting its new challenge. The success of reforms in the position of the Secretary will not be measured in terms of his contentment, but of our safety and welfare—to say nothing of the rest of the world.

The problem is basically political and constitutional in nature; if those aspects can be handled adequately, the managerial ones will follow. The Secretary must be the principal subordinate in an Administration put in office by the party vote, yet he must command nonpartisan or bipartisan support. The record of the past decade or two is encouraging in this respect; the President and the Secretary have generally found support in the Congress from members and leaders of the opposite party for their major objectives, and this has not precluded vigorous criticism and amendments of Administration proposals. It is necessary at the same time both to keep the channels of dissent and disagreement open, and to facilitate unity of action on the fundamental policies on which majority support, from both sides of the aisle, can be found.

In this process, the national leadership of the President and the Secretary is an essential part of the legislative process. If that leadership is to be effective, it must keep the public informed of its problems and its policies; as Mr. Dickey has suggested, this may argue that the Secretary should be more free to use the public affairs machinery of the Department to get information to the non-partisan organizations concerned with foreign affairs, and into the channels of mass communication. And as Mr. Elliott has noted, it would be in the interests of the responsible working of Congress as well as of the Executive if procedures could be adopted to strengthen the internal discipline of the legislative process, and to make the Congressional committees more responsible to the policies of Congress as a whole.

Within the Executive policy councils, Mr. Acheson and Mr. Bowie have pointed out, the problem is not one of passing laws to give the Secretary more authority over his colleagues, but of setting up working relationships with the other Departments in which the Secretary's opinions carry the weighty sanction of the President's confidence and support. This can be done only if the Secretary is supported by a staff which is not only subject to discipline, but itself comprehends the new nature of foreign policy and is skilled in helping to manage its relationship to domestic affairs. As Mr. Wriston has noted, this requires an effective union between the Departmental and Foreign Service, adequate training and career rewards, and a proper balance between those divisions dealing with the political, and those dealing with the economic and cultural, aspects of diplomacy.

The Department of State and the Foreign Service as they existed at the end of the second World War did not provide such a staff. They had been the victims of a vicious circle. For lack of adequate funds and support, and adequate tours of duty at home, the Foreign Service had been confined to service abroad in strictly diplomatic and consular duties. Consequently, it had no opportunity to increase its competence in the newer aspects of international policy, and looked on the foreign aid and information policy of the War period as temporary nuisances to be dropped as soon as it was possible to get back to normalcy. This attitude gave the President and the Congress further reason to distrust its sympathy with progressive policies and its ability to supply the specialized skills needed in the new diplomacy. While the Foreign Service had its faults, there was on the other side something akin to the same utopian overconfidence that had characterized the Jeffersonians; if President Roosevelt did not believe that we could dispense entirely with a diplomatic service, his attitude was probably summed up in the (perhaps apocryphal) wartime story that he had remarked that he would be satisfied if the Foreign Service would only stay neutral. It was probably inevitable, under these circumstances, that the Foreign Service would draw into itself in a self-protective attitude, would not get the support it needed for its proper development, and would find it had to adjust to the demands of an age of cold war, a scientific weapons race, long-term economic and cultural aid to the revolutionary states of Asia and Africa, and diplomacy through international organizations.

Mr. Nitze has pointed out the ways in which the new techniques of diplomacy have followed from the new nature of international relations, and how in consequence the job of the Secretary of State, like that of the Foreign Service, has had to try to adjust to the necessity of operating not as a sideshow to the nation's main political circus, but in the center ring. And the demands on the Secretary's position do not stop at the boundaries of our national political system. In some sense we are adjusting to a new system of alliances and international organizations in which the Secretary is, with the President, in the world spotlight. Whether he can do his job will be a test not only of him as a person, but of our national system of political responsibility, and its ability to fit into the international order of the future.

For while he is going to have to rely for a long time for his strength on the military and their munitions, any enduring peace will have to be built by the more complicated efforts of the missionaries of cultural and political and economic change. This will require the tying together of international as well as national programs; before we have learned to coordinate our domestic Departments we are obliged to try to lead the United Nations. We will have to find ways to help the Secretary of State to make his role effective as the principal agent of the President, and a leader of national opinion, if we are to call a free world into existence to redress the balance of the cold war.

Final Report of the Eighteenth American Assembly

At the close of their discussions, the participants in the Eighteenth American Assembly, at Arden House, Harriman, New York, October 6-9, 1960, on THE SECRETARY OF STATE, reviewed as a group the following statement. Although there was general agreement on the Final Report, it is not the practice of The American Assembly for participants to affix their signatures, and it should not be assumed that every participant necessarily subscribes to every recommendation included in the statement.

Memorandum to the Next President of The United States

The American Assembly has brought together a group of interested citizens of the United States to consider the office of one of the key officials in the American government: The Secretary of State. It has discussed that office not in terms of the men who have occupied it, nor of their policies, but of the way in which the Secretary serves, and may serve in the future, as the President's principal aide for the formulation of foreign policy and the conduct of international affairs, and the way in which he needs support if he is to serve the nation to the best of his personal abilities. And because he serves not as an independent official, but as the agent and confidant of the President, this Assembly thinks it appropriate to address its conclusions to the man to whom the American people are about to entrust the responsibilities of the Presidency for the next four years.

To you as the next President we do not need to argue the importance of this subject. Clearly our nation faces a long hard struggle to protect its security and to create conditions favorable to free values and institutions. Our success depends on strength; it depends equally on vision and ability in conducting international affairs. No neat formula can save us; to prevail we must combine public understanding, political responsibility and professional competence.

Three fundamental changes have taken place in our international activities: *first,* they are carried on not only by conventional diplomacy but also by huge and costly action programs in all parts of the globe; *second,* they are not a concern of the State Department alone, but are interwoven in the programs of virtually all executive departments and agencies as well as Congress; and *third,* they involve work through international organizations as well as by our own government. All three have greatly increased the responsibility for international activities of the Congress and the American people.

THE CENTRAL ROLE OF THE SECRETARY

More than ever the role of the Secretary of State is central. As agent of the President, to whom the Constitution entrusts ultimate Executive responsibility,

—he must bear major responsibility for the formulation of all aspects of national policy bearing on our international interests and security;

—he must take the lead in integrating our military, economic, and cultural programs with our diplomatic efforts into a coherent foreign policy, and coordinate it with activities of other nations;

—he must help inform the Congress, and develop the public consensus that must sustain and direct our public policies.

POLICY PLANNING

The first task of the Secretary, as chief advisor to the President, is to identify the crucial international problems which the nation must face and devise the general strategy to meet them. This is a matter of analyzing the basic forces which are shaping the future of the world, of framing policies by which those forces may be influenced in the national interest, and of identifying the means by which these policies may be effected. Such a systematic view of ends and means is essential for taking the initiative in building a world order congenial to free institutions.

Long-range planning depends in part on the personal judgment and leadership of the Secretary and his immediate subordinates; it also requires the most expert help. This is the task of the Policy Planning Staff. For this purpose it must be free from day-to-day operating burdens, but must be associated with current decisions closely enough to make its planning effective.

No single staff can encompass all the skills necessary to cope with the tremendous range of international problems, especially in fields involving technical matters such as disarmament and outer space. Ideas and talents should be sought out wherever they may be found. Freshness and originality will be maintained best if the Department has the authority and funds to make use of various individuals and institutions and to contract for special studies.

THE SECRETARY'S PRINCIPAL ASSOCIATES

The Secretary of State needs the support of top officials of high prestige, knowledge of international affairs, and executive ability, with a substantial number drawn from outside the career services. Their presence will strengthen the energetic leadership of the State Department and its relationship with the Congress and the public. These appointments should not be political rewards, or be restricted to members of the President's party. Status and pay should be sufficiently high to attract qualified men who should be expected to remain for substantial periods.

The Secretary's principal associates should include a Deputy Secretary of State, three Under Secretaries of State, and a series of officers charged with regional (and United Nations) responsibilities, who should have titles and authority commensurate with their relationships to the governments and organizations with which they deal.

THE AMBASSADORS

The Secretary of State needs the support, in the field, of ambassadors of outstanding ability and distinction, drawn from inside and outside the career service. As in the case of the Secretary's principal associates in Washington, these positions should not be political rewards, nor should they be restricted to members of the President's party.

In each country the ambassador should be responsible for all United States activities. He should be strong enough in his own right, and should have a staff strong enough, to assure the effective coordination of all United States programs in the country to which he is accredited.

THE CAREER FOREIGN SERVICE

Our career Foreign Service should be greatly strengthened in the following ways:

1. The admission of Foreign Service officers should be expanded, with regular and prompt induction after selection, in order to attract the most competent individuals to man effectively the increasing number of missions. This expansion should make it possible to give full effect

to the process of weeding out the least capable, and to make available adequate time for advanced education.

2. The allowances of Foreign Service officers should be high enough to permit them to serve at home and abroad without drawing on private means, in order to allow selection of the best officer for each post without regard to wealth. In particular, representation allowances are inadequate, especially in certain major posts, and the lack of living allowances for Foreign Service officers on duty in the United States can make service at home a hardship.

3. Officers should continue to be recruited from many educational institutions, with emphasis on a broad liberal education. Adequate provision should be made for scholarship assistance during college or university years, from both private and governmental sources, for declared Foreign Service officer-candidates who pass appropriate examinations. To create an undergraduate Foreign Service Academy would unduly narrow the source of recruitment and the variety of abilities and points of view drawn into the Foreign Service.

4. Special efforts should be made to recruit and to develop in the Foreign Service a larger proportion of officers qualified to serve as economists, administrators, and other specialists, especially those who can understand and help implement the relationship of policies to programs. They should be offered satisfactory opportunities for long-term careers in their respective specialities. The interchange of personnel among departments and agencies involved in foreign affairs should be further developed. Far better provision should be made for advanced training both in the Foreign Service Institute and in universities.

5. Administration of the Department and the Foreign Service should be assigned to an Under Secretary for Administration. This position should be filled by a career officer, or a highly qualified individual prepared to serve for an extended period of time.

ECONOMIC, INFORMATION AND CULTURAL PROGRAMS

The international economic and information programs should be administered by continuing agencies with a high degree of autonomy. Their directors should be acceptable to the Secretary of State, and their operations should be subject in Washington to the policy direction of the Secretary, and in the field to the authority of the ambassadors.

The position, support and coordination of our international educational aid and other cultural exchange programs, with particular emphasis on training for the less developed areas, should be substantially strengthened.

COORDINATION OF POLICY

The policies and activities of many executive departments and agencies now affect international relations. The constitutional responsibility for their direction and coordination is the President's. But with the growing importance of international affairs, he must have adequate help from his subordinates in this task. It would be inadvisable to interpose any official between the President and the Secretary in the field of international affairs. The Secretary of State should have primacy in advising on international policy. This role cannot be defined in formal terms. It must depend on the weight given by the President to the advice of the Secretary of State in the matters affecting our international interests. The Secretary of State should have the opportunity, authority, and staff to guide the foreign policy aspects of all national policies.

THE ALLOCATION OF RESOURCES

The allocation of resources for our foreign policy (including national security) should be geared more closely to policy-making. The criteria for such allocation should not be predetermined through the Budget Bureau, but should be derived from policy requirements.

CONGRESSIONAL CONSIDERATION OF FOREIGN AFFAIRS

Working with Congressional committees provides opportunity to obtain their understanding and support. Their critical scrutiny can assist in the shaping of sound programs, and make available their accumulated wisdom and experience. Candor and a willingness to discuss the difficulties and problems as well as the accomplishments of an administration are most likely to produce Congressional backing.

Congress could improve its handling of foreign affairs in several ways. Its key committees could help reduce the burden on the Secretary of State by accepting testimony from his political subordinates, once the President and the Secretary have outlined their policies. Party policy committees might play a constructive role in developing a more consistent approach to foreign policy matters by Congress and its main committees. Vigorous Congressional leadership with the support of the President should prevent national policy from being frustrated by unsympathetic chairmen of committees and sub-committees. A national sense of the increased responsibilities of Congress for the making or breaking of foreign policies and programs should strengthen the hands of leadership, to make the intention of the whole Congress prevail.

PUBLIC INFORMATION

The State Department should make more effort and have more funds to inform the public about the major issues of foreign policy and the requirements for its proper execution. It is unwise, particularly when foreign dictators have access to our own mass media, to put limits on the ability of the Department of State to keep the American people informed about foreign policies and programs. Should the Department go beyond the bounds of propriety, there are ample safeguards in Congressional procedures, and in criticism by the press and public interest organizations.

Participants in the Eighteenth American Assembly

FRANK ALTSCHUL
New York

WILLIAM BENTON
Publisher
Encyclopaedia Britannica
Connecticut

ANDREW H. BERDING
Assistant Secretary for Public Affairs
Department of State
Washington, D. C.

WILLIAM BLOCK
Publisher
Pittsburgh Post-Gazette & Sun-Telegraph
Pennsylvania

ROBERT BLUM
President
The Asia Foundation
San Francisco

ROBERT R. BOWIE
Director,
Center for International Affairs
Harvard University

DAVID K. E. BRUCE
Washington, D. C.

WRIGHT BRYAN
Editor
The Cleveland Plain Dealer
Ohio

FREDERICK BURKHARDT
President
American Council of Learned Societies
New York

HUGH CALKINS
Deputy Director
President's Commission on National Goals
Washington, D. C.

WARD M. CANADAY
Chairman
The Overland Corporation
Toledo

HOLBERT N. CARROLL
Chairman, Department of Political
    Science
University of Pittsburgh

HARLAN CLEVELAND
Dean
Maxwell Graduate School of Citizenship
    and Public Affairs
Syracuse University

During the Assembly participants heard formal addresses by Messrs. A. A. Berle, Jr. and W. Averell Harriman.

197

JAMES B. CONANT
New York

ROYDEN DANGERFIELD
Associate Provost
University of Illinois

JOHN DETWILER
Harriman Scholar
Columbia University

JOHN S. DICKEY
President
Dartmouth College

WM. H. DRAPER, JR.
Major General, U.S.A.R.
Draper, Gaither & Anderson
San Francisco

VERNON A. EAGLE
President
New World Foundation
New York

MARRINER S. ECCLES
Chairman
First Security Corporation
Salt Lake City

A. R. EDWARDS
President
The Armco International Corporation
Middletown, Ohio

WILLIAM Y. ELLIOTT
Professor of History & Political Science
Harvard University

NEVIL FORD
Cold Spring Harbor
Long Island, New York

GEORGE S. FRANKLIN, JR.
Executive Director
Council on Foreign Relations
New York

ROBERT L. GARNER
President
International Finance Corporation
Washington, D. C.

HUNTINGTON GILCHRIST
Ridgefield, Connecticut

CARTER GOODRICH
Professor of Economics
Columbia University

W. AVERELL HARRIMAN
New York

H. J. HEINZ, II
Chairman
H. J. Heinz Co.
Pittsburgh

LOY W. HENDERSON
Deputy Under Secretary for Adminis-
tration
Department of State
Washington, D. C.

JOHN HIGHTOWER
Associated Press
Washington, D. C.

JAMES T. HILL, JR.
New York

WILLIAM L. HOLLAND
Executive Secretary
American Institute of Pacific Relations
New York

JOSEPH E. JOHNSON
President
Carnegie Endowment for International
Peace
New York

ALAN G. KIRK
Admiral U.S. Navy (Ret.)
New York

KLINE, ALLAN
Western Spring, Illinois

SIGURD S. LARMON
Chairman
Young & Rubicam
New York

MARX LEVA
Fowler, Leva, Hawes & Symington
Washington, D. C.

COLONEL G. A. LINCOLN
Professor and Head of Department of
Social Sciences
United States Military Academy
West Point

ERNEST LINDLEY
Newsweek
Washington, D. C.

HARLAN LOGAN
Vice President
General Foods Corporation
White Plains, New York

JUST LUNNING
General Manager
George Jensen, Inc.
New York

C. B. MARSHALL
Arlington, Virginia

GEORGE C. McGHEE
Dallas

HANS J. MORGENTHAU
Professor of Government
Harvard University

ROBERT D. MURPHY
President
Corning Glass International
New York

LEE NEHRT
Harriman Scholar
Columbia University

BRUCE NELAN
Harriman Scholar
Columbia University

OTTO L. NELSON, JR.
Vice President
New York Life Insurance Co.
New York

PAUL H. NITZE
President
Foreign Service Educational Foundation
Washington, D. C.

LESLIE PAFFRATH
President
The Johnson Foundation
Racine, Wisconsin

HUGH B. PATTERSON, JR.
Publisher
Arkansas Gazette
Little Rock

MOREHEAD PATTERSON
Chairman
American Machine & Foundry Company
New York

HERMAN PHLEGER
Brobeck, Phleger & Harrison
San Francisco

HERMAN POLLACK
Management Officer
Department of State
Washington, D. C.

HERBERT V. PROCHNOW
Executive Vice President
First National Bank of Chicago

SAMUEL REBER
Princeton, New Jersey

MICHAEL ROSS
Director
Department of International Affairs
  AFL-CIO
Washington, D. C.

DEAN RUSK
President
The Rockefeller Foundation
New York

CHARLES E. SALTZMAN
New York

DAVID S. SMITH
Director
International Fellows Program
Columbia University

WILLIAM S. STREET
President
Frederick & Nelson Department Store
Seattle

GRAHAM STUART
Department of Political Science
Stanford University

LATANÉ TEMPLE
Southern Pine Lumber Company
Diboll, Texas

ROBERT TUFTS
Oberlin College, Ohio

JOHN M. VORYS
Vorys, Sater, Seymour & Pease
Columbus, Ohio

ALEXANDER V. WASSON
President
The First National Bank of Santa Fe
New Mexico

RONALD B. WOODYARD
President
Station WONE
Dayton, Ohio

ARNOLD ZANDER
International President
American Federation of State, County and
    Municipal Employees
Washington, D. C.

The American Assembly

S*ince its establishment by Dwight D. Eisenhower at Columbia University in 1950, The American Assembly has held assemblies of national leaders and has published books to illuminate issues of United States policy.*

The Assembly is a national, non-partisan educational institution, incorporated under the State of New York.

The Trustees of the Assembly approve a topic for presentation in a background book, authoritatively designed and written to aid deliberations at national Assembly sessions at Arden House, the Harriman Campus of Columbia University. These books are also used to support discussion at regional Assembly sessions and to evoke consideration by the general public.

All sessions of the Assembly, whether national or local, issue and publicize independent reports of conclusions and recommendations on the topic at hand. Participants in these sessions constitute a wide range of experience and competence. The following institutions have cooperated or are scheduled to cooperate with the Assembly in sponsoring regional, state or municipal sessions across the country:

Stanford University
University of California (Berkeley)
University of California (Los Angeles)
University of Wyoming
University of Denver
University of New Mexico
University of Oklahoma
Dallas Council on World Affairs
The Rice Institute
Tulane University
Southwestern at Memphis
Duke University
University of Florida
Emory University
University of Illinois
Minnesota World Affairs Center
University of Washington
University of Arizona
University of Wisconsin
Lawrence College

Cleveland Council on World Affairs
University of Missouri
Washington University
Drake University
Indiana University
University of Vermont
Tufts University
Foreign Policy Association of Pittsburgh
Southern Methodist University
University of Texas
Town Hall of Los Angeles
North Central Association
United States Air Force Academy
University of Arkansas
Michigan State University
International Relations Council of
  Kansas City
Vanderbilt University
University of Oregon
University of Puerto Rico

SPECTRUM PAPERBACKS

Other SPECTRUM Books . . . quality paperbacks that meet the highest standards of scholarship and integrity.

MR. SECRETARY Film

A documentary film shown at the Eighteenth American Assembly at Arden House presents the historical background of the Office of the Secretary of State.

Prints of this 16mm, 29-minute, black and white film, produced for National Educational Television, may be rented or purchased from:

The NET Film Service
Audio-Visual Center
Indiana University
Bloomington, Indiana

and

Center for Mass Communications
Columbia University Press
1125 Amsterdam Avenue
New York 25, New York